Jud

inspiration

Student's Book 4

CONTENTS

UNIT 1 — BODY AND MIND

			Grammar	Functions and Skills	Pronunciation	Vocabulary
	Thinking skills	6		Talking about studying		Studying Classroom activities
1	It doesn't matter	8	Verbs not usually used in continuous forms	Talking about food and drink Writing about healthy food and junk food	Syllable stress	Food and drink
2	What's it for?	10	Gerund as subject *by/for* + gerund *after/before* + participle clause	Describing objects and saying what they're for Describing a sequence of events Listening to and writing a recipe	Linking consonant sounds	Household objects Kitchen equipment Recipe
3	When people expect to get better …	12	Verb + gerund or infinitive	Talking about illness and medicine Reading an article about alternative medicine Writing a paragraph giving arguments for and against	Weak forms	Health Illness and treatment
4	Integrated Skills Discussing and correcting information	14	Expressions for correcting information	**Reading** Matching statements and paragraphs: *Reality Check* **Listening** Noting details: beliefs **Speaking** Correcting information **Writing** Writing a paragraph discussing the truth of a statement **Learner Independence** Thinking skills; Word creation: noun and adjective suffixes		Popular beliefs Natural events Useful expressions
	Inspiration *Extra!*	16	**Project** Cooking Around the World File **Sketch** The Expert **Revision & Extension** **Your Choice!**			
	Culture	18	East and West			

UNIT 2 — CREATIVITY

			Grammar	Functions and Skills	Pronunciation	Vocabulary
1	I don't think it's art!	20	Present perfect continuous with *for* and *since*	Talking about activities which continue up to now Matching texts with pictures Listening for details in a conversation Role play: a celebrity interview Writing a paragraph about recent activities	/b/ bare /p/ pair	Materials Art
2	I've been hoping …	22	Present perfect simple and continuous	Talking about recent events Reading web forum postings Writing a paragraph comparing achievements and ambitions	Syllable stress	Acting Film-making
3	I'd been reading books for a long time	24	Past perfect simple and continuous	Talking about a sequence of past events Reading a biography Listening for details: biography Writing a description of an author's life	Syllable stress	Books Story telling
4	Integrated Skills Telling a folk tale	26	Linking words: *neither … nor …*	**Reading** Connecting ideas: *The Professor and the Wise Ferryman* **Listening** Listening to check prediction **Speaking** Discussion **Writing** A folk tale **Learner Independence** Thinking skills; Word creation: noun suffix *-ment*		School subjects Folk tales Useful expressions
	Inspiration *Extra!*	28	**Project** Class Magazine **Song** Spooky **Revision & Extension** **Your Choice!**			
	Review Units 1–2	30	Grammar & Vocabulary Progress Check			

CONTENTS

UNIT 3 — SCIENCE AND DISCOVERY

		Grammar	Functions and Skills	Pronunciation	Vocabulary
1	Light travels incredibly fast	32 — Comparison of adverbs; Adverbs of degree; Position and order of adverbial phrases	Describing and comparing the way things happen; Listening for details; Writing comparisons of achievements	Numbers	Science
2	What a fantastic sight!	34 — *What (a/an) …!*; *so/such (a/an) …*; Result clauses: *so/such … that*; Order of adjectives	Making exclamations; Expressing result; Reading a blog; Writing descriptions of exciting events	Exclamations	Life underwater; Adjectives
3	It won't be cheap	36 — Future review: future simple, present simple and continuous, *going to*	Talking about future events, schedules, arrangements and plans; Listening to a tour schedule; Discussing predictions; Writing about plans and changes	Exclamations	Space flight and tourism; Phrasal verbs with *down, on* and *off*
4	Integrated Skills — Describing events and consequences	38 — Linking words: expressing cause and result	Reading Connecting ideas: *People Who Changed The World*; Listening Correcting mistakes; Speaking Giving reasons for an opinion; Writing Profile of a significant person; Learner Independence Thinking skills; Word creation: *noun* suffixes *-sion* and *-tion*		Medicine; Environment; Radio; Navigation; Useful expressions

Inspiration Extra! 40 Project Exploration File   Sketch Space Talk   Revision & Extension   Your Choice!

Culture 42 Your Culture

UNIT 4 — GETTING IT RIGHT

		Grammar	Functions and Skills	Pronunciation	Vocabulary
1	Some things won't have changed	44 — Future continuous; Future perfect	Discussing possible future lifestyles; Making predictions; Reading an article about life in the future; Writing personal predictions	List intonation	Technology; Phrasal verbs with *out*
2	Unless we take action now …	46 — First conditional with *if* and *unless*; Time clauses with *when, as soon as* and *until*	Talking about future possibility; Listening to a radio phone-in; Role play: a conversation about travelling; Writing: paragraph completion	Two-syllable words stressed differently as nouns and verbs	Global warming
3	If you could choose …	48 — Second conditional; *wish/if only* + past simple	Talking about imaginary or unlikely situations; Expressing wishes about the present; Listening to a radio programme; Writing about wishes	Sentence stress and intonation	Tourism
4	Integrated Skills — Debating an issue	50 — Linking words: adding information and giving examples	Reading For and Against: *Direct Action*; Listening Listening to a debate to complete notes; Speaking Debate; Writing A balanced account of a controversial issue; Learner Independence Thinking skills; Word creation: prefixes *anti-* and *non-*		Politics; Formal debate; Useful expressions

Inspiration Extra! 52 Project Future File   Song Every Breath You Take   Revision & Extension   Your Choice!

Review Units 3–4 54 Grammar & Vocabulary   Progress Check

CONTENTS

UNIT 5 — EXTRAORDINARY PEOPLE

		Grammar	Functions and Skills	Pronunciation	Vocabulary
1	If the plot had succeeded …	56 Third conditional *wish/if only* + past perfect	Talking about unreal or imaginary past events. Expressing regret about the past. Writing about an event which would have changed the world	Sentence stress and weak forms	Historical events
2	You don't have to be mad …	58 *must, have to* and *need to*; *don't have to, don't need to* and *needn't*	Expressing obligation and lack of obligation. Listening to a radio programme and checking details. Writing about qualifications for jobs	Contrastive stress	Routines; Qualifications
3	What could have happened to them?	60 *must have* and *can't have*; *could/may/might have*	Making deductions and speculating about the past. Writing about an unexplained mystery	Sentence stress and weak forms	Aviation; Phrasal verbs with *up*
4	Integrated Skills — Contrasting facts and ideas	62 Linking words: *whereas* and *while*	Reading Connecting ideas: magazine article about women's football. Listening Completing a text. Speaking Discussing male/female equality. Writing Paragraphs contrasting male and female situations. Learner Independence Thinking skills; Word creation: adjective suffix *-ous*		Sport; Useful expressions

Inspiration Extra! 64 Project Extraordinary Person File Sketch The Break-In Revision & Extension Your Choice!

Culture 66 Saying the right thing

UNIT 6 — ON THE MOVE

		Grammar	Functions and Skills	Pronunciation	Vocabulary
1	I promised I wouldn't forget!	68 Reported speech with various reporting verbs	Reporting what people said. Interviewing. Writing a report of interviews	Stress in two-syllable verbs	Travel; Reporting verbs
2	The waitress wanted to know if …	70 Reported questions	Reporting what people asked. Listening to an interview and checking details. Writing a report of a conversation	Sentence stress and intonation	Restaurant; Food
3	It's time that people realised …	72 *get/have something done*; *It's time* + past simple	Describing problems. Suggesting solutions. Completing a questionnaire. Writing a comparison of questionnaire results	Strong and weak forms of *have*	Shops and services; Phrasal verbs with *in/into*
4	Integrated Skills — Reporting and summarising what people said	74 Revision	Reading Topics: *Travelling with parents* interview. Listening Note-taking. Speaking Interviewing and reporting an interview. Writing A report summarising an interview. Learner Independence Thinking skills; Word creation: adjective prefix *well-*		Holidays; Useful expressions

Inspiration Extra! 76 Project Ideal Holiday File Song Hanging On The Telephone Revision & Extension Your Choice!

Review Units 5–6 78 Grammar and vocabulary Progress check

CONTENTS

UNIT 7 — GETTING THE MESSAGE ACROSS

		Grammar	Functions and Skills	Pronunciation	Vocabulary
1	Well done – keep it up!	80 Passive tenses	Describing changes and experiences Reading an article about English idioms Listening to a conversation about a kitchen makeover Doing a questionnaire	*been* and *being*	Idioms Furniture, fixtures and fittings
2	She deserves to be awarded a prize	82 Passive infinitive *either … or* *both … and*	Talking about what's right Reading an article about the discovery of DNA Role play: discussion Writing about teenage attitudes	Syllable stress	Science
3	They couldn't ring up a doctor	84 Phrasal verbs	Using the phone Role play: phone conversation Writing messages	Stress and intonation	Mobile phones Telephone language Phrasal verbs
4	Integrated Skills Discussing languages	86 Linking words *not only … but also* Non-defining relative clauses	Reading Connecting ideas: *Language Death or Language Murder?* article Listening Listening for details: debate Speaking Debate Writing Arguments for and against Learner Independence Thinking skills; Word creation: verb prefix *re-*		Languages Useful expressions

Inspiration Extra! 88 Project Advertising File Sketch Find A Friend Revision & Extension Your Choice!

Culture 90 Student Life

UNIT 8 — MAKING THE GRADE

		Grammar	Functions and Skills	Pronunciation	Vocabulary
1	He wasn't able to get a job	92 *could(n't), was(n't) able to, managed to, in order to, so that*	Talking about past ability Expressing purpose Reading an article about success stories Reading and writing a poem	Syllable stress	Achievements Examinations
2	She needn't have worried	94 Modal expressions in the past and future	Expressing obligation and ability Reading an article about school in the past and in the future Listening to interviews Completing a questionnaire	Intonation	Education
3	Let your colours shine out bright!	96 *make* and *let*	Talking about obligation, permission and prohibition Reading an interview on a website Listening to an interview about rules Doing an interview in writing	Pronunciation of *ng*	Music Family rules
4	Integrated Skills Making an application	98 Revision	Reading Topics: letter of application Listening Listening for details: telephone interviews Speaking Role play: telephone interview Writing Application form and letter of application Learner Independence Thinking skills; Word creation: noun suffix *-ness*		Volunteering Useful expressions

Inspiration Extra! 100 Project Ideal School File Song True Colours Revision & Extension Your Choice!

Review Units 7–8 102 Grammar & Vocabulary Progress Check

Congratulations 104 Communication Activities: Student A 106 Communication Activities: Student B 116
Grammar Summary 109 Word List 120 Irregular Verbs 127

1 BODY AND MIND
Thinking skills

Learning power

Thinking about how you learn is an important skill. Answer the questionnaire by writing O (Occasionally), S (Sometimes), or U (Usually) for each statement.

Learning questionnaire

1. I find it easy to concentrate.
2. I keep trying even when a task is difficult.
3. My head is full of questions.
4. When I learn I try to make links with what I know.
5. I see things in my mind's eye.
6. I work slowly and carefully.
7. I make good use of the resources around me.
8. I plan my learning carefully.
9. I keep a record of my learning.
10. I reflect on my learning to see what I could do better.
11. I work well as part of a team.
12. I can easily see other people's points of view.

Compare your answers with other students.

Memory Building

Here's an activity which you can use to improve your memory. Try it and see what you think.

Look at these 20 words for one minute and try to remember as many as possible.

happy	reggae	coconut	crime	painter	folk	doctor
lonely	prawn	kick	engine	rock	teacher	spaghetti
sad	worried	rap	cousin	pilot	melon	

How did you do? Did you notice that the words (except *crime*, *kick*, *engine* and *cousin*) are in groups: feelings, music, food, and jobs? You can use the Word List to make similar activities.

You'll find more memory building activities in the *Learner Independence* and *Your Choice!* sections.

Developing Logic

Solving puzzles helps develop your thinking skills. Try this one!

What can run but never walks,
has a mouth but never talks,
and has a bed but never sleeps?

There are brainteasers and crosswords in every unit of the Workbook and puzzles in the *Communication Activities* section.

UNIT 1

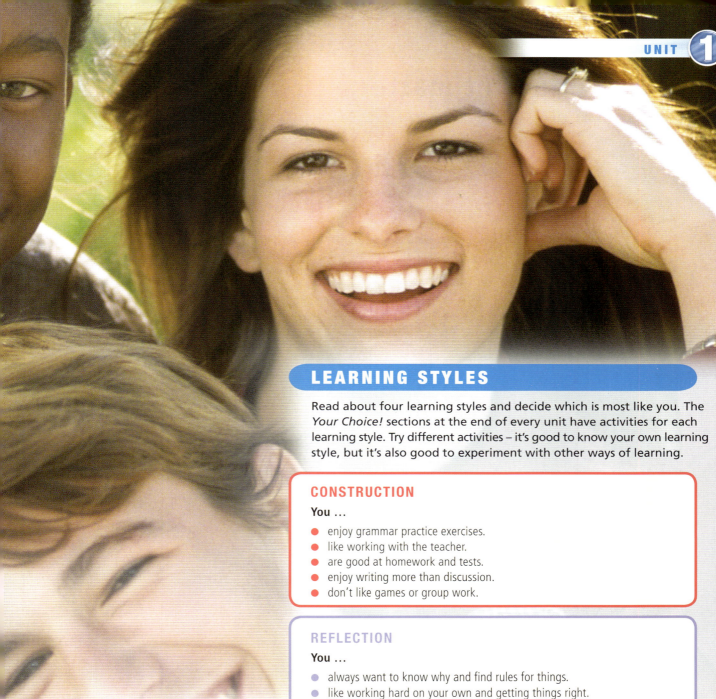

LEARNING STYLES

Read about four learning styles and decide which is most like you. The *Your Choice!* sections at the end of every unit have activities for each learning style. Try different activities – it's good to know your own learning style, but it's also good to experiment with other ways of learning.

CONSTRUCTION
You …
- enjoy grammar practice exercises.
- like working with the teacher.
- are good at homework and tests.
- enjoy writing more than discussion.
- don't like games or group work.

REFLECTION
You …
- always want to know why and find rules for things.
- like working hard on your own and getting things right.
- prefer listening, reading and writing to speaking.
- sometimes don't finish work and are unhappy if it isn't perfect.

ACTION
You …
- like listening and speaking more than reading and writing.
- enjoy fun activities and moving around more than exercises and homework.
- like doing lots of different things and working with other people.
- like games more than writing and grammar.

INTERACTION
You …
- really enjoy learning languages.
- love group and pair work and prefer speaking to writing.
- don't like exercises and rules.
- like working with others and discussing personal things.

Body and Mind

Brain power is about your body as well as your mind. Try these two techniques.

Take a break!
When you're studying at home, stop every 20–30 minutes, stand up, stretch and move around for two or three minutes. This will give you fresh energy.

Walk and breathe in time!
This simple technique helps you relax, gives you energy, and improves your breathing and therefore your voice. 'Walking meditation' is something which you can do every day on your way to or from school. Start walking with your left foot and breathe in through your nose for four steps (left, right, left, right). Then breathe out through your mouth for three steps (left, right, left). Don't breathe for one step (right), then breathe in again. Try it – you'll be amazed!

Answer to brainteaser: A river.

BODY AND MIND

1 It doesn't matter

Verbs not usually used in continuous forms
Talking about food and drink

1 Opener

What are your favourite things to eat and drink? Are they good or bad for you? How do you know?

2 Reading

Read *Food and Drink: Fact or Fiction?* and decide: true or false?

Food and Drink: Fact or Fiction?

1 Bottled water is purer than tap water.
2 A vegetarian diet is the healthiest.
3 Eating cheese gives you nightmares.
4 Dried fruit is not as healthy as fresh fruit.
5 Margarine contains less fat than butter.
6 A food label which includes the words 'low fat' indicates a healthy choice.
7 Neither fruit juice nor diet drinks are bad for your teeth.
8 Experts disagree with each other about what healthy eating is.

Now match statements 1–8 with answers A–H. Then listen and check.

A
In fact, the main messages about healthy eating have stayed the same for some time. For example, 15 years ago experts were saying that we should reduce the amount of fat that we eat. And over 50 years ago they were emphasising the importance of fruit and vegetables. They appear to disagree because the media often exaggerate when reporting scientific research.

B
In fact both are. Fruit juice contains sugar, which can damage your teeth. Diet drinks are often acidic, which means that they can cause tooth decay. The best drinks for your teeth are water or milk.

C
As part of a balanced diet we need to eat at least five portions of different fruit and vegetables a day. It doesn't matter whether they are fresh, frozen, tinned or dried (but fruit juice only counts as one portion a day). The only thing which dried fruit lacks, and fresh fruit has, is vitamin C, but both are equally healthy.

D
It often seems from advertising that this is true. However, while butter and margarine contain different kinds of fat, they both contain a similar amount of fat.

3 Comprehension

Answer the questions.

1 How many of the statements 1–8 are true, how many are false and how many could be true or false?
2 Why do experts appear to disagree about healthy eating?
3 What were experts saying 15 years ago?
4 What does advertising make us believe?
5 Why is it a bad idea to eat late in the evening?
6 What is an example of an unhealthy vegetarian diet?
7 Why do people think that 'low fat' products are OK? Are they right?
8 Why do some people prefer bottled water?

4 Grammar

Complete.

Verbs not usually used in continuous forms

Fruit juice _____ (contain) sugar.
It often _____ (seem) that this is true.
It _____ (not matter) whether they are fresh, frozen, ...
People _____ (suppose) that they are OK.
They _____ (think) that bottled water _____ (taste) better.

Many of these verbs refer to states (including mental states, eg *think*) rather than actions, or to the senses (eg *taste*). Modal verbs (eg *must*) do not have continuous forms.

 Check the answers: Grammar Summary page 109

E
It's not what you eat but when you eat that matters. Scientists agree that it's not a good idea to eat just before you go to bed. You can't relax properly while you're digesting food.

F
It depends. Vegetarian diets can be very healthy. But if your vegetarian diet consists of chips and biscuits, then that's a different matter. Make sure that your diet includes food with the protein, vitamins and minerals you normally get from meat.

G
Not at all. 'Low' products must contain 25% less fat than usual, so people suppose that they are OK. But these types of food are often very high in fat to start with. So a 'low fat' product can still have quite a high amount of fat.

H
This is a popular myth. Although some people think that bottled water tastes or smells better, there's nothing to prove that it's always purer than tap water. In fact, in the USA it's believed that 25–30% of bottled water comes from tap water. And do you realise that bottled water can cost up to 10,000 times more than tap water?

5 Grammar Practice

Which of these verbs can you find in the texts in exercise 2?

Verbs not usually used in continuous forms
agree/disagree   appear   believe   consist   contain
depend   feel   hear   include   know   lack   like/dislike
love   matter   mean   need   prefer   promise   realise
recognise   remember   see   seem   smell   sound
suppose   taste   think   understand   want

6 Speaking

Discuss these statements with another student using verbs from exercise 5.
- The best way to lose weight is to skip a meal.
- Healthy food is boring and expensive.
- I like junk food – what's wrong with that?
- I take vitamins, so I don't have to worry about what I eat.
- It's not a good idea to go swimming for an hour after a meal.
- Eating lots of carrots helps you see better in the dark.

> Some people believe in skipping meals, but they soon feel hungry and eat lots of snacks.

> I prefer to eat normally and take exercise.

7 Pronunciation

Write the words in the correct column.

biscuit   bottled   contain
decay   depend   digest   fiction
label   nightmare   portion
prefer   product   protein
reduce   relax   suppose

■ ■	■ ■
biscuit	contain

 Now listen and check. Repeat the words.

8 Speaking

Make notes for a food diary, describing what you have eaten and drunk in the last 24 hours. Then show your notes to another student and discuss them.

> You had cereal and fruit for breakfast. What did you have to drink?

> Tea – I dislike coffee. In fact, I like hot chocolate best. How about you?

> I didn't have breakfast – it doesn't matter. I can get some crisps at break.

9 Writing

Using at least five of the verbs in exercise 5, write a paragraph about the advantages and disadvantages of healthy food and junk food.

1 BODY AND MIND

2 What's it for?

Gerund as subject
by/for + gerund
after/before + participle clause
Describing objects and saying what they're for
Describing a sequence of events

1 Opener

Look at these photos of lifestyle gadgets. What do you think each item is?

What's New?

2 Reading

Read *What's New?* and match the photos with the descriptions. Then listen and check.

3 Comprehension

True or false? Correct the false sentences.

1. The key looks like a bottle opener.
2. You can't unlock your front door with the key.
3. You can charge your mobile battery by plugging in the phone charger.
4. The sandwich toaster is for roasting sandwiches.
5. By hiding somewhere in the room, Clocky makes you get out of bed.
6. Experts recommend walking a thousand steps a day.
7. The pedometer is for telling the time.
8. You can make the pedometer talk by pressing a button.

1. This looks like a door key, but in fact it's a clever gadget for opening bottles. Keep this bottle opener on your key ring, and you'll never be thirsty again when you're out and about. But when you come home, don't try to open your front door with it!

2. Keeping in touch is easy with this magic mobile phone charger. When your mobile battery is flat, you can get more power by plugging the charger into your phone and winding it up. A three-minute wind gives you about eight minutes of talking time, so you can stay in touch wherever you are. Keep one in your bag and never worry about the 'flat battery' beep again.

3. Do you like making toasted sandwiches? Then this sandwich toaster is the answer. It produces perfect toasted sandwiches and it's small enough to fit in a kitchen drawer. It comes with lots of delicious recipes and you can use it at home, on the barbecue, or when you go camping.

4. An ordinary alarm clock wakes you up, but Clocky is a furry alarm clock on wheels that also makes sure you get out of bed. When the alarm goes off and you press the snooze button, the clock rolls off the bedside table onto the floor and finds a place to hide. When the alarm clock sounds again, you have to get out of bed and look for it, so you are fully awake before turning it off. Clocky's 25-year-old inventor, Ms Gauri Nanda, is a student – she came up with the idea after struggling to get up in the morning.

5. Walking 10,000 steps a day (as recommended by experts) is great fun with this talking pedometer! Clip it onto your hip – on a belt or pocket – and it counts your footsteps. Press a button, and it will speak, telling you the number of steps you've taken, the distance you've travelled, and the current time. And you can listen to the radio while you walk!

4 Grammar

Complete.

> **Gerund as subject**
> _____ (keep) in touch is easy.
> _____ (walk) 10,000 steps a day is great fun.
>
> **by/for + gerund**
> You can get more power **by** _____ (plug) the charger into your phone.
> It's a clever gadget **for** _____ (open) bottles.
>
> **after/before + participle clause**
> She came up with the idea **after** _____ (struggle) to get up in the morning.
> You are fully awake **before** _____ (turn) it off.

➜ Check the answers: Grammar Summary page 109

5 Grammar Practice

Complete with the *-ing* form of the verb and *after, before, by* or *for* where necessary.

1. Alarm clocks are _____ _____ people up. (wake)
2. _____ _____ to sleep, I set my alarm clock. (go)
3. _____ sheep can help you go to sleep. (count)
4. You unlock the door _____ _____ the key clockwise. (turn)
5. _____ a meal is easy if you follow a recipe. (cook)
6. I often feel sleepy _____ _____ a big meal. (eat)
7. _____ to English radio programmes is a good idea. (listen)
8. You keep fit _____ _____ regular exercise. (take)

6 Vocabulary

Match the words for kitchen equipment with pictures 1–8.

> **Kitchen equipment**
> bread knife   cheese grater   coffee maker
> corkscrew   frying pan   kettle   tin opener   toaster

 Listen and check. Then ask and answer questions using these phrases.

> boil water   fry food   grate cheese   make coffee
> make toast   open bottles   open tins   slice bread

A What's number 1?
B It's a tin opener. It's for opening tins.

7 Pronunciation

🎧 Listen and repeat.

> **Linking consonant sounds**
> front‿door   eight‿minutes   flat‿battery
> bed‿side‿table   great‿fun   foot‿steps
> current‿time   bread‿knife   cork‿screw

8 Listening

🎧 Look at the recipe for Spaghetti Carbonara. The instructions A–I are in the wrong order. Try to put them in the right order. Then listen and see if you are right.

SPAGHETTI CARBONARA
Serves 4

INGREDIENTS: 350g spaghetti, 175g bacon, 2 medium onions, 50ml olive oil, 50ml white wine, 4 eggs, 100ml cream, 100g grated Parmesan cheese, salt

- A Meanwhile, boil 3–4 litres of water in a saucepan.
- B Then stir in the egg, cream and cheese mixture.
- C Chop the onions and bacon into small pieces.
- D Add the white wine and turn down the heat.
- E Sprinkle with the rest of the Parmesan cheese and serve immediately.
- F When the pasta is cooked, drain it and add the onions and bacon.
- G Put the spaghetti in the boiling water, add salt and stir for a few seconds.
- H Heat the oil in a frying pan and fry the onions and bacon slowly until the onions are almost clear.
- I While the pasta is cooking, use a fork to beat the eggs and cream together in a bowl, and then add half the Parmesan cheese.

9 Speaking

Check your answers to exercise 8 using *after/before ...ing*.

A First chop the onions and bacon into small pieces.
B After chopping the onions and bacon, fry them slowly.
A Before frying the onions and bacon, heat the oil in a frying pan.

10 Writing

Note down the ingredients for a dish that you like, and write a recipe explaining how to make it.

1 BODY AND MIND

3 When people expect to get better ...

Verb + gerund or infinitive
Talking about illness and medicine

> Much so-called alternative medicine is at best harmless and at worst dangerous.

> My father took herbal medicine when he tried to stop smoking last year. It didn't work. But that's probably his fault, because he didn't remember to take it every day.

> Research shows that patients who tried having acupuncture for bad headaches had fewer headaches and saw the doctor less often, than those who didn't try it.

> I remember going to the doctor for my first acupuncture session. I pretended to be calm, although I couldn't help feeling nervous! I didn't exactly enjoy having acupuncture, but it didn't hurt and the next day my back was much better.

Alternative Medicine
Is it all in the mind?

1 Opener

Can people who are ill get better without the help of modern medicine? Do you know people who use alternative medicine?

2 Reading

🎧 Read and listen to the text.

3 Comprehension

True or false? Correct the false sentences.

1. Patients who had acupuncture for headaches saw the doctor more often.
2. Acupuncture can help people with back pain.
3. More and more people are trying acupuncture.
4. Herbalists treat each patient as being different.
5. A company hopes to make pills which will work in the same way as acupuncture.
6. A Chinese woman had a major operation without a general anaesthetic.
7. Acupuncture needles seem to change the way the brain reacts to pain.
8. The effects on those patients who had a real knee operation and those who didn't were different.

One in five people in the UK choose to use alternative medicine every year.

Alternative medicine may be news, but it's not new. It's modern medicine that is new – for example, the first synthetic drug, aspirin, only dates from 1899. But alternative medicine goes back thousands of years. Acupuncture, inserting fine needles at selected points in the body, was used in China over 2,000 years ago and keeps growing in popularity. Herbal medicine, treating illness and pain with natural remedies, is the oldest system of medicine in the world. Herbalists are prepared to spend more time than modern doctors with patients so they can treat them as individuals.

And what's next? 'Acupuncture-in-a-pill'! A company in Singapore expects to identify the gene responsible for acupuncture healing soon. It will then make a pill for people who want to avoid having acupuncture because they can't stand the thought of all those needles.

A recent TV programme on alternative medicine showed a young Chinese woman having open-heart surgery without a general anaesthetic – but with acupuncture. There seemed to be no doubt that acupuncture stopped the woman feeling pain. Later the programme showed how the needles appeared to change the brain's reaction to pain.

Then there's the 'placebo' effect. In a major trial in the USA a group of patients had a normal operation for bad knee pain. Another group of patients with knee pain also believed they had operations. But in fact all the surgeon did was cut the knee open and close it again. Both groups had the same positive results from their 'operations'. In other words, the effect of real and fake operations was the same.

So what does this experiment tell us about medicine? Simply this: when people expect to get better they often do.

12

4 Grammar

Complete.

Verb + gerund or infinitive
Some verbs, eg *enjoy*, *dislike*, are followed by the gerund; others, eg *decide*, *want*, are followed by the infinitive. And some verbs can be followed by **either** the gerund **or** the infinitive.

Patients who tried _____ (have) acupuncture …
He tried _____ (stop) smoking last year.
try + gerund = do something to see what happens
try + infinitive = attempt something difficult

I remember _____ (go) to the doctor.
He didn't remember _____ (take) it every day.
remember/forget + gerund refers to an action in the past.
remember/forget + infinitive refers to a necessary action and looks ahead.

 Check the answers: Grammar Summary page 109

5 Grammar Practice

Find these verbs in the texts in exercise 2 and complete the chart.

avoid   appear   couldn't help   choose   expect
keep   pretend   seem   stop   want

Verb + gerund	Verb + infinitive

6 Grammar Practice

Gerund or infinitive? Complete with the correct form of the verb.

A doctor talks about alternative medicine.

'My own interest in alternative medicine goes back to when I was a medical student on a visit to China. I really enjoyed __1__ (travel) round the country. I'll never forget __2__ (go) into the operating theatre of a hospital in a small town. A woman was on the operating table with three needles in her left ear. I tried __3__ (see) if she had any other anaesthetic, but there didn't appear __4__ (be) any. I kept __5__ (think) 'They certainly didn't tell us this in medical school.' I had forgotten __6__ (take) my camera with me, so unfortunately I couldn't take a photo. When I returned to the UK I tried __7__ (find) out more about acupuncture. I remember __8__ (tell) my professor about it but he didn't really want __9__ (discuss) it.'

7 Speaking

What would you do in these situations? Complete the sentences for each situation and then tell another student.

Situations
You want to go on holiday on your own.
You want to pass the end-of-year exams.
You want to go to an all-night party.

1 I'd try to …   4 I'd avoid …
2 I wouldn't risk …   5 I'd remember to …
3 I'd promise to …

> I'd try to save up some money.
> I wouldn't risk going without telling my parents.
> I'd promise to phone home regularly.

8 Pronunciation

 Listen and repeat.

Weak forms: /ət/, /əv/, /fə/, /tə/
at best … at worst …   thousands of years
remember to take it   at selected points
acupuncture for headaches   system of medicine
a pill for people   appeared to change
pretend to be calm   a group of patients

9 Vocabulary

Make a word map for medicine. Use words from this lesson, and add other words you know.

10 Speaking

Interview three other students about their views on alternative and modern medicine and note down their answers.

> What are the differences between modern medicine and alternative medicine?
> Modern medicine is scientific.
> Alternative medicine sometimes works, but we don't know how.
> I wouldn't risk trying alternative medicine.

11 Writing

Read the text in exercise 2 again and make a list of the advantages and disadvantages of alternative medicine. Write a paragraph giving your views on alternative medicine using the list and your notes from exercise 10.

1 BODY AND MIND

4 Integrated Skills
Discussing and correcting information

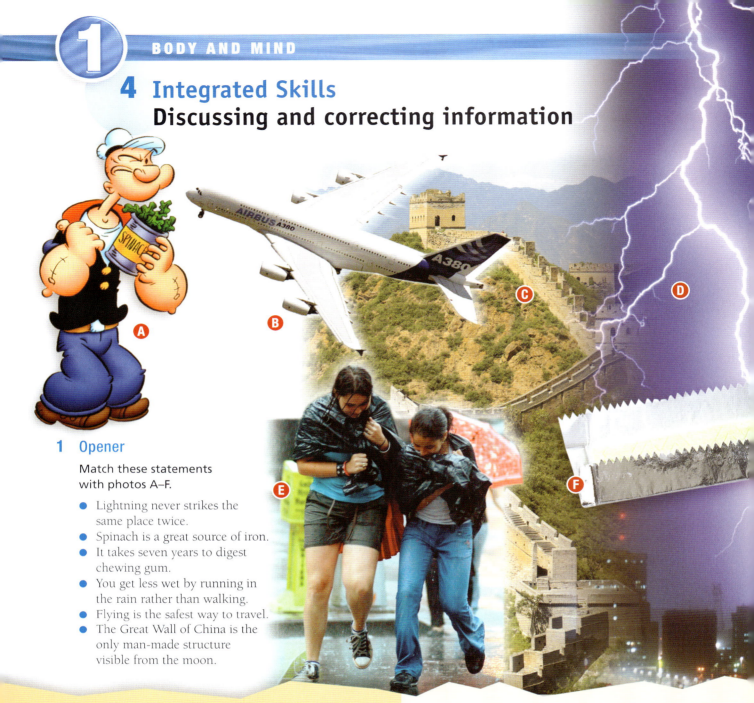

1 Opener

Match these statements with photos A–F.

- Lightning never strikes the same place twice.
- Spinach is a great source of iron.
- It takes seven years to digest chewing gum.
- You get less wet by running in the rain rather than walking.
- Flying is the safest way to travel.
- The Great Wall of China is the only man-made structure visible from the moon.

REALITY CHECK

1 This idea was probably made up to stop children swallowing gum, but it's nonsense. It may be a bit more difficult to break down than other things we eat, but actually it doesn't take very long to digest.

2 This is a common belief, but it's false. Astronauts in space can see the Great Wall before leaving the earth's orbit, as well as several other things like airports, motorways, and even bridges. But the truth is that the famous landmark is not visible from the moon.

3 This is probably true. Many people are afraid of flying because they believe it's risky, but statistics show that it's safer than crossing the road, and there is a greater chance of accidents in other forms of transport. However, the chances of surviving a plane crash are low.

4 Popeye claimed his strength came from this vegetable, but it isn't a particularly good source of iron. In fact, it contains an acid which stops the body absorbing most of the iron. However, it is a rich source of healthy things such as vitamins A, C and E.

5 This is a myth. People believe that fewer raindrops land on them if they run because they spend less time in the rain. But in reality you can get wetter by running, because more rain hits your chest when you run than when you walk. On the other hand, if you run to the nearest shelter you will get less wet. Of course, carrying an umbrella is the best way to avoid getting wet!

6 This is a famous saying, but is it a fact? On the contrary, lightning frequently hits the same place more than once. This is particularly true of high places – the Empire State Building in New York is struck 100 times every year on average, and in one storm it was struck 15 times in 15 minutes. The building is even designed as a lightning conductor to stop lightning hitting other buildings.

Reading

2 Read *Reality Check* and match the statements in exercise 1 with paragraphs 1–6.

🎧 Now listen and check. How many of the statements are actually true?

3 What do the words in *italics* refer to?

Paragraph
1 … actually *it* doesn't take very long to digest.
2 … *the famous landmark* is not visible from the moon.
3 … they believe *it's* risky …
4 … *it* is not particularly rich in iron.
5 People believe that fewer raindrops land on *them* …
6 *The building* is even designed as a lightning conductor …

Listening

4 Here are three more statements. Discuss whether each one is true or false.

1 The number of people alive today is greater than the number who have ever died.
2 It's essential to drink at least eight glasses of water a day.
3 We use only ten per cent of our brains.

🎧 Now listen to an expert discussing the statements and check.

5 Listen again and complete the notes below.

❶ *Estimated number of people who have died in the last …*
Modern humans appeared …
Experts believe the number of dead in human history is …

❷ *A lot of the water we need is provided by …*
We can take in water by drinking …
The sensible thing is to …

❸ *Brain scans and other tests show …*
We use different parts of our brain for different activities …
We don't use all our muscles at the same time, so …

6 Speaking

Look at your notes in exercise 5, and tell each other the facts about the three statements in exercise 4. You can use the phrases in the box.

Correcting information
actually   in fact

More formal
in reality   the truth is that   on the contrary

7 Writing

Choose one of the statements in exercise 4, and write a paragraph discussing it. Use your notes and the *Reality Check* article to help you.

Learner Independence

8 Thinking skills: use your brain to think about words! For each of these words from Unit 1, try to answer the questions below.

decay   delicious   frozen   nightmare
saucepan   snooze

- What does it mean? Is it a noun and/or a verb, or an adjective?
- Can you remember its context in the unit?
- What other words do you associate with it?
- What other words can you use with it?
- What does it sound like?

Now compare your answers with another student.

Which word do you think is the most useful? Why? Which word do you like best? Why?

9 Word creation: complete the chart with words from Unit 1.

Noun	Adjective
___	acidic
danger	___
harm	___
health	___
herb	___
___	ill
___	important
___	real
risk	___
sense	___
___	strong
thirst	___
___	true

10 Phrasebook

🎧 Find these useful expressions in Unit 1. Then listen and repeat.

That's a different matter.   Not at all.
Do you realise that …?   What's wrong with that?
It's not a good idea to …   It didn't work.
It's nonsense.   On the other hand …
The sensible thing is to …

Now write sentences which could come before five of the expressions.

> **Unit 1** Communication Activity
> Student **A** page 106
> Student **B** page 116

1 BODY AND MIND

Inspiration Extra!

PROJECT Cooking Around the World File

Make a file about food from different countries.

1. Work in a group and make a list of different national kinds of cooking, for example: Italian, Chinese, Mexican, Indian. Then choose three kinds and write a list of typical dishes. For each kind of cooking, choose one dish to write about. Make notes about why you chose each dish.

2. Find out information about each dish using the Internet or a library.

   What ingredients do you need to make it?
   How do you cook it?
   What does the finished dish look and taste like?
   When do people usually eat it?

3. Work together and make a Cooking Around the World File. Describe each dish and how to make it. Say why you chose it. Read the file carefully and correct any mistakes. Draw pictures or use photographs from newspapers or magazines. Show your Cooking Around the World File to the other groups.

GAME Acrosswords

- Choose a long word from this unit. Write the word across the top of a piece of paper, and down the left-hand side. Then write the same word backwards down the right-hand side of the paper.

- Make a copy and give it to another student. Both of you try to find words which begin with the letter on the left and end with the letter on the right. You can use a dictionary to help you. It doesn't matter if you can't find words for all the lines.

- Score one point for each letter. The student with the most points wins.

```
S Y N T H E T I C
Y               I
N E X           T
T A K           E
H I G           H
E X T I N C     T
T R A I         N
I D E N T I F   Y
C H A N G E     S
```

SKETCH The Expert

🎧 Read and listen.

MAN   Yes, can I help you?
WOMAN I want to dye.
MAN   I beg your pardon! What did you say? You want to die?
WOMAN I want to dye it. It's my shirt.
MAN   Diet! Ah, yes, you've come to the right man. I'm a diet expert. Now why do you want to diet? Is your shirt too small?
WOMAN It's not the size, it's the colour. I don't like it. It's white and I want it to be brown.
MAN   There's nothing wrong with your colour – you look fine. And anyway a diet won't change your colour. Try sunbathing.
WOMAN Listen! I want to dye it brown.
MAN   Sorry. I haven't got any brown diets. I've got high-energy diets, all-meat diets, fruit diets, lots of diets, but no colour diets.
WOMAN I don't want to dye the collar! I want to dye the whole shirt. And these jeans. They're the right size but the wrong colour.
MAN   You can't change your genes – you're born with them.
WOMAN No, I wasn't! I bought them last week. In a new jeans shop in the High Street.
MAN   A genes shop!
WOMAN Yes. But if you won't help me, I'll take them back to the shop and change them.
MAN   How interesting! I've always wanted to change my genes. I could be tall and have lots of hair. I think I'll come with you!

Now act out the sketch in pairs.

UNIT 1

REVISION for more practice

LESSON 1

Look at exercise 6 on page 9. Write sentences responding to the statements.

Some people believe in skipping meals, but they soon feel hungry and eat lots of snacks.

LESSON 2

Look at exercise 6 on page 11. Write sentences about the kitchen equipment.

A bread knife is for slicing bread.

LESSON 3

Look at exercise 5 on page 13. Choose five of the verbs in the box. Write five sentences about things that happened last week using the verbs + gerund or infinitive.

I couldn't help being late for school because the bus broke down.

EXTENSION for language development

LESSON 1

Look at *Food and Drink: Fact or Fiction?* on page 8. Write eight similar statements about food and drink – four true and four false. Ask another student to say which are true and which are false.

LESSON 2

Look at exercise 9 on page 11 and the recipe you wrote in exercise 10. Write sentences about the recipe using *after/before …ing*.

LESSON 3

Look at exercise 7 on page 13. Then complete sentences 1–5 below for these situations:

- You want to ask another student for a date.
- You want to ask your parents for money to buy an MP3 player.

1 I'd expect to …
2 I'd keep …
3 I wouldn't dare to …
4 I'd suggest …
5 I'd ask to …

YOUR CHOICE!

CONSTRUCTION Gerund or infinitive?

Complete with the correct form of the verb.

1 She enjoys _____ (go) to see the herbalist because he seems _____ (understand) her.
2 Acupuncture appears _____ (help) my pain so I'm going to keep _____ (have) it.
3 He decided _____ (take) aspirin because he didn't want _____ (risk) _____ (have) a headache all day.
4 Always late? Try _____ (set) your watch five minutes fast.
5 Did you remember _____ (lock) the door?
6 He'll never forget _____ (meet) Nelson Mandela.
7 She tried _____ (explain) what to do but he didn't understand.
8 I remember _____ (take) my glasses off but now I can't find them.
9 Don't forget _____ (give) me a call when you arrive.

REFLECTION Gerund and infinitive

Complete.

- *avoid*, *enjoy* and *suggest* are examples of verbs which are followed by the _____.
  appear, *expect* and *refuse* are examples of verbs which are followed by the _____.
- Some verbs like *remember*, _____ , and _____ can be followed by either gerund or infinitive, but with different meanings. For example, *remember* + _____ refers to something it is important to do in the future, while *remember* + _____ refers to something that happened in the past.
- Other verbs, for example, *hate*, *like*, *love*, and *prefer* can be followed by _____ gerund or infinitive with the _____ meaning.

ACTION Topics

- Work in a small group.
- Choose six topics from this list:
  animals   clothes   countries   environment
  feelings   food   health   home   leisure
  sport   television   travel
- Choose a letter for the group by opening a book, closing your eyes and pointing with your finger.
- Work on your own in the group. For each topic, write down as many words as you can beginning with the chosen letter. You have ten minutes.
- Then read out your lists, scoring one point for each word and two points for any words the others haven't thought of.

INTERACTION Special events and feelings

- Work in a small group.
- Tell each other about:
  Something special which happened to you recently.
  A place which is special for you.
  A number which is special for you.
- Answer the other students' questions.

17

culture
EAST AND

Mustafa (Egypt)

Wulandari (Indonesia)

We asked four teenager two questions about East and West.

What do you think of when you hear the words East and West?

Mustafa For me, the West means principally the USA, but also Europe, Canada, New Zealand, Australia and of course Japan – so it's not really a place, more a way of living.

Amanda When I hear East I think of China. I used to think of the Chinese as millions of people all doing the same thing and wearing the same clothes, but now China's a world power. I mean, it seems that everything we buy is made in China!

Wulandari The word West makes me think of other words like technology, capitalism and racism.

Tom I think of the East as a place where there are no choices – everything is decided for you. Society in the East is essentially more conservative – look at the position of women.

Mustafa Actually, East and West are only ideas. When you get to know people better, you stop seeing them as stereotypes. It's so important for people from different countries to communicate – ordinary people can always get on with each other.

Wulandari If you take religion, then East means Islam first of all, but of course there are also Hindus and Buddhists and lots of others. And there are plenty of other religions in Western countries as well as Christianity – I know there are lots of Muslims in the UK for example. But, anyway, I'm against labelling people – we're all human.

1 Vocabulary

Read the texts and match these words with their definitions.

1 principally *adv*
2 capitalism *n*
3 essentially *adv*
4 conservative *adj*
5 stereotypes *n*
6 military *adj*
7 consumption *n*
8 priority *n*
9 generous *adj*
10 independent *adj*

a something which is put first
b to do with the army
c not needing help from other people
d mainly, mostly
e basically
f fixed ideas held about people
g happy to give money or time
h not welcoming change
i use of resources
j economic system where companies are owned by people, not the government

culture

Amanda (UK)

Tom (USA)

What do you see as the principal differences between East and West?

Mustafa Some things are better in the West and some in the East. In the East we place much more importance on the family and the way in which we support each other. But I also like the freedom people have in the West to do what they want – especially women.

Amanda The truth is that the East has more natural resources, like oil, than the West. The West needs, or rather wants, these resources and uses military power to get them. Instead of taking other people's resources we should look at ways of reducing our own consumption.

Wulandari In fact, we're very different in our priorities. Muslims are very generous and give a lot to charity. But in the West people care more about their pets and possessions. At Christmas, for example, there's an enormous amount of waste on silly things.

Tom Like I said, the first thing I think of is the way women are treated in the East. In the West women are more respected and can lead independent lives. But in the East they aren't allowed to make choices.

Mustafa I think we help each other more in our culture. If there's a fire, everyone comes to help. If you see a thief running away, everyone chases him. But in the West if people see a crime, they're scared.

2 Comprehension

Complete with Amanda (A), Mustafa (M), Tom (T), or Wulandari (W).

1 _____ has a changed view of a country.
2 _____ compares eastern and western views of crime.
3 _____ and _____ think the position of women in the West is better.
4 _____ thinks that being able to choose is important.
5 _____ sees eastern society as being more traditional.
6 _____ thinks the West should consume less.
7 _____ and _____ think people are basically the same everywhere.
8 _____ believes the way people help each other is important in society.
9 _____ says that in the West people care more about animals than about people.
10 _____ sees East and West as lifestyles rather than places.

3 Speaking

Discuss these questions.

1 What do you think of when you hear the words East and West?
2 What do you see as the principal differences between East and West?
3 What stereotypes do people in your country have about East and West?
4 Whose answers do you disagree with most? Why?
5 'Some things are better in the West and some in the East.' What things?
6 Do you think differences between East and West are increasing or getting less? Why?

4 Writing

Choose one of the questions in exercise 3 and write two paragraphs answering it.

2 CREATIVITY

1 I don't think it's art!

Present perfect continuous with *for* and *since*
Talking about activities which continue up to now

1 Opener

Look at the photos of works of art. What do they show?

What materials were used to create these works? Choose from these words.

Materials
bronze   cardboard
concrete   dung   gold
ice   plaster   plastic
rubber   sand   snow
stone   wood

2 Reading

 Read and listen to information about four famous modern artists. Match them with their work in photos A–D.

1
Andy Goldsworthy has been working with natural materials to make unique sculptures since his days as an art student. He's a sculptor who is interested in 'movement, light, growth and decay'. He usually works outside and with his bare hands to create structures out of stone, snow, ice, sand, wood or brightly-coloured leaves. A striking example of his work is an ice arch, which he succeeded in building one early winter morning in Canada. As the sun became warmer the arch gradually melted and finally collapsed.

Up early
working in the dark
before the day became too warm
to complete the arch
ahead of the incoming tide
a meeting of two waters –
river and sea
FOX POINT, NOVA SCOTIA
1 February 1999

2
Since the late 1980s, Rachel Whiteread has been creating unusual sculptures of everyday domestic items – the empty spaces under chairs and staircases, around baths, and inside cupboards and rooms. One of the most famous of these was her first public sculpture, the award-winning *House* – a concrete cast of the inside of a terraced house in east London. She recently created a huge sculpture consisting of 14,000 white plastic boxes cast from ten different cardboard boxes. Whiteread also uses materials like plaster, rubber and polystyrene to define the space around or inside objects and buildings.

3
Tracey Emin's first piece of public art is *Roman Standard* in the centre of Liverpool. It's a bronze sculpture of a bird on top of a four-metre high pole. In an interview, Emin said: 'Since 1992 I've been making a series of drawings and prints of birds. I've always had the idea that birds are the angels of this earth and that they represent freedom.' Reactions to the sculpture are not all positive: 'I don't think it's art – it's a complete waste of money!' The bird is certainly small – in fact it disappears if you stand directly in front of it and only reappears if you move to the left or right.

4
For many years, prize-winning artist Chris Ofili has been using elephant dung in his paintings as a symbol of his African heritage. He also stands his paintings on elephant dung, which he gets free of charge from London Zoo. One of his best-known works is *No Woman No Cry*, the title of a Bob Marley song. The painting is a tribute to the family of Stephen Lawrence, a London teenager who was murdered by a racist gang. The boy's face can be seen in each of the crying woman's tears.

3 Comprehension

Answer the questions.

1. How long has Andy Goldsworthy been creating sculptures from natural materials?
2. What kind of materials does he use?
3. How long has Rachel Whiteread been making sculptures of everyday items?
4. What was *House* made of?
5. What other materials does Whiteread use?
6. How long has Tracey Emin been making drawings and prints of birds?
7. What's her *Roman Standard* bird made of?
8. What's unusual about Chris Ofili's work?

What do you think about the works of art in the photos?

4 Grammar

Complete.

> **Present perfect continuous**
> Since 1992 I've _____ _____ a series of drawings and prints of birds.
> For many years, Chris Ofili _____ _____ _____ elephant dung in his paintings.
> How long _____ Andy Goldsworthy _____ _____ with natural materials?
>
> We can use the present perfect continuous with *for* and *since* to talk about a continuous or repeated activity which started in the past and continues up to now.
> We can also use this tense to talk about recently completed continuous actions which have present results.
> I can tell she's been crying. (Her eyes are red.)
>
> ➡ Check the answers: Grammar Summary page 110

5 Grammar Practice

Ask questions beginning *How long …?* with the present perfect continuous, and answer them using both *for* and *since*.

A   How long has Steven Spielberg been directing feature films?
B   For … years. Since … .

1. Steven Spielberg directed his first feature film – *Duel* – in 1971.
2. Robbie Williams started performing pop songs in 1990.
3. JK Rowling wrote her first story in 1971 at the age of six.
4. George Clooney started acting in 1979.
5. Jennifer Lopez started singing in 1975, when she was five.
6. Ronaldinho started playing professional football at the age of 18 in 1998.

Now write sentences.

Steven Spielberg has been directing feature films for … years, since … .

6 Listening

Look at the photo of the statue. Is there anything unusual about it?

Now listen and find the answers to these questions.

1. How long has the woman been taking photos?
2. Has the man been standing completely still?
3. How long has he been standing there?
4. Why is he wet?
5. How long has he been performing as a living statue?
6. What has he been studying?
7. What has he been trying to do?

7 Pronunciation

Listen and repeat.

/b/ bare	/p/ pair
bowl	pole
back	pack
symbol	simple
cab	cap
bulb	pulp

Now listen and write the words you hear.

8 Role Play

Role play an interview between a journalist and a celebrity (real or imaginary). At each stage of the interview, the journalist asks follow-up questions using the present perfect continuous and notes down the celebrity's answers.

Journalist	Celebrity
Ask what the celebrity has been doing recently.	
	Talk about your recent work.
Ask what else he/she has been doing.	
	Talk about leisure activities.
Ask about his/her home and family.	
	Reply.
Ask about his/her relationships.	
	Reply.
Thank the celebrity for talking to you.	

What have you been doing recently?
I've been working on a new film.

Now change roles.

9 Writing

Write an article about the celebrity you interviewed using the present perfect continuous.

The famous actor Carol Charisma has been working hard recently. She's been making a film for six months, and she's been rehearsing a new play since last week.

2 CREATIVITY

2 I've been hoping …

Present perfect simple and continuous
Talking about recent events

1 Opener

Have you ever wanted to be in a film or on TV? One way is to become an 'extra' – someone you see in the background in a film. What do you think life is like as an extra?

2 Reading

Read and listen to the texts.

An EXTRAordinary job!

Believe it or not, Britain's most popular temporary job is being a film extra. So what's it like, and how do you find work? You start at 6 or 7am and work a nine or ten-hour day. But most of the time is spent waiting for things to happen, so be prepared to get cold, hungry and bored! Listen carefully to any instructions about how to move or look because there may be several 'takes' for each scene and you will have to do exactly the same thing each time. You may catch sight of some stars – but no autographs or photographs! To get work, you need to join an agency, which will charge 15% of the £75 or so a day you are paid. And there are more extras than jobs – many extras only work a few days a month or even a year. But in what other job can you work with a big Hollywood name and see yourself on screen a year later?

3 Comprehension

Complete with *How*, *What*, *When*, *Where*, or *Who*. Then answer the questions.

1. … do extras usually begin work?
2. … has Anastasia been doing every morning?
3. … hasn't had a job yet this year?
4. … enjoyed a screen kiss?
5. … was Den's first job last year?
6. … is surprised that others haven't had much work?
7. … is Frankie working today?
8. … has had lots of job offers?
9. … has been working on a spy film?
10. … much are extras paid?
11. … have people been calling a lot this week?
12. … do you get a job as an extra?

The EXTRAS Web Forum

TOPIC: How much work have you had this year?

17.44
I've only had two jobs so far and they were both commercials. There seems to be very little work about. Last year my first job was in February – a football film. Freezing! What's it been like for others? **Den**

19.15
I've been working on the new Bond movie this week. It's good money but there's a lot of hanging about as usual. We're on location today and we've been waiting for them to start for nearly six hours. They've been trying to get the lighting right, but every time they do it starts raining! **Frankie**

20.11
It does seem quiet. I've been calling the agencies first thing every morning but haven't had any work. Last year was very different – my best job was doubling for Penelope Cruz, so I had to kiss Martin Freeman, which was rather nice. **Anastasia**

23.50
I've been hoping to get something since I joined the agency at Christmas. But no luck yet. **Jon**

04.18
That's odd! My phone's been ringing non-stop this week (not when I'm on set of course!) and I've had plenty of offers. But some of the work has been quite badly paid. **Nicky**

UNIT 2

4 Grammar

Complete.

Present perfect simple and continuous
Some of the work _____ _____ quite badly paid.
I _____ only _____ two jobs so far.
The present perfect simple is used to describe a completed action or series of actions.

I _____ _____ _____ on the new Bond movie.
I _____ _____ _____ the agencies every morning.
The present perfect continuous is used to describe an action which continues up to now. It is also used for a repeated series of actions.

We use the present perfect simple to focus on *how many*.
I _____ _____ plenty of offers.
We use the present perfect continuous to focus on *how long* when talking about continuous temporary activities.
My phone _____ _____ _____ all week.

➡ Check the answers: Grammar Summary page 110

5 Grammar Practice

Complete with the present perfect simple or continuous.

From ex-teacher to extra!

Ex-teacher, 34-year-old Adrian Jenkins __1__ (make) a successful career as an extra and __2__ (appear) in more than 40 feature films and TV programmes. 'I __3__ (work) as an extra for over five years now and I __4__ (never be) bored. For the last two days I __5__ (do) a commercial for a bank – that finishes tomorrow. After that I don't know – something will turn up. I __6__ (just change) my agency and the new agency __7__ (work) really hard to find me jobs. They __8__ (show) my photo to lots of directors and as a result I __9__ (have) plenty of offers. So you can see that I __10__ (not sit) around at home watching daytime TV – even if I am in some of the programmes!'

6 Vocabulary

Find these words and phrases in the lesson, and match them with their definitions.

Film-making
agency   commercial   double *v*   feature film
on location   on screen   on set   take *n*

1 section of a film which is recorded without stopping
2 in the cinema or on TV
3 act in the place of another actor in a film
4 business that helps people find work
5 where a film is shot, often in a studio
6 advertising film
7 where a film is shot, not in a studio
8 long film made for the cinema

7 Pronunciation

🎧 Listen and check your answers to exercise 6. Repeat the words and mark the stress.

8 Speaking

Make lists of five things you've always wanted to do and have done this year, and of five things you've been looking forward to doing but haven't done yet. Think about:

books to read   films to see   places to visit
activities to do   food to try   things to get
people to meet   skills to learn   things to do better

Compare your lists with another student and discuss them.

> You've always wanted to get up early and watch the sun rise, and you did it last Sunday.
>
> I've been looking forward to learning to drive. And I'm going to start lessons next week!

9 Writing

Look at the lists you made in exercise 8. Write a paragraph comparing your lists with another student's.

2 CREATIVITY

3 I'd been reading books for a long time

Past perfect simple and continuous
Talking about a sequence of past events

Philip Pullman, storyteller

'Stories are the most important thing in the world. Without stories, we wouldn't be human beings at all.'

Philip Pullman is the author of the award-winning and best-selling *His Dark Materials* trilogy. The three books follow the progress of a young girl called Lyra and her friend Will on their journey into unknown worlds. *His Dark Materials* is much more than an adventure story – it's about growing up, or innocence and experience, and it explores the major themes of truth, love and death.

Pullman himself spent a great deal of his childhood travelling abroad because both his father and stepfather were pilots in the Royal Air Force. As a child he went on several long sea voyages and he lived in Africa and in Australia. 'Before I was 11 I had been to eight different schools.'

'In Australia I made a great discovery. TV hadn't reached Australia yet, but everyone listened to the radio. I remember listening to gangster serials, and cowboy serials, and best of all – Superman! When I first saw a Superman comic, it changed my life. I'd been reading books for a long time, but I'd never known comics before. Soon afterwards I discovered Batman too, whom I loved even more.'

Pullman started writing his first novel the day after he had finished his final exams at Oxford University. 'I discovered after about an hour that it was much harder than I'd expected. It still is! I found that the amount I could write comfortably every day was about three pages, so that's what I've done ever since.'

Before he became a full-time writer, Pullman had been teaching for many years. 'What I enjoyed most in that difficult and valuable profession was telling stories, telling folk tales and ghost stories and Greek myths, over and over, until I knew them as well as I knew my own life.' He had always loved telling stories – as a schoolboy he had entertained his friends by reading ghost stories to them, or by making up his own.

One day he was delighted to get a letter which had arrived at his door even though the writer didn't know his address. The envelope said 'Philip Pullman, The Storyteller, Oxford.'

'I couldn't ask for anything better,' he said.

1 Opener

Who is the most popular writer of novels for teenagers in your country? Who is your favourite author?

2 Reading

Read and listen to the text.

3 Comprehension

True, false, or no information? Correct the false sentences.

1. *His Dark Materials* is simply an adventure story.
2. Philip Pullman travelled to South Africa when he was a child.
3. He hadn't read any comics before he went to Australia.
4. He liked Superman more than Batman.
5. He started writing his first novel before he'd finished his final exams.
6. Writing a novel was easier than he had expected.
7. He still writes about three pages every day.
8. He had been teaching in secondary schools before he became a full-time writer.
9. As a schoolboy, he had made up stories.
10. He's very happy to be known as a storyteller.

4 Grammar

Complete.

Past perfect simple and continuous

Past perfect simple Past simple NOW

Past perfect continuous – – – →

Before I **was** 11 I **had been** to eight different schools.
It _____ (be) much harder than I _____ _____ (expect).
TV _____ n't _____ (reach) Australia yet.
I _____ _____ _____ (read) books for a long time, but I _____ never _____ (know) comics before.
Before he _____ (become) a full-time writer, Pullman _____ _____ _____ (teach) for many years.

We use the past perfect to describe the earlier of two past events. We use the _____ _____ _____ to talk about a continuous or repeated earlier activity.

➡ Check the answers: Grammar Summary page 110

5 Grammar Practice

Complete with past simple and past perfect tenses, using the past perfect continuous where possible.

1. By the time he _____ (be) 11, Philip Pullman _____ (be) on several sea voyages.
2. He _____ (read) books for years before he _____ (discover) comics.
3. He _____ (come) across Batman after he _____ (discover) Superman.
4. After he _____ (write) a couple of novels for adults, he _____ (start) writing for children.
5. The ideas for some of his novels _____ (come) from plays he _____ (create) for his school pupils.
6. He _____ (tell) stories ever since he _____ (be) a child.

6 Speaking

Look at the picture. Say what had been happening before the girl's boyfriend arrived in the café. Talk about the girl, her boyfriend, the artist and the waiter using these verbs in the past perfect continuous.

do draw drink eat look
read run shop wait wash

> The girl had been reading a book.

7 Listening

🎧 Listen to a short biography of another best-selling author and complete the information in the chart.

Roald Dahl

1916	Born in _____. Norwegian parents.
_____	Left school. Started working for Shell in _____.
1938	Sent by Shell to _____.
_____	Second World War started. Dahl joined the RAF in _____.
1940	Crash-landed and badly injured. Spent _____ _____ in hospital.
_____	Fighter _____ in Greece and Syria.
1942	Sent to _____. Started writing stories for _____.
_____	*Over to You* published (first collection of stories).
1953	Married _____ _____ Patricia Neal. Had _____ children.
_____	Started writing books for _____.
1960	Family moved to _____.
1990	Dahl died on _____.

Now check your answers. Use the past perfect simple and continuous to link events.

> Dahl was born in Wales in 1916.

> After he'd left school in 1934, he started working for Shell …

8 Pronunciation

Count the syllables and mark the stress.

abroad adventure author childhood
discovery entertain envelope experience
innocence publish trilogy university voyage

■ *abroad*   2

🎧 Now listen and check. Repeat the words.

9 Writing

Find out information about another popular author. Make notes about the author's life, similar to the chart in exercise 7. Then write two or three paragraphs about him/her using the text in exercise 2 to help you.

JK Rowling, author of the best-selling Harry Potter books, was born in …

2 CREATIVITY

4 Integrated Skills
Telling a folk tale

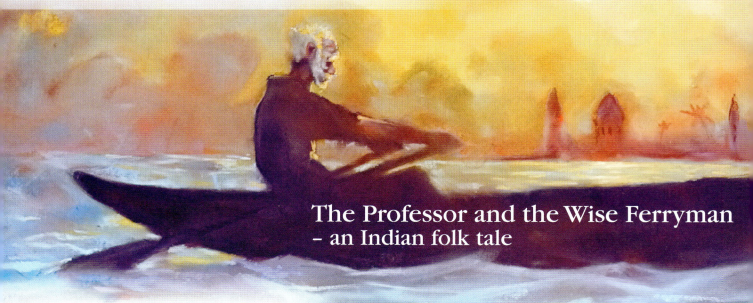

The Professor and the Wise Ferryman – an Indian folk tale

1 Opener

Every country has folk tales – stories which children often hear from their parents. For example, the Swiss story of William Tell, his son and the apple is told in many countries. What folk tales are there in your country?

Reading

2 Read and complete the text with phrases a–i.

a which he had never learnt
b and so had his grandfather before him
c and well-polished shoes
d so I haven't learnt any history
e but couldn't understand why people chose to live there
f the countries, mountains and rivers
g and think about things
h and had been doing it ever since
i and got the same answer

Now listen and check. Which words in the phrases helped you to complete the text?

3 Find the highlighted words in the text which mean:

1 important university teacher n
2 hurrying, moving very quickly v
3 great surprise n
4 almost not adv
5 with a bright surface adj
6 complained v

There was once an old ferryman who lived in a hut by the River Ganges in India. For as long as anyone could remember his family had rowed people across the river. His father had been a ferryman __1__.

Like all the people from his village the ferryman was poor. The money he made from the ferry was hardly enough to feed his family. He had taken over the job when he was a young boy __2__. Although life was hard, he never grumbled and was pleased to help his passengers.

The ferryman had learnt a lot about life by listening to his passengers. He had heard about life in the city, __3__. It seemed to him that city people spent all their lives rushing about with no time to think. The ferryman rowed slowly and was in no hurry. He had time to talk __4__. People said that he was wise and often asked his advice.

One day a well-dressed professor from the city with a shiny briefcase climbed into his boat. He was wearing a smart suit __5__. Slowly the ferryman began to row his passenger across the river. After a while the professor spoke.

'Have you studied any history?' he asked.

'No, sir,' said the ferryman.

'What!' said the professor in surprise. 'You haven't studied history? Aren't you proud of your country? Why don't you know any history?'

'Well, sir,' the ferryman replied, 'I've never been to school. I've been rowing people across the river all my life, __6__.'

'There's no excuse for not learning,' said the professor. 'And I suppose you haven't studied geography either.'

'No, sir,' the ferryman replied.

'Geography tells us about the world,' the professor said almost angrily. 'Don't you know anything about the world – __7__?'

'I haven't been to school, sir,' the ferryman replied. 'I don't know anything about these things.'

After a few minutes the professor asked if the ferryman had studied science, __8__. 'You've studied neither geography nor history, and you haven't heard about science!' he shouted in amazement. 'Scientists are the most important people in the world today. Look at me. I'm a professor of science. Do you see my briefcase? It's full of important books and papers. If you don't know about science, you don't know about the world. You have learnt nothing! And if you don't know anything, you might as well be dead.'

The ferryman looked sad. No one had ever spoken to him like this before. He felt terrible. There was so much knowledge hidden in books __9__.

4 Answer the questions.

1 What do we know about the ferryman and the professor?
2 What reasons did the professor give for learning history, geography and science? Do you agree?
3 Do you think the ferryman really knew nothing about history, geography and science? Why/Why not?
4 What do you think will happen next?

5 Linking words: *neither … nor …*

Find an example of *neither … nor …* in *The Professor and the Wise Ferryman*. Rewrite these sentences using *neither … nor …* .

1 The ferryman didn't have a suit or a briefcase.
2 The ferryman hadn't been to school or university.
3 The ferryman hadn't studied history or science.
4 The ferryman and the professor didn't know what was going to happen next.

6 Listening

Listen to the end of the story and see if you were right. Answer the questions.

1 What happened to the ferryman and the professor?
2 Does the story have a message? What can we learn from it?

Speaking

7 Discuss these questions.

1 Is what you learn in school more important than what you learn out of school? Why/Why not?
2 Which school subjects are the most and least important to you?
3 Some people are said to know a lot, some are said to be wise. What do you need to know to be wise? What does 'wise' mean?

8 Think about folk tales from your country and choose one. Tell each other the tale and say what it means – what its message is.

9 Writing

Write one of the folk tales from your country.

Learner Independence

10 Thinking skills: complete this chart each week to help you think about your learning.

This week the lessons were about:	
What I learnt was:	
This week I used my English to:	
This week I read these things in English:	
This week I made these mistakes when writing:	
A problem for me at the moment is:	
I would like to be able to:	
Next week I plan to:	

11 Word creation: add the suffix *-ment* to these verbs and use five of them to complete the sentences.

advertise   amaze   argue   arrange
equip   move   pay   treat

1 To her _____ she got a job as an extra.
2 I don't want to have an _____, so let's agree to disagree.
3 The agency took 15% of the _____ she received for the work.
4 He was an extra in a TV _____ for a new car.
5 As an artist he's interested in _____ and light.

12 Phrasebook

Find these useful expressions in Unit 2. Then listen and repeat.

So what's it like?   No luck yet.   That's odd!
It's a complete waste of money!   It changed my life.
It still is!   over and over
I couldn't ask for anything better.
There's no excuse for …   You might as well …

Which expression means …?

a That's strange.
b I'm still waiting for something to happen.
c many times
d Nothing has been the same since.

> **Unit 2** Communication Activity
> Student **A** page 106
> Student **B** page 116

2 CREATIVITY
Inspiration Extra!

PROJECT Class Magazine

Write a collection of articles for a class magazine.

1 Work in a group and make a list of articles about creative subjects which you could contribute to a magazine. For example, articles or interviews with interesting people (either real interviews with people in your school or town or imaginary interviews with famous people), reviews giving your personal opinion of the best and worst new films, TV programmes, books, gigs, music CDs, etc. Then choose two or three people or topics to write about.

2 Find out information for your articles from newspapers, magazines and the Internet and make notes:

> **Interview with or article about a person:**
> Why do you think the person is interesting?
> What has he/she done recently?
> What do you think readers would like to know about the person?
>
> **Review:**
> Describe the film, TV programme, book, CD etc.
> What is your personal opinion of it?
> Would you recommend it to readers? Why/Why not?

3 Work together and write the articles. Read them carefully and correct any mistakes. Find photos from magazines or newspapers to illustrate them. Show your magazine articles to other groups, and put them all together in a file to make a class magazine.

GAME Alibi

Yesterday evening, some time between 6 and 10pm, a valuable painting was stolen from an art gallery in your town. Police detectives want to interview two suspects who were together yesterday evening.

- Choose two suspects. The rest of the class are detectives.

  Suspects A and B
  You were together from 6 to 10pm yesterday evening. The detectives are going to ask you questions about your activities. Where did you go? What did you do? And after that? Work together to prepare your alibi in detail.

  Detectives
  Prepare questions to ask the suspects about what they did yesterday evening: ask about places, times and sequence of events. Where did you go? What time did you …? What did you do after you'd … ?

- Suspect B leaves the room. The detectives ask Suspect A questions and note down the answers.
- Then Suspect B returns and the detectives ask the same questions.
- Do the suspects' stories match? The detectives decide whether they are innocent or guilty!

SONG

Read and try to guess the missing words.

Spooky

In the cool of the evening
When everything is getting kind of groovy
You call me up and ___1___ me
Would I like to go with you and see a ___2___?
First I say no, I've got some plans for tonight
And then I stop and say all ___3___
Love is kind of crazy with a spooky little boy like you

You always keep me guessing
I never seem to know what you are ___4___
And if a girl looks at you
It's for sure your little eye will be a-winking
I get confused, I never know where I stand
And then you smile and hold my ___5___
Love is kind of crazy with a spooky little boy like you
Spooky

If you decide some day
To stop this little ___6___ that you are playing
I'm gonna tell you all the things
My heart's been a-dying to be ___7___
Just like a ___8___ you've been haunting my dreams
But now I know you're not what you seem
Love is kind of crazy with a spooky little boy like you
Spooky

🎧 Now listen and check.

UNIT 2

REVISION for more practice

LESSON 1

Write sentences about yourself using the present perfect continuous with *for* and *since*. Use these phrases to help you.

> learn English   use this book   come to this school
> play (*sport*)   watch (*TV series*)

My favourite sport is basketball. I've been playing basketball for ...

LESSON 2

Look at exercise 8 on page 23. Write sentences about things you've done this year, and about things you haven't done yet.

I've seen several films, but I haven't seen the latest James Bond movie yet.

LESSON 3

Look at your completed chart about Roald Dahl in exercise 7 on page 25 and write a paragraph about his life.

Roald Dahl was born in ...

EXTENSION for language development

LESSON 1

Read the texts about artists in exercise 2 on page 20 again. Now find out information about another living artist and write a similar paragraph about his/her work.

LESSON 2

Look at the *Extras Web Forum* in exercise 2 on page 22 again. Imagine you are a film extra. Write a posting to the forum saying what you have been doing this week.

LESSON 3

Answer these questions using the past perfect continuous. Use your imagination!

1 *Because he'd been speeding.*

1 Why did the police stop the motorcyclist?
2 Why did the man have a black eye?
3 Why was the girl crying?
4 Why was everything white outside?
5 Why were the boys' clothes dirty?
6 Why was the girl angry with her boyfriend?

YOUR CHOICE!

CONSTRUCTION   Past perfect simple or continuous?

Complete with the correct form of the verbs, using the past perfect continuous where possible.

Superman's first film appearance was in an animated cartoon series in 1941, but he __1__ (rescue) people for several years before that. The character __2__ (first appear) in comics in 1938. Superman, who __3__ (arrive) on Earth as a baby from the planet Krypton, was created by writer Jerry Siegel and artist Joe Shuster. They __4__ (come) up with the idea in 1933, but it __5__ (take) them five years to sell the story of their superhero.
   Superman __6__ (not be) around for long when Batman appeared in 1939, created by artist Bob Kane and writer Bill Finger. By the end of 1952, Batman and Superman __7__ (meet) each other in a Superman comic story. The two superheroes __8__ (live) separate lives, but now they regularly worked together in a series of adventures.

INTERACTION   It means a lot to me

- Work in a small group.
- Think about a favourite possession that means a lot to you. What's special about it? How long have you had it? How did you feel when you got it?
- Take turns to ask and answer questions about each other's favourite possessions.
  A How long have you had your guitar?
  B Who gave it to you?

REFLECTION   Present perfect continuous

Match the examples a–f with language functions 1–3.

The present perfect continuous is used to talk about …
1 a continuous or repeated activity which started in the past and is still continuing
2 a continuous or repeated activity which started in the past and has just finished
3 a completed continuous activity which has present results.

a There you are at last! I've been waiting for ages.
b We've been living here for 10 years.
c Her hair is wet because she's been swimming.
d I can't concentrate with this noise – they've been playing loud music all evening.
e He's been singing so loudly that he's lost his voice!
f It's been raining since I woke up this morning.

ACTION   Freeze frame game

- Work in a small group.
- You are in a film on video/DVD. In turn, perform an activity, but don't say what it is. After 5–10 seconds, someone says 'Pause!' and you're caught in freeze frame.
- The rest of the group asks Yes/No questions to find out what you've been doing.
  A Have you been riding a motorbike?
  B Have you been driving a car?

REVIEW UNITS 1-2

1 Read and complete. For each number 1–12, choose word or phrase A, B or C.

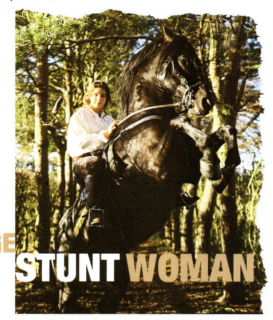

TEENAGE STUNT WOMAN

Angelina Jolie __1__ like the perfect horsewoman in *Tomb Raider 2*. But in reality, no matter how comfortable on a horse movie stars are, they all __2__ a little help – especially when the film __3__ dangerous stunts.

__4__ horses is something 19-year-old Camilla Naprous knows all about. She __5__ her father to advise movie stars since she was eight and it is a big part of her life now.

'I really enjoy __6__ on feature films like *Tomb Raider*,' Camilla says. 'I remember __7__ to Angelina's house every day for a month. She was a lovely woman and a great rider who wanted __8__ everything. I doubled her for one difficult scene in the film but she did all the other stunts herself.'

Camilla __9__ since she was able to walk – not surprising as her father was a well-known movie stunt rider. By the time she was 18 she __10__ performing in public for ten years and __11__ a member of her father's team of riders, 'The Devil's Horsemen'.

'Horses and movies,' Camilla says, '__12__ the most important things in my life.'

1	A looks	B is looking	C was looking
2	A need	B needs	C are needing
3	A includes	B has included	C is including
4	A Ride	B To ride	C Riding
5	A helped	B has been helping	C was helping
6	A works	B to work	C working
7	A go	B going	C to go
8	A to try	B try	C trying
9	A rides	B has been riding	C rode
10	A was	B has been	C had been
11	A become	B has become	C had become
12	A are always	B were always	C have always been

2 Write sentences using the infinitive or gerund of the verbs.

1. I enjoyed (apply) for jobs as a film extra, but didn't dare (hope) that I would get one.
2. I remember (get) the email asking me to a screen test. Of course I agreed (go).
3. I tried not (look) nervous during the screen test and managed (stay) calm.
4. I can't stand (be) disappointed and really didn't expect (get) the job. But I did.
5. I'll never forget (arrive) at the film studio the next day – Brad Pitt was there!
6. I pretended not (see) him, but it was no use.
7. The director wanted me (double) the role of Brad's co-star in a love scene. Half of me wanted to refuse (do) it – the other half wanted (see) what it would be like.
8. However, I dislike (be) looked at, so I decided (say) no. That was the end of my job as an extra!

3 Complete with the present perfect continuous of these verbs and *for* or *since*.

collect consider get talk use visit walk

A visitor to a Cambridge museum has smashed three hugely valuable Chinese vases. The 300-year-old vases had stood in a window on a staircase __1__ over 20 years. Nick Flynn, 42, slipped on the stairs and fell onto the vases. __2__ the accident happened, the museum __3__ the thousands of small pieces. They __4__ a digital camera to photograph the pieces, and they __5__ to experts about mending the vases. Mr Flynn was unhurt but angry when he got a letter from the museum asking him not to go there 'in the near future'. 'I __6__ the museum __7__ years,' said Mr Flynn. 'It's not my fault that I slipped.' The museum says Mr Flynn misunderstood the letter. 'We __8__ lots of calls __9__ the accident from journalists asking for his name – we wanted to protect him,' the museum director said. 'It was just an accident. People __10__ past those vases __11__ many years and this has never happened before. But __12__ the accident we __13__ how best to display the vases when they are mended.'

4 Complete with the present perfect simple or continuous of these verbs.

answer develop get give let
ring sell show start win work

Masa Tateno, 30, the exciting Japanese artist, __1__ his work for over ten years now, but in the last year his paintings __2__ to attract international attention. 'I __3__ my own style since I left art school,' he says. Now that I __4__ a few prizes people are beginning to notice me. Also I __5__ several paintings recently, which __6__ me confidence.' Tateno appeared on worldwide TV last month and since then he __7__ lots of media attention. 'It's hard' he says. 'Lots of times I __8__ on a picture when the phone __9__. Sometimes I __10__ and other times I __11__ it ring!'

UNITS 1-2 REVIEW

5 Complete with the past perfect simple or continuous of the verbs.

Many years ago in Greece there was a painting competition. The judge, who in the past __1__ (be) the best artist in the country, told two artists to paint a picture which was as true to life as possible in three months. The artists returned when they __2__ (finish) their pictures, each of which was covered with a curtain. The judge __3__ (invite) a large crowd, which __4__ (arrive) early in the morning. By midday they __5__ (wait) for several hours when the first painter pulled back his curtain. The picture was of a bunch of grapes and was so beautiful and lifelike that some birds which __6__ (fly) past tried to eat the grapes. Then the judge asked the other painter to pull his curtain back. But the second painter did nothing. The crowd and the judge were impatient because they __7__ (wait) for three months. So the judge tried to pull the curtain. But he couldn't. 'There is no curtain here,' he said to the crowd. 'It is a painting of a curtain.' One painting __8__ (fool) the birds and the other __9__ (fool) the people. Which painting did the judge choose? The second one. The crowd cheered because they __10__ (find) out who was the best painter. Or had they?

Vocabulary

6 Complete with the correct words.

chop/shop   clip/clap   clouds/crowds   cream/crime
diet/doubt   ferry/furry leaves/lives   maths/myths
needles/noodles scan/scene sneeze/snooze
taste/toast

1 She was very tired so she had a quick _____.
2 Some people _____ their key ring to their belt.
3 Greek _____ are stories about gods and heroes.
4 Chinese medicine uses a lot of _____.
5 There was no bridge, so they took a _____ across the river.
6 In an experiment a patient was given a brain _____ while having acupuncture.
7 It was a holiday and there were _____ of people in the street.
8 People often lose weight when they're on a _____.
9 First _____ the onions and then fry them.
10 In autumn there are lots of _____ on the ground.
11 Some people like _____ in their coffee but I prefer milk.
12 You need bread if you're going to make _____.

7 Match the verbs in list A with the words and phrases in list B. Then write sentences using four of the expressions.

A	B
1 beat	in touch
2 catch	with cheese
3 come	the eggs
4 keep	vitamins
5 react	up with an idea
6 skip	sight of something
7 sprinkle	a meal
8 take	to pain

8 Match these words with their definitions.

anaesthetic   domestic   gang   grater   heritage
margarine   mineral   racist   struggle   tribute

1 yellow substance which looks like butter
2 natural substance in food or in the earth, eg iron
3 try very hard to do something difficult
4 something that cuts food into very small pieces
5 important art, buildings, traditions and beliefs from the past
6 someone who believes that, eg, one skin colour is better than another
7 something you do or say to show you respect someone
8 about people's homes and family life
9 group of people who spend time together and may cause trouble
10 drug given before an operation to stop a patient feeling pain

9 Find the odd word.

1 dried   fresh   frozen   tinned
2 mineral juice   protein   vitamin
3 consist feel   smell   taste
4 boil   roast   cook   fry
5 fake   false   natural   synthetic
6 agency   commercial   feature film   TV series
7 bronze   gold   iron   wood
8 comic   ghost story   folk tale   myth

PROGRESS CHECK

Now you can ...

1 Talk about food and drink
2 Describe objects and say what they are for
3 Describe a sequence of events
4 Talk about illness and medicine
5 Talk about activities which continue up to now
6 Talk about recent events
7 Talk about a sequence of past events

Look back at Units 1 and 2 and write an example for 1–7.

1 Margarine contains less fat than butter.

How good are you? Tick a box.

★★★ Fine ☐   ★★ OK ☐   ★ Not sure ☐

Not sure about something? Look back through the lesson again.

3 SCIENCE AND DISCOVERY

1 Light travels incredibly fast

Comparison of adverbs
Adverbs of degree
Position and order of adverbial phrases
Describing and comparing the way things happen

1 Opener

Have you heard of the Big Bang?
What was it and when did it happen?

2 Reading

Read and answer the quiz.

QUIZ How much do you know about the world you live in?

1. Approximately how old is the universe?
   A 13.7 billion years. B 13.7 million years.
2. Which travels faster?
   A Light. B Lightning.
3. When did life on earth begin?
   A Four billion years ago. B Four million years ago.
4. Which began later?
   A Life on land. B Life in the sea.
5. Which distance is further?
   A From New York to Moscow. B From the surface to the centre of the Earth.
6. Where does the Earth rotate most quickly?
   A At the Equator. B At the North Pole.
7. Which contains a higher percentage of water?
   A A potato. B A human.

3 Comprehension

 Read and listen to *What on Earth?*, and check your answers to the quiz. How well did you do?

What on Earth?

Scientists disagree about exactly when the Big Bang, which created the universe, happened. But we know that it was between ten and twenty billion years ago. The universe has been expanding extremely rapidly ever since, and is a million million million million miles across. We can also measure distances in space in light years, the distance travelled in one year at the speed of light. And light travels incredibly fast! The speed of light is an amazing 300,000 kilometres a second. Lightning also travels really quickly and can heat the air around it to 28,000°C. But it travels more slowly than light, up to 150,000 kilometres a second.

The Earth itself is four and a half billion years old and scientists believe that life began suddenly in the sea soon after that. Life developed extremely slowly after this quick start. It was only four hundred million years ago that organisms began to breathe oxygen and live on land. People believe that apes started to walk on two feet between three and seven million years ago. However, we can say more accurately that humans appeared on Earth two million years ago.

It's believed that the Earth weighs an astonishing six billion trillion tonnes. And at 6,380 kilometres, the distance from the surface of the Earth to the centre is nearly as far as from New York to Moscow. The Earth rotates most quickly at 1,675 kilometres an hour at the Equator, more slowly at about 900 kilometres an hour in Paris and London, and doesn't rotate at all at the exact North or South Pole.

Perhaps we ought to call our planet Water, because most of its surface is ocean. And animals and plants are largely made up of water – a tomato is 95% water, a potato 80% and a human 65%.

4 Grammar

Complete.

> **Comparison of adverbs**
> Lightning travels _____ slowly than light.
> Which began _____: life on land or in the sea?
> Where does the Earth rotate _____ quickly?
>
> Adverbs ending in -ly take *more/most*. Adverbs with the same form as adjectives add *-er/-est*.
>
> **Irregular forms**
> well   better   _____
> badly worse   worst
> far   further furthest
>
> **Adverbs of degree**
> *quite really extremely incredibly*
> The universe has been expanding _____ rapidly.
> Lightning also travels _____ quickly.
>
> **Position and order of adverbial phrases**
> Life began **suddenly** *in the sea* after that.
>   **Manner** → *Place* → **Time**
>
> ➡ Check the answers: Grammar Summary pages 110 – 111

5 Grammar Practice

Complete with the correct adverbs.

1. Since the Big Bang the universe has been getting bigger _____ _____. (incredible/quick)
2. Light travels _____ than lightning. (fast)
3. We know _____ when humans appeared than when apes first walked. (exact)
4. The Earth rotates _____ at the Equator. (rapid)
5. The Earth turns _____ as you move _____ away from the Equator. (slow, far)
6. Tomatoes are almost _____ made up of water. (complete)

6 Grammar Practice

Put the adverbial phrases in the correct order.

1. The Big Bang happened …
   (over 13 million years ago/suddenly)
2. Life developed …
   (in the sea/for billions of years/slowly)
3. Organisms started to breathe oxygen …
   (400,000,000 years ago/on land)
4. Apes walked …
   (over 3,000,000 years ago/on two feet)
5. The Earth rotates …
   (in both London and Paris/at roughly the same speed)

7 Listening

 Listen and complete the text.

SPACEFLIGHT RECORDS

● The three astronauts who have been in space longest are all Russian: Sergei Krikalev with a total of _____ days, Sergei Avdeyev, 747 days, and Valeri Polyakov, _____ days.
● The two astronauts who have flown most often (_____ flights each) are Franklin Chang-Diaz and Jerry L. Ross, both from the USA.
● The first two spacewalks took place in 1965. In March Alexei Leonov left his spacecraft for _____ minutes and in June Edward White did the same for _____ minutes.
● The first moonwalk was from Apollo 11 on 21 July 1969, when Neil Armstrong and Buzz Aldrin walked on the surface of the Moon for _____ hours, 31 minutes and 40 seconds. Soon after, on 19 November 1969, Pete Conrad and Alan Bean left their spacecraft, Apollo 12, for a walk which lasted _____ hours, 56 minutes and three seconds.

Now make sentences comparing the astronauts.

> … was in space longest.
>
> Krikalev flew in space longer than …
>
> … have made the most space flights.
>
> Conrad and Bean walked on the Moon longer than …

8 Pronunciation

Listen and repeat.

> 13.7 billion years   four and a half billion years
> 300,000 kilometres a second   1,675 kilometres an hour
> 28,000°C   95%   six billion trillion tonnes
> two hours, 31 minutes and 40 seconds

9 Speaking

Ask three other students these questions and note down their answers.

● How fast can you say the alphabet backwards in English?
● How far can you throw a tennis ball?
● How high can you reach?
● How far do you travel to school?
● How early do you get up on Saturdays?

Now make comparisons between yourself and the other students.

> Sasha can say the alphabet backwards in 45 seconds. That's faster than me.
>
> I get up at eight on Saturdays. That's earlier than you.

10 Writing

Look at your notes from exercise 9. Write a paragraph using comparative and superlative adverbs.

Helena and Monika can both reach 2.2 metres, but Stefan can reach the highest.

3 SCIENCE AND DISCOVERY

2 What a fantastic sight!

What (a/an) …! so/such (a/an) …
Result clauses: so/such … that
Order of adjectives
Making exclamations
Expressing result

1 Opener

Read *Deep Sea Fact File*. Did any of the facts surprise you?

2 Reading

 Read and listen to scientist Petra Hardy's blog.

DEEP·SEA·FACT·FILE

97% of all the water on Earth is in the sea and the average depth is 3.86 kilometres. But until recently what was beneath the waves was a mystery. In 1930 Charles William Beebe and Otis Barton set a world record by descending 183 metres. Beebe wrote: 'As I peered down I realised I was looking toward a world of life almost as unknown as that of Mars.'

Thirty years later a two-man US Navy team in the *Trieste* dived 10,916 metres to the Challenger Deep in the Mariana Trench in the western Pacific, the deepest underwater point on Earth. It was so deep that they didn't expect to see any life, but when their submersible touched the bottom it disturbed a fish.

Greetings from a research ship in the Azores in the western Atlantic. One of science's great questions is why the sea doesn't get saltier when millions of litres of water evaporate every day. The answer lies 2,400 metres below me on the sea bed and I'm going down in a submersible to see it. I'm taking my laptop with me and will continue the blog underwater.

We're diving in a comfortable, spacious, modern Russian submersible. The three of us – the pilot, myself and another observer – are having such an amazing time as we go deeper and deeper! We're heading towards hydrothermal vents called the Rainbow Vents – they're a kind of underwater volcano.

We're over 2,000 metres down now, and everything is dark because no sunlight comes this far. Now we're near the sea bed. The pilot puts on the submersible's lights and we can see the Rainbow Vents. What a fantastic sight! It's so unexpected! The bottom is covered with 'chimneys' up to 20 metres high and from the chimneys comes black, white and clear water. The chimneys themselves are yellow, red, orange, green, blue and black – you can see why they are called rainbows.

The most incredible thing is that the water from the chimneys is at a temperature of 400°C, while the rest of the water down here is only 1°C. People had thought that the water was so cold that nothing could live at this depth. But thousands of shrimps, crabs, mussels and fish live around the chimneys. There are so many different kinds that I can't count them. I've just seen a beautiful small flat blue fish and I'm sure it's a new species.

What has this got to do with salt? Well, there are hydrothermal vents all over the world where new rock has pushed up the sea bed. Water goes slowly down through tiny cracks in the sea bed. Then a kilometre below the sea bed the water meets molten rock, is heated, and comes back up again. During this process the salt is removed. It's not quick though – it can take ten million years. And until 1977 no one knew that hydrothermal vents existed! What a discovery!

Today I've seen the vents for myself and after ten hours we're returning to the surface. It's been such an exciting dive that I haven't noticed the time. But now I'm starting to get hungry!

UNIT 3

3 Comprehension

Complete the questions with *What, When, Where, How* or *How many*. Then match the questions with the answers.

1 _____ is the research ship?
2 _____ is one of science's greatest questions?
3 _____ metres below the ship is the sea bed?
4 _____ people are there in the submersible?
5 _____ did the Rainbow Vents get their name?
6 _____ temperature is the water in the chimneys?
7 _____ far below the sea bed is the hot rock?
8 _____ is removed from the water in the hydrothermal vents?
9 _____ were hydrothermal vents first discovered?
10 _____ hours did Petra's dive last?

a 2,400. b 10. c 400°C. d Salt.
e In the Azores. f Three. g In 1977.
h They are multi-coloured. i One kilometre.
j Why doesn't the sea get saltier?

4 Grammar

Complete.

What (a/an) ... so/such (a/an) ...
_____ a discovery!
The three of us are having _____ an amazing time.
It's _____ unexpected!

Result clauses: so/such ... that
It was _____ deep _____ they didn't expect to see any life.
It's been _____ an exciting dive _____ I haven't noticed the time.

Order of adjectives
I've just seen a ___ ___ ___ ___ fish.
         Opinion Size Shape Colour
... a ___ , ___ , ___ submersible.
    Opinion Size Age Origin

Opinion → Size → Age → Shape → Colour → Origin

➡ Check the answers: Grammar Summary page 111

5 Grammar Practice

Read Petra Hardy's blog again and complete.

1 The sea bed was at such a depth that sunlight ...
2 It was so dark on the sea bed that the pilot had to ...
3 The chimneys are so colourful that ...
4 There are so many different species around hydrothermal vents that you ...
5 Until 1977 people thought the water on the sea bed was so cold that ...
6 The rock a kilometre below the sea bed is at such a high temperature that ...

6 Grammar Practice

Write these adjectives under the correct heading:

Opinion	Size	Age	Shape	Colour	Origin

average beautiful blue Brazilian Chinese
comfortable enormous fantastic flat French
giant great green grey huge Italian long
modern narrow new old purple red round
Russian small spacious Spanish square thin
tiny unknown white young

7 Pronunciation

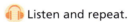 Listen and repeat.

Exclamations
What a fantastic sight!
What a discovery!
It's so unexpected!
We're having such an amazing time!
It's such a high temperature!
It's been such an exciting dive!

8 Speaking

Make notes about real or imaginary exciting events in your life and the life of someone you know. Tell another student about the events: say what happened and what the reactions were.

> I was out shopping and a TV crew wanted to interview me about clothes. I got so excited that I couldn't think of anything to say!

> I was with Sue when she heard that she had passed the exams. She was so happy that she cried.

9 Writing

Use your notes from exercise 8 to write descriptions of five exciting events.

3 SCIENCE AND DISCOVERY

3 It won't be cheap

Future review: future simple, present simple and continuous, *going to*
Talking about future events, schedules, arrangements and plans

1 Opener

You are going to read about space tourism. Which of these words do you expect to find in the text?

> astronaut   flight   helicopter   honeymoon
> lightning   orbit   passenger   spaceship
> speed   weightlessness

2 Reading

 Read and listen to the text.

3 Comprehension

Answer the questions.

1. What will be the highlights of the Virgin Galactic Spaceship flight?
2. What else will the $200,000 fare include?
3. Who are going to be among the first passengers?
4. How will ordinary travellers be able to afford space tourism?
5. The man says 'Forget it!' – what is he not going to do?

Would you like to be a space tourist? Why/Why not?

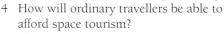

All you ever wanted to know about Space Tourism

People have been talking about space tourism ever since astronauts first landed on the moon. Will the dream ever become reality?

Believe it or not, we're counting down to the first space tourist flight. The Virgin Galactic Spaceship is due for lift-off soon, and there are rumours that Angelina Jolie and Brad Pitt are among those who have put their names down to fly.

How exciting! I'm going to book a ticket!

Hang on, it won't be cheap – each passenger will pay US$200,000 for the three-hour flight.

Over a thousand dollars a minute – that's extremely expensive!

Yes, but the space tourists will fly at three times the speed of sound, they'll experience four to five minutes of weightlessness and they'll be able to look down on Earth. 'Every passenger will have a spectacular view; they will have large windows and luxurious seats,' says Virgin boss Sir Richard Branson, who's going to travel on the first flight with members of his family. And the holiday will include pre-flight training and three days' luxury accommodation at the Virgin Galactic space camp. Initially, the spaceships will take off from the Mojave Desert near Los Angeles, but later there'll be a spaceport in New Mexico.

And what about people who don't have thousands of dollars?

I'm sure the cost of space flights will come down, and one day ordinary travellers will be able to go on trips into space. So perhaps our grandchildren will spend their holidays on the moon, and have honeymoons in a hotel orbiting Venus. But meanwhile, you can book a spaceship flight online at www.virgingalactic.com with a deposit of US$20,000.

Forget it! I've got to go – I'm flying to Florida today and I'm visiting the Kennedy Space Center tomorrow. The tour starts at 9.45am …

4 Grammar

Complete.

> **Talking about the future**
> We use the future simple (will/won't) to give information about future events and to make predictions.
> Every passenger _____ have a spectacular view.
> I'm sure the cost of space flights _____ come down.
> It _____ be cheap.
> _____ the dream ever become reality?
>
> We use the present simple to talk about schedules and timetables.
> The tour _____ at 9.45am.
>
> We use the present continuous to talk about fixed arrangements.
> I _____ _____ the Kennedy Space Center tomorrow.
>
> We use going to to talk about plans and intentions.
> Branson _____ _____ to travel on the first flight.
> I _____ _____ to book a ticket!

➡ Check the answers: Grammar Summary page 111

5 Grammar Practice

Complete with the most suitable form of the verbs: future simple, present simple or present continuous.

1. Each Virgin Galactic spaceship _____ (carry) six passengers.
2. I'm scared of flying, so I definitely _____ (not be) a space tourist.
3. My friends _____ (fly) to Florida at the weekend.
4. Their flight _____ (depart) at 6pm on Saturday.
5. They've booked a hotel in Orlando and they _____ (stay) there for a week.
6. Do you think lots of people _____ (travel) in space?
7. Where _____ (you go) for your next holiday?
8. Can you tell me what time the tour _____ (end)?

6 Listening

 Listen and complete the tour schedule with the times.

Kennedy Space Center Tour

9:45 am	Arrive at the Kennedy Space Center
_____ am	See an IMAX space movie
_____ am	Visit the Astronaut Hall of Fame and ride a spaceflight simulator
_____ pm	Meet an astronaut during lunch at the Space Center
_____ pm	Take the NASA bus tour, which stops at the International Space Station
_____ pm	Return to the Kennedy Space Center
_____ pm	Depart from the Kennedy Space Center

Now imagine you are going on the Kennedy Space Center Tour. Ask and answer questions about the schedule using the present simple.

> What time do we arrive at the Space Center?

7 Pronunciation

Complete the exclamations with cold, exciting, expensive, fast.

> It costs over a million dollars.
> That's extremely _____!
> It flies at three times the speed of sound.
> That's incredibly _____!
> The temperature is minus 30°C.
> That's terribly _____!
> We're going to meet an astronaut.
> How _____!

Now listen and check. Repeat the exclamations.

8 Speaking

Below are some predictions by a major British telecommunications company. Do you agree or disagree with the predictions? Say what you think about them.

A Do you think there'll be a hotel in space by 2017?
B Yes, it's possible. But I'm not going to stay in it because it'll be too expensive!

THE FUTURE IN SPACE

2013–2017
Hotel in space

2016–2020
Mining on moon

2020s
First manned mission to Mars
Space factories for commercial production

2030s
Space elevator to moon

2040s
Moon base the size of small village
Colony on Mars

From 2051
Contact with extra-terrestrial beings.

9 Vocabulary

Find these phrasal verbs in the text about space tourism, and match them with their meanings a–f.

1. come down
2. count down
3. hang on
4. look down
5. put down
6. take off

a. wait a minute
b. write someone's name on a list
c. fall or become less
d. opposite of land
e. 10-9-8-7-6-5-4-3-2-1!
f. drop your eyes

10 Writing

You are on a spaceship which has been away from Earth for ten years. Now you are returning to Earth and will land there tomorrow.

What are you going to do when you land? Write about your plans.

What changes do you think there will be on Earth?

3 SCIENCE AND DISCOVERY

4 Integrated Skills
Describing events and consequences

1 Opener

This lesson is about people who changed the world. Which people do you think changed the world?

Reading

2 Read *People Who Changed The World* and complete the text with six of the phrases a–h. There are two extra phrases.

a and to reduce environmental damage
b which led to his 'germ theory of disease'
c since the beginning of the century
d in the air and at sea
e by boiling and then cooling the liquid
f published in 1962
g which will be extremely difficult
h from England to France in 1899

Now listen and check. Which words in the phrases helped you to complete the text?

3 Find words in the text which mean:

1 disease that can pass from one person to another *adj*
2 idea which explains how or why something happens *n*
3 causing discussion and disagreement *adj*
4 chemicals used to kill insects *n*
5 effect *n*
6 damage caused to the air, water or land, eg by chemicals *n*
7 growing crops on farms *n*
8 someone who studies physics *n*
9 across the Atlantic Ocean *adj*
10 send out an electronic signal *v*

People Who Changed The World

The French chemist and biologist **Louis Pasteur** (1822–1895) made one of the most important discoveries in medical history. He discovered that there were germs called bacteria in the air which caused liquids to turn sour, so he developed the process called 'pasteurisation': killing the bacteria __1__. Because of Pasteur's research, most dairy products today are pasteurised. Pasteur then realised that most infectious diseases are caused by germs in the air, __2__. He used this theory to explain how vaccination worked and showed how doctors could prevent some illnesses by injecting weak forms of the disease. Pasteur's pioneering work has protected millions of people from disease, thanks to pasteurisation and vaccination.

The American writer and biologist, **Rachel Carson** (1907–1964) started the modern environmental movement when she wrote a controversial book about the destructive effects of pesticides on the chain of life. *Silent Spring*, __3__, is one of the few books that have changed the way people view the natural world. Its impact was so enormous that it was compared with Charles Darwin's theory of evolution. As a result, Carson was attacked by the chemical industry, but *Silent Spring* also caused a massive protest against environmental pollution. Consequently, the US government started to take action to control the use of pesticides in agriculture __4__. And thanks to Rachel Carson, there is now a worldwide movement to protect the environment.

The Italian physicist, **Guglielmo Marconi** (1874–1937) made the first ever transatlantic radio transmission on 12 December 1901. A transmitter in south-west England signalled the letter S – three dots in Morse code – and the signal was picked up in Newfoundland, 3,500km away. This achievement was so extraordinary that at first people didn't believe it. Marconi had already successfully transmitted a message over 50km __5__. But most scientists believed that radio waves would not follow the curve of the Earth and could, therefore, never transmit signals across an ocean. It was such a long way that it seemed completely impossible. Marconi proved them wrong. As a result of his achievement, we have seen the development of broadcasting, communications satellites, radar, the telephone and the Internet. Marconi's genius has also helped to save thousands of lives on land, __6__ – when the *Titanic* sank in 1912, an estimated 700 lives were saved thanks to SOS signals from a Marconi transmitter.

4 Linking words: expressing cause and result

We can use these phrases to express reason or cause.

> as a result of ...   because (of) ...   thanks to ...

We can use these words and phrases to express consequence or result.

> as a result   consequently   so   so ... that
> such ... that   therefore

Find examples of all these words and phrases in *People Who Changed The World* and notice how they are used.

5 Listening

There are ten mistakes in the text. Can you guess what they are? Then listen and correct the mistakes.

The English engineer **John Harrison** (1693–1776) solved one of the greatest scientific problems of his time. Ships sailing across rivers didn't know their exact position at sea because they couldn't measure longitude – how far the ship had travelled east-west round the sun. It was easy to work out latitude (position up or down the globe) by looking at the sky, but sailors could only guess approximate longitude by measuring the ship's direction and size. As a result, thousands had lost their lives at sea.

In 1714 the British government offered a prize of £20,000 (several hundred pounds in today's money) to anyone who came up with a solution. After many weeks of work, in 1759 Harrison succeeded in making a sea clock that told sailors the exact date at their port of origin. His clock was so accurate that it kept perfect time at sea. Thanks to Harrison's clock, soldiers could use the time difference to calculate longitude. For example: out at sea the moon is at its noon high-point but the London clock says 1pm, so there's a time difference of one minute. Therefore the ship must be 15 degrees west of London.

But Harrison was an old man when, in 1772, he finally received the prize money for solving the 'longitude problem'.

6 Speaking

Which of the people in this lesson changed the world the most? Tell each other your opinion and give reasons for your choice.

7 Writing

Find out information about another person who you think changed the world and make notes.

- What did the person do and when?
- Why was his/her achievement so important?
- What were the consequences?

Now write one or two paragraphs about the person. Use the texts in exercises 2 and 5 to help you, and some of the linking words and phrases from exercise 4.

Learner Independence

8

Thinking skills: look at this list of nouns for one minute and try to remember them all.

> satellite   astronaut   shrimp   spaceship   chimney
> damage   theory   distance   solution   impact

Now cover the list and write down all the words you can remember. Then compare your list with another student. Which words were easier to remember?

Nouns which refer to things you can see or touch are often easier to remember than abstract nouns – words for ideas, feelings or qualities. Try to associate abstract nouns with things you can see or touch, for example *damage – car*.

9

Word creation: make nouns ending in *-sion* or *-tion* from these verbs and use six of them to complete the sentences.

> act   create   decide   discuss   evolve   pasteurise
> permit   pollute   possess   produce   revise   solve
> transmit   vaccinate

1 Cars cause serious _____ in cities.
2 The class had an interesting _____ about the media.
3 My arm hurts because I've just had a _____.
4 You should ask the teacher for _____ to leave early.
5 Broadband _____ makes Internet use faster.
6 Everyone can take _____ to protect the environment.

10 Phrasebook

Find these useful expressions in Unit 3. Then listen and repeat.

> What a fantastic sight!   It's so unexpected!
> The most incredible thing is …
> What has this got to do with …?   Hang on.
> How exciting!   Forget it!   as a result   thanks to …

Now think of other situations where you could use each of the four exclamations.

'What a fantastic sight!' *Looking at Earth from space.*

> **Unit 3** Communication Activity
> Student **A** page 107
> Student **B** page 117

3 SCIENCE AND DISCOVERY
Inspiration *Extra!*

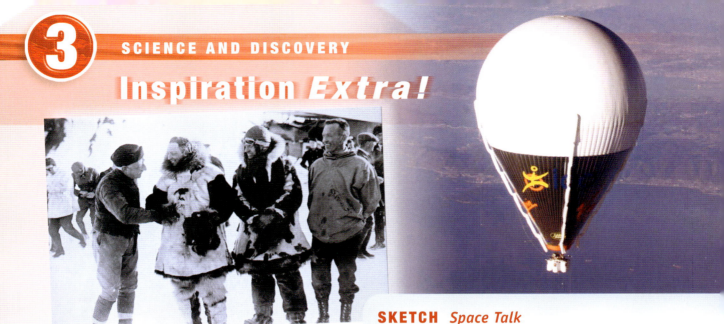

PROJECT *Exploration File*

Make a file about exploration on Earth, in the sea, in the sky, or in space.

1. Work in a group and make a list of recent and past explorers and expeditions. For example, think about expeditions to the North and South Poles, early attempts to sail to the Far East, flying around the world, or the first men on the moon. Then choose one or two explorers or expeditions to write about.

2. Find out about your chosen explorers or expeditions using books or the Internet. Make notes and copy or print pictures.

   > Where did they go, how, when and why?
   > What problems were there?
   > Were they successful?
   > What happened afterwards – what were the results of the expedition?

3. Work together and make an Exploration File using your notes and pictures. Read it carefully and correct any mistakes. Show your Exploration File to the other groups.

GAME *Mystery Word*

- Play in pairs. The aim is to discover the other player's mystery word.
- Student A writes down a word from this unit of four to six letters, and says how many letters the word has.
- Student B tries to guess the word by saying a word with the same number of letters.
- Student A then says how many letters are the same as in the mystery word and what those letters are. For example, if the mystery word is *flight* and Student B says *planet*, Student A replies 'Two letters: *l* and *t*'.
- The game continues until Student B guesses the word. If Student B hasn't guessed the word after ten tries, Student A wins. Then Student B writes down a mystery word.

SKETCH *Space Talk*

🎧 Read and listen.

CAPTAIN   What a great day, Number 1! Today we're going to break the world spacewalk record.

NUMBER 1   Excuse me sir, but don't you mean the space spacewalk record? After all we are in space, not on Earth. And what's all that equipment for?

CAPTAIN   Number 1. I know best – that's why I'm the captain. I need this equipment to show that we broke the record. I'll go first. Oh, no! I can't get through the door. Give me a push.

NUMBER 1   I can't, sir. We're weightless. There's nothing to push against, sir.

CAPTAIN   Put your back against the door so that you can push me out.

NUMBER 1   But sir, what will happen when you …

CAPTAIN   Push! There, you see, it worked! Now come and join me.

* * *

CAPTAIN   Right, Number 1. That's a new world record!

NUMBER 1   Yes, sir. Now it's time to get back in the spaceship.

CAPTAIN   Not yet, Number 1. We're going to set a record that no one can beat.

NUMBER 1   But sir, in a few minutes the computer will close the door and fire the rockets to return to Earth.

CAPTAIN   Oh, very well then. But I can't get through the door!

NUMBER 1   Let me get in first, sir, and I can pull you in.

CAPTAIN   Good idea, Number 1. There, you go in first. Now take my hands and pull.

NUMBER 1   Oh no, sir! The computer's closing the door. It's going to fire the rockets. I'll have to let you go. I'm sorry, sir. The next spaceship will be here in a week's time. Goodbye, sir!

CAPTAIN   Help! Help …

NUMBER 1   Spaceship to Ground Control. Can you hear me? Returning to Earth now. Captain is staying in space to attempt a new record.

Now act out the sketch in pairs.

UNIT 3

REVISION for more practice

LESSON 1

Look at the questionnaire and *What on Earth?* text on page 32. Write five similar questions about the text and ask another student to answer them.

1 *How big is the universe?*
   a) twenty billion miles across
   b) a million million million million miles across

LESSON 2

Choose six words from the blog in exercise 2 on page 34, and use your dictionary to help you write definitions. Ask another student to match your words with your definitions.

LESSON 3

Look at exercises 2 and 3 on page 36. Write five more questions about the space tourism text and answer them.

How much will each passenger pay for the Virgin Galactic spaceship flight?
$200,000.

EXTENSION for language development

LESSON 1

Look at *Spaceflight Records* on page 33. Write six questions about the text beginning with *Who, When, How long, What*, and *Where*. Ask another student to answer the questions.

LESSON 2

Look at the blog in exercise 2 on page 34. When Petra gets to the surface she phones a friend in the USA and describes her dive. Her friend asks lots of questions. Write the conversation between Petra and her friend.

Petra   Hi! I've just had such a fantastic experience.
Friend   Really? What have you been doing?

LESSON 3

Write about your future.
What are you doing next week? Write about your arrangements.
What are you going to do in the next five years? Write about your plans.
What else do you think you'll do in the future?

YOUR CHOICE!

CONSTRUCTION Order of adjectives

Put the adjectives in the right order.
1 The first submersible was Beebe's (round/small/uncomfortable) 'bathysphere'.
2 The *Alvin* is the (American/modern/round) submersible which explored the wreck of the *Titanic*, the (famous/old) passenger ship.
3 Around the hydrothermal vents there are (long/red and white/spectacular) worms, (pink/small/strange) fish, and (unusual/white) crabs.
4 By the hot vents there are also (black/giant/unknown) mussels and (5cm-long/white) shrimps.

REFLECTION so or such?

Complete.
We use _____ before *a/an* + _____ + noun.
It was such a deep dive.

We don't use _____ after _____.
It was a ~~so~~ huge ship.

_____ is followed by an adjective without a noun.
It was _____ dark that they didn't expect to find anything.

_____ can be followed by *a/an* + noun,
or by *a/an* + adjective + noun.
It was _____ a (big) surprise that she couldn't believe it.

ACTION Move in order

- Work in two groups of five or six.
- Each group chooses a different lesson from this unit, and then chooses a paragraph from the text(s). They copy the first few sentences out, each on a separate piece of paper.
- Group A gives their mixed up pieces of paper to group B, one to each student.
- The members of group B read their sentences aloud.
- Then they try to stand in a line to show the order of the sentences in the paragraph.
- When group B is ready, group A shows them the original paragraph. Then group B gives group A their mixed-up pieces of paper.

INTERACTION Fortune teller

- Work in a small group.
- Each student writes three questions to ask the fortune teller: one each about his/her life one, three, and ten years from now.
- One student plays the role of the fortune teller and the other students ask their questions. The fortune teller always replies in the same way.

Fortune teller: What do you want to know about your life three years from now?
Student: Will I be at university?
Fortune teller: Tell me the answer you want and it will come true.
Student: I want to go to university and study English.
Fortune teller: Yes, you will go to university and you will study English.

culture Your Culture

Every country, and often each area in a country, has its own distinctive culture. Here's a guide to help you create something which reflects the culture of your country or area. It could be a story, a song, a poem or a video. Follow the guide and learn how to get creative ideas and develop them.

Get inspired!

Brainstorming is a great way of getting loads of ideas in a short time. You can brainstorm on your own or in a group.
- Be clear about your aim – what kind of ideas are you trying to come up with?
- Anything goes – the sillier the ideas the better, because you never know where they may lead.
- Jot all the ideas down – a good way of doing this is on separate pieces of paper so you can re-arrange them afterwards.
- No criticism or evaluation – criticism blocks creativity.

Can't get started? Use an Ideas Box!

- Draw a chart with categories across the top and fill in as many options as you can for each category. Then mix and match options to form new combinations.
- So from the example below you could create a ghost story set in a theatre with a dancer and a pop star which begins with a phone ringing. What happens next?

IDEAS BOX

Kind of story	Place	Character 1	Character 2	Event
Thriller	Hotel	Police officer	Tourist	A car crashes
Science fiction	Theatre	Doctor	Teenager	A phone rings
Horror	Park	Robot	Pop star	There's an explosion
Ghost story	Shop	Murderer	Taxi driver	A stranger arrives
Romance	Train	Dancer	Child	Someone gets ill

Use a creativity notebook to plan and develop your ideas

- Always have it with you – you never know when inspiration will arrive!
- Use drawings as well as words to explain your ideas.
- You can write anything in your notebook: thoughts, feelings, or things you see or hear.
- Your mind is very creative while you're asleep, so keep your notebook by the bed. Note down your dreams and how you feel about them.
- When you're stuck for an idea, look through your notebook for inspiration.

Action! Start writing

- To plan a video, create a storyboard with drawings of the scenes and the dialogue underneath.
- When writing a song or poem, say the words aloud as you write them.
- In a story, always stop before the end of a paragraph. Then when you start again it's much easier to continue.
- Don't be afraid to show friends or family what you've written. Let them ask you questions about it. Don't be defensive in your answers.

Presentation

- Take care over the appearance of your work and check it carefully.
- Show or read out what you've written to someone whose opinion you value.
- You may want to post your work on a website or message board.
- Listen to any criticism and take notes.
- Don't take criticism personally – it's your work that's under discussion, not you!
- Finally, reflect on what you've done. Were there problems? Did you find solutions? What did you learn? How will you do better next time?

1 Vocabulary

Read the guide and match these words and expressions with their definitions.

1 anything goes   a react badly to criticism
2 jot down   b think about something carefully
3 block v   c everything is possible
4 mix and match   d put on the Internet
5 stuck   e prevent
6 be defensive   f make a quick note
7 take care   g put different things together
8 post on a website   h unable to do something
9 reflect on   i be careful

2 Comprehension

Answer the questions.

1 What should you do before you start brainstorming?
2 Why are silly ideas good in a brainstorm?
3 What shouldn't you do when brainstorming?
4 In what situation is it a good idea to use the Ideas Box?
5 What should you always keep with you?
6 What technique helps you to continue writing a story?
7 What's the first thing to do when you've finished writing?
8 What should you do after you've shown people your work and listened to any criticisms?

3 Listening

Your creative space is where you generate ideas, put them together and make them into something real. Look at the list below and listen to artist Andy March. For each item on the list, choose which alternative he prefers.

Your creative space

Think about where you work best. What helps you be creative?

- well lit or softly lit?
- noisy or quiet?
- cool or warm?
- alone or with others?
- space to move around or not?
- tidy or untidy?
- morning, afternoon, evening or night?
- music or silence?

How about you? Where do you work best? Compare your views with other students.

4 Writing

Use the guide to help you create a story, a song, a poem or a plan for a video. Share what you have created with the other students.

43

4 GETTING IT RIGHT

1 Some things won't have changed

Future continuous
Future perfect
Discussing possible future lifestyles

2020 Vision

Earrings which read our pulse rates and glasses which show videos, or a life expectancy of 120, and cats that glow in the dark? Different experts have different views on how we'll be living in 2020. Some things won't have changed much – people will still have to work, but they'll be working longer and retiring later. Other areas of our life will have changed completely.

Craig Cormick, of Biotechnology Australia, believes that people will live until they're 120 thanks to advances in medicine. 'The main difference between life now and then,' he says, 'is that doctors won't be treating diseases any longer.' Cormick sees a world where we'll be able to wipe out disease by eating a banana. 'We'll be growing crops with vitamins and vaccines in them to prevent health problems.'

'You'll also be able to change the colour of your cat or dog. We can already carry out operations to put genes into rabbits and fish and make them glow,' Cormick points out. 'So it will be perfectly possible to create a glow-in-the-dark cat or a designer dog.'

Nearly all researchers agree that wireless technology will have developed. Anything large enough to carry a microchip will have one. Scientists will have invented earrings which take our pulses, and glasses on which we watch videos. Instead of wristwatches, we'll be wearing gadgets which will combine the functions of a phone, camera, MP3 player and computer. In the home, household equipment will have improved – there'll be fridges which read the use-by date on milk cartons and order new milk when necessary. On the road, we won't have got rid of cars, but we will have keyless electric cars which we can talk to.

Will we get the balance right? Will we have created a bright new future, or will we all be living longer, but no more happily? Only time will tell.

1 Opener

Is it possible to predict the future? Here are some famous 'bad' predictions.

Radio has no future. Heavier-than-air flying machines are impossible. X-rays will prove to be a hoax.
Lord Kelvin, British scientist, 1899

There is not the slightest indication that nuclear energy will ever be obtainable. Albert Einstein, 1932

There will never be a bigger plane.
Boeing engineer after the first Boeing 247 flight, 1933

We don't like their sound and guitar music is on the way out.
Decca Records executive who missed out on signing the Beatles, 1962

What do you think life will be like in 2020?

2 Reading

Read and listen to *2020 Vision* and see if your predictions are the same as those of the experts.

3 Comprehension

Answer the questions.

1 What won't have changed in 2020?
2 Will people be retiring earlier in 2020?
3 What won't doctors be treating then?
4 How will food keep people well?
5 What idea is shared by most thinkers about the future?
6 What will we be wearing on our wrists in 2020?
7 How will fridges know when to order new milk?
8 What won't the cars of the future have?

UNIT 4

4 Grammar
Complete.

Future continuous
They _____ _____ _____ (work) longer.
Doctors _____ _____ _____ (treat) diseases any longer.
_____ we all _____ _____ (live) longer?

Future perfect
Scientists _____ have _____ (invent) earrings which take our pulses.
We _____ _____ _____ (get) rid of cars.
_____ we _____ _____ (create) a bright new future?

We use the future _____ to talk about events that will be in progress at a particular time in the future.
We can also use the future continuous to talk about future arrangements.
We use the future _____ to talk about something which will/won't have finished by a certain time in the future.

➡ Check the answers: Grammar Summary page 111

5 Grammar Practice
Complete these predictions with the future continuous or future perfect of eight of these verbs.

become   believe   create   invent   learn
live   retire   talk   watch   wear

By 2020
1 Scientists _____ the world's first designer dog.
2 People _____ to their cars.
3 Fridges _____ intelligent.
4 People (not) _____ from work earlier.
5 We _____ multi-function gadgets on our wrists.
6 People _____ videos on their glasses.
7 People _____ about 40 years longer than today.
8 But _____ we _____ to live together more happily?

6 Speaking
Interview two other students and note down their answers. Ask questions about what they will be doing, and what they will have done, in three months' time.

What will you be doing in three months' time?
Will you be …

- wearing the same clothes?
- listening to different music?
- texting the same friends?
- watching the same TV programmes?
- supporting a different football team?
- looking forward to the holidays?
- eating different food for breakfast?
- worrying about the exams?
- feeling happier than you are now?

If the answer is 'No', ask 'So what/who will you be …ing?'

What will you have done in three months' time?
Will you have …

- been on holiday? Where?
- learnt a new skill? What?
- saved some money? How much?
- been to a party? Whose?
- made a journey? Where?
- bought something new? What?
- given someone a present? What?
- done something you've always wanted to? What?
- done something you haven't wanted to do at all? What?

7 Vocabulary
How many of these phrasal verbs can you find in this lesson? Match the verbs with their meanings a–e.

1 carry out   a calculate
2 miss out on   b destroy
3 point out   c do a particular piece of work
4 wipe out   d fail to take the chance to do something
5 work out   e tell someone something they should know

8 Pronunciation
🎧 Listen and repeat this sentence, copying the stress and intonation closely.

Life in 2020 will have changed because of better medicine, later retirement, less disease, fewer health problems, wireless technology, more microchips, and improved household equipment.

9 Writing
Look at the questions in exercise 6 again. Write two paragraphs about yourself saying what you will be doing in three months' time, and what you will have done in three months' time.

45

4 GETTING IT RIGHT

2 Unless we take action now ...

First conditional with *if* and *unless*
Time clauses with *when, as soon as* and *until*
Talking about future possibility

1 Opener

Look at the photo. What does it show and what problem does it highlight?

2 Reading

 Read and listen to the text.

3 Comprehension

True or false? Correct the false sentences.

1. Air pollution will increase when carbon emissions decrease.
2. We will reduce the impact of global warming if we take action now.
3. We won't halt global warming if we stop flying.
4. If we travel by train, we'll only produce a quarter of the emissions of a flight.
5. If you fly from London to Montreal, you will produce 1.46 tonnes of CO_2.
6. We'll have to pay a carbon tax when we fly in the future.
7. Carbon offset projects will solve the problem of global warming.
8. The situation will improve if we all work together.

A Question of Balance

Global warming is no longer a threat – it is a reality. Most global warming has been caused by the production of greenhouse gases, in particular, carbon dioxide (CO_2). Whenever we turn on the TV, drive a car or take a flight, we add more CO_2 to the atmosphere. Today we talk to environmental campaigner Gina Freeman about carbon emissions.

Is it too late to do something about carbon emissions?	No, it isn't. And as soon as carbon emissions decrease, air pollution will decrease. But unless we take action now, we won't reduce the impact of global warming.
You're particularly concerned about the increase in air travel – why?	Air travel is a major source of carbon emissions. It's estimated that by 2020 it will be the single biggest cause of global warming. I believe that we won't halt global warming until we stop flying.
So what can we do?	Take holidays closer to home. If we don't travel so far, we'll reduce carbon emissions. And if we travel by train, we'll only produce 12.5% of the emissions of a flight.
But how do I visit my grandparents in Canada? I can't get there by train!	One solution is to 'offset', or balance, carbon emissions. For example, if you take a return London-Montreal flight, you will produce 1.46 tonnes of CO_2. If you pay an organisation to reduce CO_2 in the atmosphere by the same amount, you will offset your carbon emissions. There are several organisations which fund carbon offset projects.
What kind of projects?	For example, planting trees, which absorb CO_2 from the atmosphere.
So it will be OK for me to fly if I plant enough trees.	It's better not to fly at all. But if you can't avoid producing carbon, the next best thing is to offset it. In the future when we fly, we'll pay a compulsory carbon tax.
Will carbon offset projects solve the problem of global warming?	No, they won't. But the situation won't improve unless we all work together. And the future will look brighter when all governments agree to reduce carbon emissions.

4 Grammar

Complete.

First conditional
***if/unless* + present simple, future simple**
If we _____ (not travel) so far, we _____ (reduce) carbon emissions.
It _____ (be) OK for me to fly if I _____ (plant) enough trees.
The situation _____ (not improve) unless we all _____ (work) together.

***when/as soon as/until* + present simple, future simple**
In the future when we _____ (fly), we _____ (pay) a compulsory carbon tax.
As soon as carbon emissions _____ (decrease), air pollution _____ (decrease).
We _____ (not halt) global warming until we _____ (stop) flying.

➡ Check the answers: Grammar Summary page 111

5 Grammar Practice

Complete with the present or future simple form of the verb.

1 If we _____ (continue) flying so much, global warming _____ (get) worse.
2 People _____ (not stop) flying until train travel _____ (become) cheaper.
3 When flights _____ (get) more expensive, people _____ (use) other means of transport.
4 Governments _____ (have) to work together if they _____ (want) to reduce carbon emissions.
5 There _____ (be) serious climate change unless we _____ (take) action soon.
6 As soon as everyone _____ (take) global warming seriously, the situation _____ (improve).

6 Listening

Listen to three people talking to Gina on a radio phone-in programme and complete the chart.

Montse	Barcelona – _____
Purpose	_____
Distance	_____ km
CO_2 emissions	_____ tonnes

Adam	Warsaw – _____
Purpose	_____
Distance	_____ km
CO_2 emissions	_____ tonnes

Claudia	Rome – _____
Purpose	_____
Distance	_____ km
CO_2 emissions	_____ tonnes

Now check your answers with another student.

- Where does Montse want to fly to?
- Why does she want to go there?
- If she takes a return flight, how far will she travel?
- How much CO_2 will her flight produce?

How else could Montse, Adam and Claudia travel?

7 Pronunciation

Many English words are both nouns and verbs. The following two-syllable words have first-syllable stress when they are nouns, and second-syllable stress when they are verbs.

decrease   desert   export   import
increase   permit   produce   suspect

Mark the stressed syllable on the highlighted words in these sentences.

1 There will be a decrease in pollution when carbon emissions decrease.
2 Our problems increase with the increase in global warming.
3 The soldier deserted the army in the desert.
4 The UK imports a lot of food but also sells food exports.
5 The police suspect the money was stolen and are questioning a suspect.
6 You aren't permitted to work there without a work permit.

Now listen and check. Repeat the sentences.

8 Role Play

Role play a conversation between two backpackers about travelling.

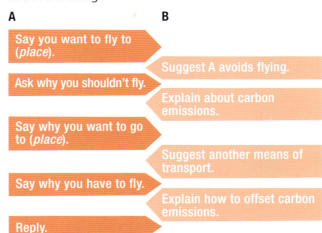

A
- Say you want to fly to (*place*).
- Ask why you shouldn't fly.
- Say why you want to go to (*place*).
- Say why you have to fly.
- Reply.

B
- Suggest A avoids flying.
- Explain about carbon emissions.
- Suggest another means of transport.
- Explain how to offset carbon emissions.

9 Writing

Complete this paragraph in your own words to explain why we should reduce carbon emissions.

Climate change will continue unless … . Global temperatures will increase if … . The polar ice caps will melt if … . The sea level will rise when … . Many islands will disappear if … . There will be droughts and floods unless … . As soon as there is a serious energy crisis … . We won't reduce global warming until … . We'll save the planet if … .

3 If you could choose …

Second conditional
wish/if only + past simple
Talking about imaginary or unlikely situations
Expressing wishes about the present

1 Opener

You are going to read about travel. Which of these words do you expect to find in the text?

> autograph guesthouse hostel
> microchip out-of-date overland
> performance satellite scenery
> traditional trekking

2 Reading

 Read and listen to the text.

3 Comprehension

Match the beginnings with the endings. There are three extra endings.

1 Hippies used to travel
2 It's still possible to travel
3 Vic has visited
4 He would stay
5 He wishes that people
6 He wouldn't stay
7 Nepal is a great place
8 Vic wouldn't take

a in London drank a lot of tea.
b his friends with him.
c to meet mad people in.
d Kathmandu at least once before.
e in Kathmandu if he was on a long visit.
f overland to Nepal but it isn't very safe.
g to Nepal lots of times.
h if you like walking long distances.
i in London lived at a slower pace.
j in the same hostel because of the garden.
k overland to Nepal in the 1960s.

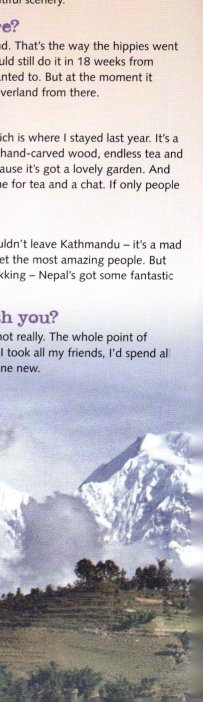

If you could choose …
Vic Gerrard, student, London

If you could choose … where would you be now?
In Kathmandu, in Nepal. It's a magical place with the world's highest mountains and some of the most beautiful scenery.

how would you get there?
If I had enough time, I'd travel overland. That's the way the hippies went there in the 60s. And in theory you could still do it in 18 weeks from London to Kathmandu if you really wanted to. But at the moment it would be safer to fly to India and go overland from there.

where would you stay?
I'd stay in the International Hostel, which is where I stayed last year. It's a traditional Nepali guesthouse – lots of hand-carved wood, endless tea and no TV. If I could, I'd go back there because it's got a lovely garden. And the guy who runs it has always got time for tea and a chat. If only people were like that in London!

what would you do?
If I was in Nepal for a short time, I wouldn't leave Kathmandu – it's a mad mixture of East and West, and you meet the most amazing people. But if I had more time, I'd definitely go trekking – Nepal's got some fantastic walking country.

who would you take with you?
I wish I could take all my friends! No, not really. The whole point of travelling is meeting new people. So if I took all my friends, I'd spend all my time with them and not meet anyone new.

4 Grammar

Complete.

Second conditional
If I _____ enough time, I _____ travel overland.
If I _____ in Nepal for a short time, I _____ (not) leave Kathmandu.
If you _____ choose, where _____ you stay?

wish + past simple
I wish I _____ take all my friends!

if only + past simple
If only people _____ like that in London.

We use the _____ conditional to talk about imaginary present or unlikely future situations.
We use _____ only or _____ + past simple to express a hope or desire for something in the present to be different. With the verb *be* we can use either *was* or *were* after *I/he/she/it*.

➡ Check the answers: Grammar Summary page 112

5 Grammar Practice

Complete with the correct form of these verbs.

be   can   have   know   look

1. It's raining. I wish I _____ my umbrella.
2. She feels lonely and miserable. She wishes she _____ at home.
3. He doesn't speak French. He wishes he _____ what they were saying.
4. I want to buy that jacket so much. If only I _____ enough money!
5. What a car! I wish I _____ how to drive.
6. She has to log on to the computer now. If only she _____ remember the password!
7. They love pets. They wish they _____ a dog.
8. She wishes her new boyfriend _____ like Brad Pitt.

6 Listening

🎧 Listen to a radio phone-in called *Secret Wishes* and complete the chart.

Name	Problem	Secret Wish: would like …
Karen	People don't talk to _____. They all talk to her _____.	to be an _____ _____.
Will	Spends all his time on _____. Feels sick when he _____ _____ _____.	to _____ _____ _____ _____.
Alice	Has too many _____. Never has time for _____.	to be _____ _____.
Sally and Frank	Their _____ aren't happy with their relationship.	them to _____ what they mean to each other.

Now tell another student what the callers' secret wishes are.

> Karen wishes she was …

Then tell each other what the callers believe. Do you agree?

> Karen believes that if she was … , people would … .

Listen to each caller's final words again. Can you complete the presenter's final sentence to each caller?

7 Pronunciation

🎧 Listen and repeat these sentences from exercise 6. Mark the stressed words.

> It's hard. Really hard.
> It takes ages. Absolutely ages.
> It sounds silly. Extremely silly.
> They get angry. Very angry.

8 Speaking

Interview three other students using these questions from exercise 2 and take notes.

> If you could choose …
> where would you be now?
> how would you get there?
> where would you stay?
> what would you do?
> who would you take with you?

9 Writing

Use your notes to write one paragraph each about two of the interviews.

If Sylvia could choose, she'd be in Spain now. She'd travel there in a minibus with lots of friends.

4 GETTING IT RIGHT

4 Integrated Skills
Debating an issue

1 Opener

What's happening in the photo above? What other issues do people protest about?

Reading

2 Read and complete the text with six of the phrases a–g. There is one extra phrase.

a who are too young to vote
b as has happened in anti-globalisation demonstrations
c and act
d and not on the streets
e and attacked the police
f who feel strongly about a particular issue
g and generated enormous publicity

🎧 Now listen and check. Which words in the phrases helped you to complete the text?

3 Find the highlighted words in the text which mean:

1 to do with right and wrong *adj*
2 take control of something (eg a plane) illegally *v*
3 protests in the streets by a large number of people *n*
4 extremely important *adj*
5 with changed genes *adj*
6 protests where people refuse to eat for a long period *n*
7 start fighting *v*
8 separation of black and white people *n*
9 well-balanced *adj*
10 protests where people take over a building *n*

DIRECT ACTION

For three famous people, Mahatma Gandhi, Martin Luther King and Emmeline Pankhurst, direct action was the only way to achieve their aims. They organised **demonstrations** and marches, **sit-ins** and **hunger strikes**, __1__. Largely as a result of their direct action, India became independent (1947), **racial segregation** ended in the USA (1964 and 1965), and women in Britain got the vote (partly in 1918 and fully in 1928).

'Happiness is when what you think, what you say, and what you do are **in harmony**.' *Mahatma Gandhi*

'Non-violence is the answer to the **crucial** political and **moral** questions of our time.' *Martin Luther King*

'We have to free half of the human race, the women, so that they ca help free the other half' *Emmeline Pankhurst*

So what are the arguments for and against direct action?

Supporters of direct action say that their methods get results. For example, they claim that anti-GM food demonstrations have made people aware of the danger of **genetically modified** food. And the world knows about the cruelty of whale hunting thanks to direct action against Japanese and Norwegian whaling ships. They also argue that direct action involves people who can't or don't vote in elections, such as those who are not registered or __2__. What's more, they say there is evidence that when the media report direct action, for instance a millio people on an anti-war march, politicians listen __3__.

Opponents of direct action point out that non-violent protest can lead to violen as protestors and police **clash**, __4__. They also claim that it is easy for small groups of protestors __5__ to '**hijack**' demonstrations. In addition, they argue th the whole point of a democracy is that we elect representatives to take decisions for us. If we feel strongly about an issue, we should make our case with the elect representatives __6__.

4 Do you agree with the ideas in the quotations from Gandhi, King and Pankhurst?

5 Linking words: adding information and giving examples

Find *also, in addition, what's more* in the text. Which two of these expressions usually come at the start of a sentence?

Find *for example, for instance, such as* in the text. Which one of these expressions can't come at the start of a sentence?

6 Listening

Listen to the debate. What is the result? Then listen again and complete the speakers' notes and the details of the voting.

Introduction
CHAIR Hello, my name's Jan and I'm chairing this debate. The motion today is: 'If necessary, we should take direct action to protect the environment'. Tim is proposing the motion and Helen is opposing it. Tim, would you like to start?

Tim's notes for the start of his speech

> What I'm going to argue is that direct action can be necessary. Firstly, because big business is so __1__ that even governments can't stop it. Secondly, because direct action makes people aware of problems, take __2__ for example. And thirdly, because it is often the only way to save an animal or the environment before it is __3__.

Helen's notes for the end of her speech

> What I've argued is this. Firstly, if __4__ looked after their own environment we wouldn't need direct action. Secondly, many protestors are better at getting __5__ than actually changing anything. And thirdly, that political action is better than direct action - the environment is too important to be left to __6__.

Conclusion
CHAIR Thank you both very much. Now you have one sentence each to sum up your argument before we have a vote.
TIM We've only got one world. Let's use direct action to save it.
HELEN Show by the way you live your life that you care about the environment.
CHAIR And now raise your hands to vote. Those in favour of the motion? Thank you. And those against? Thank you. The result is __7__ votes for the motion and __8__ votes against.

7 Speaking

Have a class or group debate. Choose a chair and two speakers. Look at exercise 6 again and use this structure:

The Chair says what the motion is and introduces the speakers. Each speaker:
1 says what he/she is going to say.
2 makes three points about the motion.
3 summarises what he/she has said.

The Chair asks each speaker for a one-sentence statement of their views and then there is a vote.

Choose your own topic or one of these:
- People should be able to vote when they are 16.
- Mobile phones are dangerous and should be banned.
- A woman's place is in the home.

8 Writing

Look at exercise 2 again. Write two paragraphs giving the arguments for and against the topic of your debate, or one of the topics in exercise 7.

Learner Independence

9 Thinking skills: learning new words and phrases
- Write the new words and phrases on cards and place them around your room.
- Walk around the room looking at each card. Say each word or phrase aloud and remember its position. Look at the cards the next time you move around the room.
- Take the cards away. The next day, walk around the room and try to remember what was on each card.

10 Word creation: add the prefix *anti-* or *non-* to these words and complete the sentences.

> fiction   iron   spam   terrorism   violent   war

1 The government has introduced new _____ laws.
2 This new shirt is great – it's completely _____.
3 I read some novels but I prefer _____.
4 Gandhi was in favour of _____ protest.
5 There was a large _____ demonstration on Saturday.
6 I've got a new _____ program for my computer.

11 Phrasebook

Find these useful expressions in Unit 4. Then listen and repeat.

> Only time will tell.   So what can we do?
> But what if I …?   If only people were like that …
> You meet the most amazing people.
> The whole point is …   It takes ages.
> It sounds silly.   What's more …

Now write a five-line dialogue using three of the expressions.

Unit 4 Communication Activity
Student **A** page 107
Student **B** page 117

4 GETTING IT RIGHT
Inspiration Extra!

PROJECT *Future File*
Make a file of your predictions about life in the future.

1. Work in a group and make a list of aspects of our lives that will probably be different in the future, for example: transport, environment, fashion, music, food, money, communications, education, work. Choose a year in the future, and choose two or three topics to make predictions about.

2. Make notes about each topic:

   What will we be doing in (*year*)?
   What will we have stopped doing?
   What will we have invented/discovered/built?
   Will our lives be better or worse because of these changes? Why?

3. Work together and make a Future File. Read it carefully and correct any mistakes. Draw pictures or use illustrations from magazines or newspapers. Show your Future File to the other groups.

GAME *Word square*

- Work in pairs.
- Write down as many English words as possible, using pairs of letters from anywhere in the square, eg FU + TU + RE, FU + LL.
- Score 1 point for a four-letter word, 2 points for a six-letter word, 4 points for an eight-letter word.
- The pair with the most points is the winner.

FU	EL	LL	CO	AL
TU	LI	FE	HE	AT
RE	AC	TI	ON	NA
PO	RT	ME	TE	ST
TH	EN	ER	GY	CA

SONG
Read and complete with these words. Four words are used more than once.

> cold   day   face   heart   lost
> make   play   say   see   take

Every Breath You Take

Every breath you take
And every move you __1__
Every bond you break, every step you __2__
I'll be watching you

Every single __3__
And every word you __4__
Every game you __5__, every night you stay
I'll be watching you

Oh, can't you __6__
You belong to me
How my poor __7__ aches
With every step you __8__
Every move you __9__
And every vow you break
Every smile you fake, every claim you stake
I'll be watching you

Since you've gone I've been __10__ without a trace
I dream at night, I can only see your __11__
I look around but it's you I can't replace
I feel so __12__ and I long for your embrace
I keep crying, baby, baby, please

Oh, can't you __13__
You belong to me
How my poor __14__ aches
With every step you __15__
Every move you __16__
And every vow you break
Every smile you fake, every claim you stake
I'll be watching you
Every move you __17__, every step you __18__
I'll be watching you

🎧 Now listen and check.

UNIT 4

REVISION for more practice

LESSON 1

Look at exercise 6 on page 45. Write sentences about one of the students you interviewed.

In three months' time, Jon won't be wearing the same clothes. He'll have bought some new jeans.

LESSON 2

Look at your completed chart in exercise 6 on page 47. Write sentences about Montse, Adam and Claudia.

Montse wants to go to Geneva for a skiing holiday. If she flies, ...

LESSON 3

Look at your completed *Secret Wishes* chart in exercise 6 on page 49.

What did the callers say? Write two or three sentences for each person.

Karen: People don't talk to me. I wish I was an only child. If my sister wasn't there, people would talk to me.

EXTENSION for language development

LESSON 1

Imagine yourself in ten years' time. Write two paragraphs saying what you will be doing and what you will have done.

In ten years' time, I'll be working ...

LESSON 2

Complete these sentences about yourself.

1 When I leave school, I …
2 If I go to university, I …
3 … unless I work hard.
4 As soon as I have enough money, …
5 I won't get married until …

LESSON 3

Imagine you're alone in a strange place with no map or mobile phone. You're hungry and thirsty but you don't have any money. Write sentences:

I wish/If only …   If I …, I would(n't) …

I wish I wasn't alone. If I wasn't alone, I wouldn't feel so nervous.

YOUR CHOICE!

CONSTRUCTION   Conditional sentences with *if* and *unless*

Rewrite the sentences with the verbs in the negative.

1 You won't catch the train if you don't run.

1 You'll catch the train if you run.
2 I'd buy a car if I passed my driving test.
3 We'll have a picnic if the weather is fine.
4 They'll see the Pyramids if they go to Cairo.
5 He'd have Greek lessons if he went to Greece.
6 I'll phone you if I need help.
7 She'll go to the party if she feels better.
8 They'd call the police if they were really worried.

Now rewrite the sentences using *unless*.

1 You won't catch the train unless you run.

REFLECTION   Present or past?

Complete the rules and examples.
We form the future continuous with *will/won't be* +_____ participle.
This time tomorrow, she'll be on a plane. She'll _____ _____ to Australia!
We form the future perfect with *will/won't have* + _____ participle.
I'm sorry, but I won't _____ _____ my homework by tomorrow.
In first conditional sentences, the verb in the *if* clause is in the _____ tense.
If you _____ at people, they'll smile back at you.
In second conditional sentences, the verb in the *if* clause is in the _____ tense.
We wouldn't be lost if we _____ a map.

ACTION   Mime game

- Work in a small group.
- Take turns to choose a word from Unit 4. Say the number of letters in the word, but don't say what it is! Then mime words which begin with each letter in your chosen word. For example, if your word is *COAL*, you could mime *Cat*, *Open*, *Angry*, *Love*. You can make noises, but don't say anything.
- The rest of the group guess and write down each letter until they have the complete word.

INTERACTION   *I wish …*

- Work in a small group.
- Tell each other about:
  something you wish you could do.
  something you wish you had.
  something you wish you didn't feel.
- Explain why you wish these things and answer other students' questions.

53

REVIEW UNITS 3–4

Grammar

1 Read and complete. For each number 1–10, choose word or phrase A, B or C.

EXPANDING CITIES

This boy lives in Mumbai, India, where an estimated 300 people arrive every day from the countryside. They come to look for work. But they also need somewhere to live. While Mumbai is expanding really quickly, other cities are growing even __1__. Where are all these new arrivals __2__? Until we take this question seriously, the problem __3__ worse.

Every day almost 180,000 people around the world move into cities from the countryside – that's about 70 million people a year. A recent report predicts that two billion more people __4__ to cities by 2030. __5__ something is done, up to half of these __6__ in the worst kind of housing: slums. In 2005 one billion people were living in slums worldwide – about a third of the people who live in cities. By 2030 it is predicted that a further billion __7__ in slums.

If people were more aware of the situation, they __8__ their governments to act. But poor housing receives little media attention. If only the TV and newspapers __9__ as much attention to world poverty as they give to sport. Until they __10__, the situation can only get worse.

1	**A** more rapid	**B** more rapidly	**C** rapid
2	**A** live	**B** living	**C** going to live
3	**A** will get	**B** is getting	**C** gets
4	**A** have moved	**B** are moving	**C** will have moved
5	**A** Unless	**B** As long as	**C** If
6	**A** live	**B** will live	**C** will have lived
7	**A** live	**B** are living	**C** will be living
8	**A** will get	**B** would get	**C** will have got
9	**A** gave	**B** give	**C** are giving
10	**A** are doing	**B** do	**C** will do

2 Complete with the correct adverbs, using the information in *Expanding Cities* where necessary.

1. The number of new arrivals in Mumbai has been growing ____ ____. (incredible/quick)
2. But other cities are expanding even ____ than Mumbai. (fast)
3. We must take this problem ____ than we do. (serious)
4. 'Which city in Africa is growing ____?' 'Lagos.' (rapid)
5. Nearly half the people of Jakarta, the capital of Indonesia, are living ____ ____ (extreme/miserable) in slums.
6. The media could be ____ at informing people about poor housing. (good)

3 Complete with *so* or *such* and match the beginnings with the endings.

1. The sea bed is ____ dark that
2. Submersibles are ____ expensive things to build that
3. The water around a 'chimney' is ____ different from the rest of the ocean that
4. The molten rock deep in the Earth is ____ hot that
5. Hydrothermal vents are ____ a recent discovery that

a. we still don't know how many new species there are around them.
b. submersibles need very thick walls and windows.
c. the animals that live around it are unique.
d. there are still only a few of them in the world.
e. submersibles need to have powerful lights.

4 Complete with the most suitable form of the verbs: future simple, present simple or present continuous.

One day, spaceships __1__ (fly) from Europe to Australia in half an hour. People __2__ (have) conversations like this:

KIM   What __3__ (you/do) this afternoon?
CATHY Oh, I __4__ (fly) to Australia after lunch on one of the new spaceships.
KIM   When __5__ (it/leave)?
CATHY At three o'clock and it __6__ (get) there at half past three our time.
KIM   But what __7__ (be) the time in Australia?
CATHY Er, half past midnight.
KIM   So all the shops __8__ (be) closed and everyone __9__ (be) asleep.
CATHY I know. But I __10__ (only go) for the ride. I __11__ (come) back on the next flight.
KIM   And when __12__ (that/leave)?
CATHY At 1am Australia time. So it __13__ (arrive) back here at half past four our time.
KIM   I see. So what __14__ (do) this evening?

5 Complete with the future continuous or future perfect of the verbs.

- Louis Pasteur's theory of germs is ridiculous fiction. Soon we __1__ (inject) ourselves with diseases in order to get better! Whatever next!
  French professor, 1872.
- By the time he is 70 the average American __2__ (eat) 2,400 animals – 2,287 chickens, 70 turkeys, 31 pigs and 12 cows.
- The average teenager __3__ (eat) his or her own weight in additives – things added to food to make it look or taste good – by the time she or he is 17.
- The 'telephone' has too many problems for us to take it seriously. In 100 years' time we __4__ (still send) messages by hand.
  US company executive, 1876.
- Worldwide, the number of robots in people's homes __5__ (pass) twenty million by 2020.
- We __6__ (not use) planes to fight wars in the future – they are just interesting things to play with.
  French general, 1898.

UNITS 3-4 REVIEW

6 Complete with the past simple of the verb or *would*, and answer the questions for yourself.

Everyday nightmares
1 What _____ (you/do) if you _____ (drop) your mobile down the toilet?
2 If the police _____ (arrest) you, who _____ (you/phone) from the police station?
3 How _____ (you/get) home if you _____ (not have) enough money for the bus?
4 If you _____ (have to) choose, which _____ (you/give up): being able to see or being able to hear?
5 If you _____ (be) on holiday and lost your passport, who _____ (you/ask) for help?
6 What _____ (you/do) if you _____ (be) in a shop and there was a robbery?
7 If you _____ (have to) go into hospital, what three things _____ (you/take) with you?
8 What problems _____ (you/have) if you always _____ (have to) tell the truth?
9 What _____ (you/say) if a stranger _____ (ask) you for money?
10 _____ (you/panic) if _____ (you/be) at home alone and _____ (hear) footsteps?

7 Complete with the correct form of these verbs.

be can grow have realise spend try

Six wishes for a better world
1 I wish people _____ to understand each other better.
2 Everyone wishes there _____ peace on Earth.
3 We wish that we _____ do more to help with the AIDS crisis in Africa.
4 If only countries _____ less money on guns and _____ more food.
5 If only people _____ that the future of the world is in their own hands.
6 We wish that everyone _____ enough to eat and somewhere safe to sleep.

Vocabulary

8 Complete with these words.

atmosphere balance expectancy flood march
protestors retire rotate wireless

1 Women have a longer life _____ than men.
2 There were lots of _____ at the anti-war demonstration.
3 Air travel causes serious pollution in the _____.
4 My computer is _____, so I can use it anywhere.
5 At the moment in Britain, many people _____ from work at the age of 65.
6 How fast does Earth _____ at the Equator?
7 There is a _____ in central London today to protest about GM food.
8 After heavy rain the river rose and there was a _____ in the town.
9 You can _____ or offset your carbon emissions by planting trees.

9 Match these words with their definitions.

absorb compulsory crisis decrease
glow hoax molten pulse

1 when you are tricked into believing something that isn't true
2 take in, eg, gas or liquid
3 when you do something because you have to
4 difficult or dangerous situation
5 become less, get smaller
6 shine with a soft light
7 regular movement of blood around the body
8 very hot rock, metal or glass which is liquid

10 Match the verbs in list A with the phrases in list B. Then write sentences using four of the expressions.

A	B
1 achieve	publicity
2 fund	a case
3 generate	in an election
4 make	an aim
5 play	a project
6 reduce	a part
7 travel	the impact of something
8 vote	overland

11 Find the odd word or phrase.

1 carbon dioxide carbon emissions global warming greenhouse gas
2 demonstration protestor march sit-in
3 biologist chemist scientist physicist
4 approximate accurate exact perfect
5 argue oppose predict propose
6 bacteria disease illness sickness

PROGRESS CHECK

Now you can …
1 Describe and compare the way things happen
2 Make exclamations
3 Express result
4 Talk about future events, schedules, arrangements and plans
5 Discuss possible future lifestyles
6 Talk about future possibility
7 Talk about imaginary or unlikely situations
8 Express wishes about the present

Look back at Units 3 and 4 and write an example for 1–8.

1 Life developed extremely slowly.

How good are you? Tick a box.
★★★ Fine ☐   ★★ OK ☐   ★ Not sure ☐
Not sure about something? Ask your teacher.

5 EXTRAORDINARY PEOPLE

1 If the plot had succeeded …

Third conditional
wish/if only + past perfect
Talking about unreal or imaginary past events
Expressing regret about the past

1 Opener

Look at the pictures on this page, which illustrate a famous British event. What do you know about it?

Which of these words and phrases do you expect to find in the text?

> blow up   bonfire   cellars
> electricity   environment   explosion
> fireworks   flood   gunpowder plot
> king   parliament

2 Reading

🎧 Read and listen to *Remember the fifth of November*.

REMEMBER THE FIFTH OF NOVEMBER

Over 400 years ago, a gang led by Guido Fawkes – now known as Guy Fawkes – attempted to blow up King James I and his government in London. Fawkes and his gang were Catholics, who were persecuted in England at that time. They filled the cellars of the Houses of Parliament with barrels containing 2,500kg of gunpowder, but their plot was discovered. Fawkes was caught red-handed just before he set light to the explosive, and 5 November 1605 became a memorable date in history.

After his arrest, Fawkes said, 'I wish I had succeeded. If only they hadn't caught me!' Some people still wish he had got away with it. But what would have happened if the gunpowder had exploded? Calculations show that the explosion would have flattened a large part of central London. There would have been total destruction of all buildings within 42 metres. Walls and roofs of buildings up to over 100 metres away would have collapsed, while up to 500 metres away ceilings would have fallen and glass would have cracked or broken. What's more, if the plot had succeeded, the king and all the nobles, bishops and MPs in parliament would have died. Would London – and England – have ever recovered?

Fawkes and the other conspirators were all executed. Today, people in Britain still celebrate the failure of the 'Gunpowder Plot' with bonfires and fireworks on 5 November. But in a recent BBC poll, Guy Fawkes was voted a hero. He was listed in the top 100 Great Britons among Charles Darwin, Isaac Newton, Florence Nightingale, Emmeline Pankhurst, William Shakespeare – and Robbie Williams!

3 Comprehension

Match the beginnings with the endings. There are two extra endings.

1. Guy Fawkes and his gang tried to
2. The plot was discovered before
3. If the gunpowder had exploded,
4. The explosion would have caused serious damage
5. If Fawkes' plot hadn't failed,
6. Fawkes was executed because
7. People in Britain celebrate 5 November
8. Fawkes was recently included

a. he would have killed lots of people.
b. in a list of the top 100 Great Britons.
c. blow up the Houses of Parliament in 1605.
d. Guy Fawkes set light to the gunpowder.
e. he wouldn't have killed the king.
f. with bonfires and fireworks.
g. he tried to blow up parliament.
h. to buildings over 500 metres away.
i. it would have destroyed much of the centre of London.
j. to buildings within 100 metres.

Do *you* think Guy Fawkes was a hero?

4 Grammar

Complete.

> **Third conditional**
> If the plot _____ succeeded, the king _____ _____ died.
> What _____ _____ happened if the gunpowder _____ exploded?
>
> **wish/if only + past perfect**
> I wish I _____ succeeded.
> Some people still wish he _____ _____ away with it.
> If only they _____ n't _____ me!
>
> We use the _____ conditional to talk about unreal or imaginary past events.
> We use _____ only or _____ + past perfect to express regret about the past.
>
> ➡ Check the answers: Grammar Summary page 112

5 Pronunciation

Listen and repeat the conditional sentences from the Grammar box. Mark the four stressed words in each sentence. What happens to *have* and *had* in these sentences?

6 Grammar Practice

Complete the quotations with the correct form of the verb: past perfect or *would(n't) have*.

1 'If I _____ (know) I was going to live this long, I _____ (take) better care of myself.'
   Eubie Blake, jazz musician
2 'If I _____ (not start) painting, I _____ (raise) chickens.'
   Grandma Moses, artist
3 'If it _____ (not be) for the Cold War, Russia and America _____ (not send) people into space.'
   James Lovelock, scientist
4 'If God _____ (intend) us to fly, he _____ (give) us wings.'
   Father of Orville and Wilbur Wright
5 'I don't know what _____ (happen) to me if I _____ (not be) able to hear.'
   Ray Charles, singer
6 'If I _____ (not be) President of the United States, I probably _____ (end) up a piano player …'
   Harry S. Truman, US president

7 Grammar Practice

Rewrite the sentences using the words in brackets.

I'm sorry I forgot your birthday. (wish)
I wish I hadn't forgotten your birthday.

1 I'm really sorry he failed his exams. (If only)
2 She's sorry she didn't get the message in time. (wish)
3 I shouldn't have eaten so much! (wish)
4 You should have listened to me! (If only)
5 He regrets not learning to play an instrument. (wish)
6 What a shame he lost his job. (If only)

8 Speaking

What are these people thinking? Complete using the past perfect.

9 Listening

Two years ago, Sally King won the lottery. Listen to her talking about how her life changed. Tick the things she actually did, and put a cross by the things she didn't do.

a give up her job ✓
b carry on working
c sell her flat
d buy a farmhouse
e stay in Manchester
f moved to Italy
g meet Giorgio
h take up painting

Now check your answers with another student.

A She gave up her job.
B She wouldn't have given up her job if she hadn't won the lottery.

10 Writing

If the Gunpowder Plot had succeeded, it would have changed the course of history. Choose another event and write sentences saying what would and wouldn't have happened if things had turned out differently.

If Columbus hadn't sailed across the Atlantic Ocean, …
If terrorists hadn't attacked the World Trade Center in New York, …
If someone hadn't invented the wheel, …

5 EXTRAORDINARY PEOPLE

2 You don't have to be mad …

must, *have to* and *need to*
don't have to, *don't need to* and *needn't*
Expressing obligation and lack of obligation

Fun is their business!

Meet three people who work behind the scenes at top British tourist attractions.

1 Jo Kinsey, hair and colour artist

In the quiet afternoon sunshine, Jo Kinsey, 28, runs her hands over Gérard Depardieu's hair. A radio plays softly somewhere and a cup of coffee sits half-drunk on the table. As Kinsey stands in front of Gérard, Richard Branson looks on, his eyes not moving.

Kinsey works at Madame Tussaud's in London. Starting at 7.30am, two hours before the crowds arrive, she moves through the museum, checking that all the models are undamaged. 'Richard Branson had a broken nose this morning,' she says. 'And Hitler had a broken ear. He's had several lately, I don't know why.'

Her main responsibility is hair. If the hair looks a bit dirty, she takes off the head and washes it. 'I put it in the sink, use the shower, then dry it – not too hot, of course, because of the wax. We don't want to melt it.' This week she's working on Depardieu, Branson and Chris Evans.

'It's usually ones with elaborate hairstyles that need work,' says Kinsey. Each model has a reference file with 400 photographs and measurements. It costs £52,000 to make a model and the hair alone takes up to five weeks.

2 Jeanette Ewart, shark tank cleaner

'Sharks definitely have characters,' Jeanette Ewart says firmly. 'We work with them every day, so we get to know them. You have to watch their swim patterns and notice any changes. George is the largest shark in there – she's the boss of the tank – and sometimes when you're diving, you notice her dropping lower in the water and looking right at you.'

'The first day I went into the shark tank, I was excited but nervous. I had to tell myself to stay calm. But we're always careful – there are strict guidelines for aquarium diving, so there's always a diver, a stand-by diver in the tank, and someone supervising from the edge. You needn't worry about me – I've never had any scary moments.'

For 18 months, 23-year-old Ewart has been part of a team that keeps the aquarium clean and the fish healthy and well-fed (the sharks are fed three times a week). The team needs to clean the inside of the tank walls regularly so that visitors can see the fish clearly.

'Where else can you work in London and scuba dive for a living?' Ewart asks, grinning.

3 Mark Shepherd, smell-maker

'It sticks to your clothes,' says Mark Shepherd. 'You get accustomed to it, but you go home and people can smell it on you. Which isn't a good thing, really.'

He's referring to the smells he creates at the Jorvik Viking Centre in York. Shepherd is responsible for the nine smells that fill the noses of visitors – from farmyard smells to burnt wood, to rubbish and a fish market. He creates the smells two or three times a week. 'It's oil, basically, with the smell in it. A machine heats the oil, releasing the smell.'

The strength of the smells is important. 'You have to be careful because some people are more sensitive than others. Kids who've been round the museum have been sick.'

1 Opener

Look at the photos of people working at three famous British tourist attractions. Match them with these places.

> Jorvik Viking Centre
> The London Aquarium
> Madame Tussaud's

2 Reading

 Read and listen to *Fun is their business!*

3 Comprehension

Answer the questions.
1 Why don't Richard Branson's eyes move?
2 What does Jo do on arrival at work every morning?
3 Why mustn't Jo use a very hot hairdryer?
4 What sticks to Mark's clothes?
5 Does Mark have to create new smells every day?
6 Why doesn't Mark have to heat the oil himself?
7 What is unusual about the largest shark's name?
8 Why does Jeanette say we needn't worry about her?
9 Why do the team have to clean the tank wall regularly?

4 Grammar

Complete.

> **Obligation**
> *must, have to* and *need to*
> Why _____ Jo be very careful?
> You _____ _____ watch their swim patterns.
> The team _____ _____ clean the tank walls regularly.
>
> *mustn't* means that something is not allowed.
>
> **Past forms:** *had to* and *needed to*
> I _____ _____ tell myself to stay calm.
>
> **Lack of obligation**
> *don't have to, don't need to* and *needn't*
> Why _____ n't Mark _____ _____ heat the oil himself?
> You _____ n't worry about me.
>
> **Past forms:** *didn't have to* and *didn't need to*
>
> *needn't* (= *don't need to*) is a modal auxiliary verb. We can't use *need* as a modal auxiliary in affirmative statements; instead we use *need to*. But note that *need* can also be a main verb with an object:
> The elaborate hairstyles need work.
>
> ➡ Check the answers: Grammar Summary page 112

5 Grammar Practice

Complete with the correct form of the verb in brackets.
1 You _____ pay for the most valuable things in life like love and friendship. (have to)
2 A bad dancer _____ say it's the fault of the floor. (must)
3 You can't stop trouble coming, but you _____ give it a chair to sit on. (need)
4 The sign on the office wall says 'You _____ be mad to work here but it helps'. (have to)
5 My father used to say that you _____ learn to walk before you could run. (have to)
6 In Japan people used to say that if you wanted to catch a tiger, you _____ go into the tiger's cave. (need)
7 A British saying is that if you want to eat the fruit, you _____ first climb the tree. (must)
8 You _____ be afraid of a noisy dog, but you should be afraid of a quiet one. (need)

6 Listening

 Listen and complete the chart.

have to ✓   mustn't ✗ ✗   needn't ✗

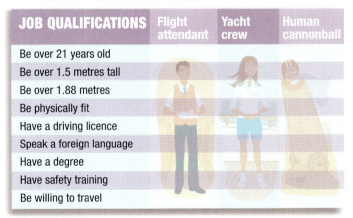

Now talk about the qualifications for the three jobs.

> Flight attendants mustn't be under 21 and they have to be over 1.5 metres tall.

7 Pronunciation

 Make sentences correcting these statements about *Fun is their business!* and say them aloud. Then listen and check the stress.

> Jo Kinsey works in *London*, not *York*.

1 Jo Kinsey works in York.
2 Richard Branson had a broken leg.
3 There are 200 photographs of each model.
4 Mark Shepherd creates sounds.
5 George is the smallest shark.
6 Jeanette Ewart is 25 years old.

8 Writing

Write two paragraphs about the qualifications needed for two of the jobs in exercise 6.

Flight attendants have to be over 1.5 metres tall.

5 EXTRAORDINARY PEOPLE

3 What could have happened to them?

must have and *can't have*
could/may/might have
Making deductions and speculating about the past

Amelia Earhart
PIONEER IN THE SKY

Born in 1897, Amelia Earhart was a record-breaking American pilot, who in 1932 became the first woman to make a solo flight across the Atlantic. The flight was difficult and dangerous. She flew through strong winds and a lightning storm, and once almost crashed into the ocean. It took her 13½ hours to make the trip from Newfoundland to Ireland, where she had to make an emergency landing in a field. But she had completed the crossing – and set a new world record. Earhart was also the first person to fly solo across the Pacific Ocean, when she flew from Hawaii to California in 1935. Every previous attempt had failed, not least because the distance is greater than a transatlantic crossing.

Her most daring journey was in 1937, when she attempted to fly round the world with navigator Frederick Noonan. But after they had completed three-quarters of the trip, their plane disappeared during the flight from New Guinea to tiny Howland Island in the Pacific. No trace of the aircraft or Earhart and Noonan was ever found.

What could have happened to them? There has been a great deal of speculation. Many believe the plane must have run out of fuel and crashed into the Pacific Ocean – Earhart had reported over the radio that they were short of fuel. But there was a massive search operation, so why wasn't the plane found? It can't have blown up in mid-air because it had used up most of its fuel. Some people think that Earhart and Noonan may have been US spies on a secret mission, and the Japanese might have shot down their plane. Others think that they could have ended up on a desert island, or even that aliens might have abducted them. Or did Earhart and Noonan simply get lost? Neither of them knew much about using the radio equipment on the aircraft.

Their disappearance remains a mystery. Whatever happened, Earhart may have died as she had wished. 'When I go,' she often said, 'I'd like best to go in my plane.'

1 Opener

Look at the photo and the map. You are going to read about a brave woman pilot. What do you think she did?

2 Reading

 Read and listen to the text.

3 Comprehension

True, false or no information? Correct the false sentences.

1. Amelia Earhart was the first person to fly solo across the Atlantic.
2. She flew from Newfoundland to Ireland in under 14 hours.
3. She beat the previous transatlantic record by three hours.
4. Her flight from Hawaii to California took longer than her transatlantic flight.
5. Earhart and Noonan disappeared over the Atlantic Ocean.
6. Earhart had reported over the radio that they were short of fuel.
7. Although there was a major search for their plane, it was never found.
8. The plane could have blown up in mid-air.
9. Earhart and Noonan were probably US spies.
10. Earhart wanted to die in her plane.

4 Grammar

Complete.

> **Deduction**
> *must have* and *can't have* + past participle
> The plane _____ _____ run out of fuel.
> It _____ _____ blown up in mid-air.
>
> **Speculation**
> *could/may/might have* + past participle
> What could _____ happened to them?
> They could _____ _____ up on a desert island.
> Earhart and Noonan may _____ _____ US spies.
> Aliens _____ _____ abducted them.
>
> We use _____ _____ when we are sure something happened.
> We use _____ _____ when we are sure something didn't happen.
> We use *could/may/might have* to talk about what possibly happened.
>
> ➡ Check the answers: Grammar Summary page 112

5 Pronunciation

 Listen and repeat the sentences from the Grammar box. Mark the stressed words in each sentence. What happens to *have* in these sentences?

6 Grammar Practice

Rewrite the sentences using the verb in brackets.

1. Amelia Earhart was certainly very brave. (must)
2. I'm sure she didn't sleep during her solo flight. (can't)
3. It's possible that Earhart and Noonan survived. (might)
4. Perhaps they landed on a desert island. (could)
5. I'm sure aliens didn't abduct them. (can't)
6. Maybe the plane came down in the sea. (could)
7. It's possible that they got lost. (may)
8. I'm sure Earhart loved flying. (must)

What do you think happened to Earhart and Noonan?

7 Vocabulary

Complete with the correct form of these verbs.

> blow   end   grow   make   sum   take   use   wake

1. We've run out of milk – we've _____ it all up.
2. My little sister wants to be a pilot when she _____ up.
3. Guy Fawkes failed to _____ up parliament.
4. I don't believe his story – I think he _____ it up.
5. After travelling round the world, he _____ up in Brazil.
6. Now I'd like to _____ up what I've just said.
7. A loud noise _____ me up in the middle of the night.
8. Earhart _____ up flying when she was a young woman.

Which of these phrasal verbs with *up* can you find in the text in exercise 2?

8 Speaking

Discuss these stories about unexplained mysteries, and say what you think happened in each case.

A Carolyn must/can't have …
B She could/may/might have …

Mystery island

In June 1974, pilot Carolyn Cascio was flying to Grand Turk Island in the Bahamas. When she flew over Grand Turk, people on the island could see her plane, but she sent a radio message: 'There is nothing down there!' Then Cascio's plane suddenly disappeared and she was never seen again.

Tunnel vision

In the winter of 1975, Mr and Mrs Wright were driving to New York City in a snowstorm. When they reached the Lincoln Tunnel, they stopped to clean snow off the car windows. Mrs Wright went to clean the back window – and she disappeared for ever.

Foreign visitor

In 1905, a man was arrested in Paris because he was a pickpocket. He spoke a completely unknown language, but finally he found a way to communicate with people. He said he came from a city called Lisbian – which doesn't exist.

Time travel

A National Airlines 727 plane was flying to Miami in 1969 when it suddenly lost contact with air traffic control. Ten minutes later, it reappeared on the radar screen. No one on the plane had noticed anything unusual, but when the plane landed on time, the watches of all the passengers and crew were ten minutes slow.

9 Writing

Write about an unexplained mystery from this lesson or another mystery that interests you. If you like, you can make one up. Describe the event and say what you think happened, giving your reasons.

5 EXTRAORDINARY PEOPLE

4 Integrated Skills
Contrasting facts and ideas

1 Opener

Look at the photo. How popular is women's football in your country? Are there other sports which more men than women play? Are there sports which more women than men play?

'Is it a man's game?' asks Marigol

1. Mexico's star woman footballer, Maribel Dominguez, is known as 'Marigol' because she scores so often – 46 goals in 49 international matches. But life isn't, and hasn't been, easy for her in a man's world – football.

2. Maribel started to play when she was nine years old on wasteland near her new home in Mexico City. But she played with boys. The short-haired new arrival was soon accepted into the group of boys. They called her Mario.

3. 'I tricked them for years,' Maribel confesses. 'They only found out I wasn't a boy when they saw my picture in the paper. I'd got into a junior national team. They went to my house and asked if I was a girl. They were pretty shocked.'

4. Maribel was 20 when she joined the Mexican national team and played in the Women's World Cup in the USA in 1999. The team lost all their matches, but Maribel was soon playing for a professional women's team in Atlanta in the USA. Then came the 2004 Athens Olympics and the Mexican women's team reached the quarter-finals, while the men's team were knocked out in the first round. By now Maribel was famous and also lucky that she had escaped serious injuries.

5. 'Maribel really is very, very good,' says Nora Herrera, one of a few women football journalists in Mexico. 'She has an incredible nose for a goal, she can smell it, and she's fast and courageous, and surprisingly strong too.'

6. In 2005 Maribel shocked the Mexican football world by joining a second-division club called Celaya, which was looking for a centre forward. It was a men's club. The Mexican Football Association said it had no problem with her playing in a male team, but they had to ask FIFA, the world football organisation. Just before Christmas 2005 FIFA announced its decision: 'There must be a clear separation between men's and women's football.' In other words, no!

7. 'I just wanted to be given the chance to try,' said Maribel. 'If I had failed, I would have been the first to say that I couldn't do it. But at least I would have tried.' So Maribel moved to Europe to play professional women's football for Barcelona.

8. Her dream is to play in another World Cup and another Olympics. Then she wants to start a football school for girls. She's saving money for it, but women footballers are paid much much less than men. In Mexico Maribel got £600 a month, whereas a top male player got £60,000. 'To play in one of those competitions feels fabulous. It's the best thing for a woman. The very best. Well, for a female footballer it's the best thing that can happen. For a man, maybe earning a million dollars a month is better. I don't know.'

Reading

2 Read *'Is it a man's game?' asks Marigol* and match these topics with the paragraphs.

> A discovery   A review   The future
> A surprise decision   Her career   Introducing Marigol
> A new continent   Early days

3 Find the highlighted words in the text which mean:
1. woman *adj*
2. says that he/she has done something wrong *v*
3. series of games in a competition *n*
4. man *adj*
5. unused open ground *n*
6. last four games between eight players or teams in a competition *n*
7. put out of a competition after losing a game *v*
8. brave *adj*
9. group of teams who play against each other *n*

4 Linking words: *whereas* and *while*

We can use *whereas* or *while* to contrast two facts or ideas. Find an example of each in the text.

5 Listening

Read and complete as much of the text as you can for Maribel. Then listen and take notes so you can complete the text for Hanna as well.

Both Maribel Dominguez and Hanna Ljungberg are international __1__. Maribel has scored __2__ goals in __3__ international matches, whereas Hanna has scored __4__ goals in __5__ internationals. Maribel started playing when she was __6__, while Hanna started when she was __7__. Maribel joined the Mexican team when she was __8__ whereas Hanna joined the Swedish team when she was __9__. Maribel played in the __10__ World Cup in the USA, while Hanna __11__. Maribel __12__ had a lot of serious injuries, while Hanna has __13__ been injured. Both women are __14__ footballers and both were asked to play for __15__ teams. Neither did.

Now listen and check your answers.

Hanna Ljungberg, Umeå IK, Sweden

6 Speaking

FIFA say that boys and girls can play football together until they are 13, but after that there must be separate male and female teams. Do you agree? And why are men footballers paid so much more than women?

In what other areas of life do men and women have different opportunities and pay? Think about sport, education and jobs. Discuss your ideas with other students.

7 Writing

Write three paragraphs contrasting the situations of men and women in your country. Is it easier to be a man or a woman – what are the advantages and disadvantages?

Learner Independence

8 Thinking skills: revising groups of words or phrases

- Make a word map of a group of words or phrases you want to revise, for example words to do with sport, on a big piece of paper.
- Stick the piece of paper on your door and look at it every time you leave your room.
- After a week take the paper down, and make a new word map for another topic.
- You can save the papers for last-minute revision.

9 Word creation: make adjectives ending in *-ous* from these nouns and complete the sentences.

> courage   danger   infection   luxury
> nerve   poison   space   superstition

1. She's very _____ – she's not afraid of anything.
2. The hotel was really _____ – I've never stayed anywhere as nice.
3. It's not safe – in fact it's quite _____.
4. People who believe in magic are often _____.
5. My cold's getting better – I don't think I'm _____ now.
6. All footballers get _____ before a match.
7. The room is very _____ – it can hold up to fifty people.
8. Those mushrooms are _____, so you mustn't eat them.

10 Phrasebook

Find these useful expressions in Unit 5. Then listen and repeat.

> I wish I hadn't forgotten …   I don't know why.
> Which isn't a good thing, really.   You needn't worry.
> What could have happened?
> She really is very, very good.   In other words …
> I just wanted to be given the chance.

Now write a six-line dialogue using at least three of these expressions.

Unit 5 Communication Activity
Student **A** page 107
Student **B** page 117

5 EXTRAORDINARY PEOPLE
Inspiration Extra!

PROJECT Extraordinary Person File

Make a file about an extraordinary person.

1. Work in a group and make a list of extraordinary people like those in this unit. They could be historical figures like Guy Fawkes, ordinary people in unusual jobs like the people in Lesson 2, or people with unusual skills or hobbies. They could be famous inventors, adventurers like Amelia Earhart, or sports stars like Maribel Dominguez. They don't have to be well-known – the important thing is that there is something extraordinary about them. Then choose one person to write about.

2. Find out as much as you can about the person from books or the Internet. If the person is still alive and lives in your town, why not make a list of questions and go and interview her/him? If you can find out an email address, you could do an email interview.

3. Work together and make an Extraordinary Person File. Read it carefully and correct any mistakes. Use your own photographs or ones from magazines or the Web to illustrate your file. Show your Extraordinary Person File to the other groups.

GAME Link-up

- Form two teams.
- One team chooses a letter square from the game board. The teacher asks a question about a word beginning with the letter. If the team guesses the word, they win the square.
- Then the other team chooses a letter square …
- The first team to win a line of *linked* squares from top to bottom or from left to right is the winner. You can go in any direction, but all your squares must touch!

SKETCH The Break-In

🎧 Read and listen.

A couple have just walked into their apartment after a holiday.

WOMAN Oh, no – what a terrible mess!
MAN There must have been a break-in! Burglars!
WOMAN They could have got in through the window – look, it's broken.
MAN They can't have come in through the window. We're on the 15th floor!
WOMAN Then they must have come through the door.
MAN They can't have – the door was locked.
WOMAN They might have had a key. Perhaps it was someone we know.
MAN I can't believe that. But what's missing? What have they taken?
WOMAN They haven't taken the computer. What about the TV?
MAN Let's check the sitting room.
WOMAN Oh, heavens – it's total chaos in here.
MAN Look! There's a body under a blanket on the sofa!
WOMAN Is it alive?
MAN I don't know. We'd better call the police.

The person on the sofa throws off the blanket.

SAM Oh, hi Mum, hi Dad.
WOMAN Sam!!! Are you all right?
SAM Yes, of course I'm all right. I'm just a bit tired, that's all.
MAN But there's been a break-in, hasn't there? What on earth happened?
SAM Ah, sorry about the mess. A few friends came round last night. If I'd known you were coming home today, I'd have tidied the place up.

Now act out the sketch in groups of three.

UNIT 5

REVISION for more practice

LESSON 1

Look at exercise 7 on page 57 and write new sentences using this extra information.

1 If only he hadn't passed his exams.

1 He passed his exams and has to leave school. He loves school and doesn't want to leave. (If only)
2 She got the message and it was bad news. (wish)
3 There wasn't much food and I wanted more. (wish)
4 I took your advice and everything went wrong. (If only)
5 He learnt to play the guitar and now people keep asking him to play at parties. (wish)
6 He stayed in his job and hated it. (If only)

LESSON 2

Look at exercise 6 on page 59 and write about the qualifications needed for the job you didn't write about in exercise 8.

LESSON 3

The famous footballer Terry Wayne has disappeared. Rewrite the sentences using the verb in brackets.

1 What do you think has happened to him? (can)
2 I'm sure he was tired of publicity. (must)
3 Perhaps he's gone to stay with friends. (may)
4 It's possible that he's had an accident. (might)
5 Perhaps he wanted a holiday. (could)
6 I'm sure he hasn't decided to give up football. (can't)

EXTENSION for language development

LESSON 1

Look at exercise 9 on page 57. Think of an event that changed your life or the life of someone you know. Write a paragraph saying what would/wouldn't have happened if things had been different.

My mother met my father when she was a nurse in hospital. She was working overtime and he was brought in after breaking his leg in a football match. If he hadn't ...

LESSON 2

Look at exercise 2 on page 58. Write a conversation between Jo Kinsey and Jeanette Ewart in which they compare their jobs.

LESSON 3

Read about the mystery voyage of the *Mary Celeste*. Then write sentences making deductions and speculating about what happened to the people on the ship.

On 7 November 1872, the *Mary Celeste* set out from New York to sail to Italy with a cargo of wine. On 4 December, the *Mary Celeste* was found sailing off the coast of Portugal. There was no one on board and the lifeboat was missing. The captain and crew had apparently left in a hurry, and they were never seen again. But everything on the ship was tidy, and there was plenty of food and water.

YOUR CHOICE!

CONSTRUCTION *needn't* or *don't have to*?

Complete with *needn't* or *don't have*.

A You mustn't miss your train. Let me drive you to the station.
B Thanks but you __1__ bother. There's plenty of time and I __2__ to catch this train. Anyway, you've got lots to do.
A You __3__ worry about me – I can always finish my work tomorrow. I __4__ to finish it today.
B I know that I __5__ worry about you – you __6__ to keep reminding me!
A I know I __7__ drive you but I thought I'd offer! Never again!
B You __8__ to get angry with me!

ACTION Picture flash

- You need a number of magazine pictures on card. The pictures can be of people, places or objects.
- Student A holds a picture upside down with its back to the other students. Holding the picture at the sides with both hands, he/she flashes it so that the other students only see it for less than a second.
- The other students say what they think the picture *must/may/could/might/can't have been*.
- Student A flashes the picture again until one student guesses correctly.
- That student flashes the next picture card.

REFLECTION Modal verbs

Match the examples a–i with language functions 1–4.

1 Obligation   2 Lack of obligation   3 Deduction   4 Speculation

a You mustn't take everything I say seriously.
b It might have been your boyfriend on the phone.
c You have to wear a safety belt in the car.
d It can't have been my boyfriend – he's lost his phone!
e She could have got lost – she doesn't know the city well.
f You must turn off your phone in the cinema.
g You don't have to pay to get into the museum.
h I may have been wrong – I don't know.
i You don't have to thank me – I was happy to help.

INTERACTION My favourite English words

- Work in a small group.
- On your own, think of five English words which you like for a special reason – it could be the sound of the word, or something it makes you think of, for example.
- Share your words with the rest of the group, saying why each word is special to you.
- Listen and ask questions as other students tell you about their favourite English words.

culture

1 Reading

Read and answer the *Shopping Skills* questionnaire.

Saying the right thing

SHOPPING SKILLS

Brush up your shopping skills! Choose the best answers.

1 You're in a shop but you aren't planning to buy anything. An assistant asks if you want any help. What do you say?

A I don't want to buy anything.
B No, thanks. You can't help me.
C No, thank you, I'm just looking.

2 You find a pair of jeans, and want to see if they fit. What do you say to the assistant?

A Excuse me, can I wear them?
B Excuse me, could I try these on, please?
C Do you mind if I put them on?

3 The jeans are too tight. What do you say?

A Do you have them in a larger size?
B Do you have a larger one?
C Do you have a smaller pair?

4 The assistant shows you a lime green jacket, saying 'This is the latest colour'. It makes you look ill. What do you say?

A It doesn't really suit me.
B I don't think it fits properly.
C It doesn't match very well.

5 The assistant shows you a jacket which you can't afford. What do you say?

A I'm afraid that's more expensive.
B Sorry, that's a bit too expensive for me.
C I wonder if you could knock £20 off.

6 You haven't got enough money to buy something. You ask a friend politely to lend you £5. What do you say?

A Give me a fiver, will you?
B Could you possibly borrow five pounds?
C Would you mind lending me five pounds?

Now listen and check. Then turn to page 119 and read the explanations.

Culture

2 Vocabulary

Complete the sentences with verbs from the questionnaire.

1. It's very cold today – _____ on a coat before you go out.
2. It's important to buy shoes that _____ properly.
3. The shirt is a nice colour but it doesn't _____ my trousers.
4. I need some new clothes – I haven't got a thing to _____!
5. Black doesn't really _____ you – it makes you look pale.
6. It's sensible to _____ on clothes before you buy them.

3 Speaking

Make and respond to requests using expressions from the box. Remember: the bigger the request, the more important it is to ask your partner politely!

> Can I borrow a pen, please?

1. Ask to borrow a pen.
2. Ask to borrow his/her iPod.
3. Ask him/her to open the window.
4. Ask him/her to help with your homework.
5. Ask to share his/her book.
6. Ask if you can use his/her mobile.
7. Ask if you can use his/her mobile to phone New York.
8. Ask him/her to look after your dog while you're on holiday.
9. Ask him/her to help you paint your room.

Making requests	Responding to requests
Will you …?	Yes, of course. ☺
Would you …?	I'd rather not. ☹
Can I/you …?	No problem. ☺
Could I/you …?	I'm afraid not. ☹
More polite	
Would you mind __ing …?	No, of course not. ☺
Do you mind if I …?	Not at all. Go ahead. ☺
I wonder if I/you could …	Yes, certainly. ☺
Could I possibly …?	I'd rather you didn't. ☹

4 Listening

You are going to hear a tourist in three different situations. First, try to match the sentences below with these places.

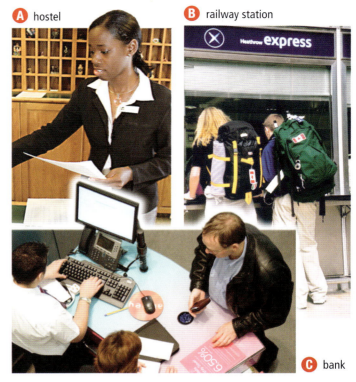

A hostel **B** railway station **C** bank

1. Could I change 100 dollars into euros?
2. I'd like a room for tonight, please.
3. How would you like the money?
4. Single or return?
5. Have you made a reservation?
6. Single or double?
7. Tens and twenties, please.
8. A day return, please.
9. Single, please, with a shower if possible.
10. Here's your change.
11. There's one in five minutes.
12. Here's your receipt for the exchange.
13. Which platform does it leave from?
14. Would you mind filling in this form, please?
15. Do I have to change?

Now decide which sentences the tourist says, and which sentences the tourist hears.

🎧 Listen and check.

5 Role Play

Choose one of the situations in exercise 4: changing money, buying a train ticket or booking a room. Act out a similar conversation between a tourist and a bank/booking clerk or a receptionist.

Now change roles and situations.

6 Writing

Write a dialogue based on one of your role plays from exercise 5.

6 ON THE MOVE

1 I promised I wouldn't forget!

Reported speech with various reporting verbs
Reporting what people said

1 Opener

Look at the photos of Kerala in India. What advice would you give to someone travelling there?

2 Reading

Laura is 16 and lives in Edinburgh. Read and listen to her email to a friend.

Hi Susanna

You'll never guess what – I'm going to India for the holidays!

Nisha – she's my best friend at school – is going to visit her grandparents in Kerala and yesterday she invited me to go with her! I replied that I'd have to ask my parents, and I hoped they'd say yes. At first they refused to let me go – Dad said it was out of the question. I explained that we wouldn't be on our own because Nisha's parents were coming too. Then Mum pointed out that I didn't like Indian food, but I told her I'd changed my mind and I loved it. In the end they agreed to let me go!

Dad told me to keep in touch and I promised to send loads of emails. Mum reminded me that I had to have injections before I left, and that I needed to take malaria tablets. Dad warned me that I could get malaria if I forgot to take them regularly. I promised I wouldn't forget! Then Mum suggested inviting Nisha and her parents for supper to talk it over – they're coming round this evening.

I'm so excited!

Laura xxxx

PS I'm attaching two photos of Kerala – doesn't it look brilliant?!

3 Comprehension

Match these sentences in direct speech with the reported speech in Laura's email. Then number sentences A–M of the dialogue in the right order.

A I've changed my mind, I love Indian food. Please let me go.
B We won't be on our own – Nisha's parents are going too.
C I promise I won't forget.
D Would you like to go to India with me in the holidays?
E But you don't like Indian food. Last time we had an Indian meal, you complained it was too spicy.
F Why don't we invite Nisha and her parents for supper? Then we can talk it over with them.
G No, you can't go to India.
H Remember, you must have injections before you leave. And you need to take malaria tablets.
I Oh, all right – you can go. But you must keep in touch.
J Oh wow! I'll have to ask my parents – I hope they'll say yes.
K Yes, you could get malaria if you forget to take them regularly.
L It's out of the question – two young girls travelling halfway round the world on their own.
M Of course, I'll send loads of emails.

Now listen and check.

4 Grammar

Complete.

> **Reported speech with various reporting verbs**
> **Verb + infinitive**
> agree   ask   hope   offer   promise   refuse
> They agreed _____ _____ me go.
> I promised _____ _____ loads of emails.
>
> **Verb + object + infinitive**
> advise   ask   invite   promise   tell   warn
> She invited _____ _____ _____ with her.
> Dad told _____ _____ _____ in touch.
>
> **Verb + (that) clause**
> agree   explain   complain   hope   point out   promise
> reply   say   suggest   warn
> Mum pointed out that I _____n't like Indian food.
> You complained it _____ too spicy.
>
> **Verb + object + (that) clause**
> promise   remind   tell   warn
> Mum reminded _____ that I _____ to have injections.
>
> **suggest + -ing**
> Mum suggested _____ Nisha and her parents for supper.

➡ Check the answers: Grammar Summary page 113

5 Pronunciation

Mark the stress on these two-syllable reporting verbs. Which two verbs are different?

> agree   offer   promise   refuse   advise   invite
> explain   complain   reply   suggest   remind

 Now listen and check. Repeat the words.

6 Grammar Practice

Write these sentences in reported speech using the verb in brackets.

1 Laura invited Nisha ...

1 Laura: 'Nisha, would you like to come to dinner?' (invite)
2 Father: 'The plane ticket will be quite expensive.' (point out)
3 Nisha: 'Don't forget your passport, Laura.' (remind)
4 Mother: 'Laura, you mustn't get sunburnt.' (warn)
5 Laura: 'I'll be very careful!' (promise)
6 Nisha: 'Let's go to the travel agency tomorrow.' (suggest)
7 Laura: 'Kerala is in the south-east of India.' (explain)
8 Father: 'Laura is a very lucky girl!' (say)
9 Nisha: 'Laura, shall I lend you a book about India?' (offer)
10 Laura: 'I haven't got any nice clothes to wear!' (complain)

7 Grammar Practice

Laura asked for travel tips on a website forum. Read the replies and write the answers to these questions.

1 What did Jackie tell Laura to do?
2 What did Kim explain?
3 What did Sandy warn Laura not to do?
4 What did Roger advise her to do?
5 What did Sara suggest?
6 What did Peter remind her to do?

> Take more money and fewer clothes than you think you'll need.
> **Jackie**

> Carry a local newspaper under your arm so you don't look like a tourist.
> **Roger**

> It's best to book an aisle seat on the plane, so you can easily get up and walk about.
> **Kim**

> If I were you, I'd buy a cotton sarong in India. You can wear it as a skirt, and you can also use it as a towel, a sheet, or a bag.
> **Sara**

> You shouldn't take more luggage than you can run with!
> **Sandy**

> Don't forget to take some insect spray to keep the mosquitoes away!
> **Peter**

8 Speaking

Interview two other students. Ask them about the situations in the *What do you say?* questionnaire and note down their answers.

> **Questionnaire** *What do you say?*
> 1 You're playing music in your room, and your parents complain that it's too loud.
> 2 You order a meal in a restaurant but when the waiter brings your food, it's cold.
> 3 A friend tells you he is very nervous about an exam tomorrow.
> 4 Your teacher asks you why you were late for school this morning.
> 5 A friend of yours has very bad toothache.
> 6 You see a woman on the bus with her bag open.
> 7 A friend tells you she is going on a snowboarding holiday.
> 8 You're going to a party, and your parents tell you to be home by 11pm.
> 9 A friend is miserable because her boyfriend is going out with another girl.

9 Writing

Use your notes from the questionnaire to report the answers of the two students you interviewed. Use as many reporting verbs as possible.

Peter agreed that the music was too loud and said he would turn it down, but Tania refused to turn it down!

6 ON THE MOVE

2 The waitress wanted to know if ...

Reported questions
Reporting what people asked

1 Opener

How much do you know about your own country? What would be the best way to find out more?

2 Reading

Read and listen to *You're welcome*.

You're welcome

Bill Bryson, an American writer who had lived in Britain for ten years, returned to the USA to rediscover his homeland. He borrowed his mother's old Chevrolet and drove 13,978 miles through 38 states, keeping mainly to side roads and small towns. This is Bryson's description of a meal in a town called Littleton in New Hampshire.

It was the friendliest little place I had ever seen. I went into the Topic of the Town restaurant. The other customers smiled at me, the lady at the cash register showed me where to put my jacket, and the waitress, a plump little lady, couldn't do enough for me.

She brought me a menu and I made the mistake of saying thank you. 'You're welcome,' she said. Once you start this there's no stopping. She came and wiped the table with a damp cloth. 'Thank you,' I said. 'You're welcome,' she said. She brought me some cutlery wrapped in a paper napkin. I hesitated but I couldn't stop myself. 'Thank you,' I said. 'You're welcome,' she said.

I ordered the fried chicken special. As I waited I became uncomfortably aware that the people at the next table were watching me and smiling at me in a slightly mad way. The waitress was watching me too. Every few minutes she came over and asked if everything was all right. Then she filled my glass with iced water and told me my food would only be a minute.

'Thank you,' I said.
'You're welcome,' she said.
Finally the waitress came out of the kitchen with a tray the size of a table-top and started putting plates of food in front of me – soup, a salad, a plate of chicken, a basket of hot bread rolls. It all looked delicious. Suddenly I realised I was starving.

The waitress wanted to know if she could get me anything else.
'No, this is just fine, thank you.' I answered with my knife and fork ready to attack the food.
'Would you like some ketchup?'
'No thank you.'
'Would you like some more dressing for your salad?'
'No thank you.'
'Have you got enough gravy?'
There was enough gravy to drown a horse. 'Yes, plenty of gravy, thank you.'
'How about a cup of coffee?'
'Really I'm fine.'
'You're sure there's nothing I can do for you?'
'Well you might just push off and let me eat my dinner,' I wanted to say, but I didn't of course. I just smiled sweetly and said no thank you.

3 Comprehension

Match the beginnings (1–10) with the endings (a–l). There are two extra endings.

1 After living abroad for a long time, Bryson wanted to
2 He feels that once you've started saying thank you, you
3 He was uncomfortable about the way people
4 When the food came he wanted to
5 The waitress asked if he would
6 She wanted to know if he
7 She asked if he had
8 She wondered if she could
9 Bryson was sure there was nothing the waitress
10 He didn't really tell the waitress to

a bring him some coffee.
b looked at him.
c like some ketchup.
d got enough gravy.
e ask for some more.
f could do for him.

g go away.
h have to continue.
i eat, not talk.
j like some more chicken.
k get to know the USA again.
l would like some more dressing.

UNIT 6

4 Grammar

Complete.

Reported questions

Direct speech	Reported speech
'Is everything all right?'	She asked _____ everything _____ all right.
'Can I get you anything else?'	She wanted to know _____ she _____ get him anything else.
'Would you like some ketchup?'	She wondered _____ he _____ like some ketchup.

In reported questions, the word order is the same as in statements. We _____ use a question mark after reported questions. Modal verbs *could*, *should*, _____, *might* do not change.

Check the answers: Grammar Summary page 113

5 Grammar Practice

Match the direct questions 1–5 with the reported questions a–e.

1 How much do you know about our country?
2 What parts of our country have you visited?
3 What places would you like to visit?
4 Have you travelled around by bus, train, car or plane?
5 Have you stayed in a hotel or with friends or family when you've been away from home?

a I asked if he/she had stayed in a hotel or with friends or family when he/she had been away from home.
b I wanted to know what parts of our country he/she had visited.
c I asked if he/she had travelled around by bus, train, car or plane.
d I wondered how much he/she knew about our country.
e I wanted to know what places he/she would like to visit.

Now ask another student the questions and write sentences reporting the questions and answers.

I asked how much Jan knew about our country. He said that he had visited the south and west, but didn't know the rest of it very well.

6 Listening

 Listen to an interview with Bill Bryson and decide: true or false? Correct the false sentences.

1 The interviewer remarked that Bryson's books weren't very funny.
2 He pointed out that Bryson could be very hard on people.
3 He asked if Bryson was someone who saw the good in everything.
4 Bryson replied that he was very easily disappointed.
5 Bryson quoted from one of his books: 'Other countries create civilisations, we build shopping malls.'
6 The interviewer wanted to know if it was true that Bryson didn't like writing to people.

7 Vocabulary

Find these words and phrases in this lesson, and match them with their definitions a–h.

Restaurant
bread roll   cash register
cutlery   dressing *n*   gravy
ketchup   napkin   special *n*

a dish of the day
b knife, fork and spoon
c individual portion of bread, like a very small loaf
d tomato sauce
e kind of sauce for salad
f machine where you pay in a shop or restaurant
g juice of cooked meat
h you use it to protect your clothes when eating

8 Pronunciation

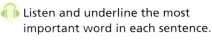 Listen and underline the most important word in each sentence.

1 Would you like some more chicken?
   No thank you, but I'd like some more chips.
2 Have you got enough gravy?
   Yes, thanks. But I'd like some more bread.
3 Would you like some ketchup?
   No thank you, but I'd like some dressing.
4 How about some coffee?
   Yes, please, and some cheesecake.

Now listen again and repeat.

9 Writing

Ask another student about what they did on holiday last year and note down the answers. Ask about:

Time	When did you …?
Place	Where did you …?
Activities	What did you …?
	Did you …?
People	Who did you …?
Food	What did you …?
	Did you …?
Enjoyment	What did you … most/least?

Now write sentences reporting the questions and answers.

I asked Sara when she had gone on holiday last year. She told me that she had gone on holiday in July.

71

6 ON THE MOVE

3 It's time that people realised ...

get/have something done
It's time + past simple
Describing problems
Suggesting solutions

1 Opener

Do many tourists visit your country? Where do they come from and how do they behave? Do some nationalities behave better than others?

2 Reading

Read and listen to *The British – the world's worst tourists*.

3 Comprehension

True, false or no information? Correct the false statements.

1 Of the 17 countries in the survey, the Germans came first.
2 The survey shows that the Germans were more polite than the Americans.
3 Jens Kees has lots of experience of tourists from different countries.
4 Jens thinks the British sleep too long in the mornings.
5 When they're abroad the British are ready to solve their own problems.
6 When you're planning a long drive across Europe, you get your car serviced first.
7 It's a good idea to go to the dentist before travelling around the world.
8 People think the British are rude because they don't respect the local culture.
9 Jens wants the Germans to be more like the British.

The British –
the world's worst tourists

A recent survey shows that the British are seen as the world's worst tourists. Tourist offices in 17 countries worldwide were asked to fill in a questionnaire including these topics: behaviour, politeness, tipping, learning the language and trying local food.

Overall the British came in last of 24 nations after the Indians, Irish and Israelis. The survey claims that the British were the worst-behaved and the Germans the best-behaved.

Tourist guide Jens Kees takes mixed-nationality groups to some of the remotest parts of the world. What does he make of the survey? 'It's time the British woke up to reality!' he says. 'Just because they speak English it doesn't mean that they own the planet. And they're never properly prepared. When something goes wrong a long way from home they expect to have everything done for them. Why? If you're taking your car across Europe, you have it serviced before you go. It's the same with your body. Before you go on a round-the-world trip it makes sense to get your eyes tested and your teeth checked. Because it may not be so easy to do these things in the middle of the Kalahari Desert!'

The survey also found the British to be the worst at learning the local language as well as the rudest tourists.

The Germans weren't the best at everything, however – they gave the worst tips and were described as the meanest nation (closely followed by the British).

'It's time that people realised that their behaviour abroad is important. It's up to each individual to behave responsibly,' says Jens. 'I don't expect the British to turn into perfect tourists overnight. But they could take in this feedback and start to change.'

TOP TOURISTS
1st Germans
2nd Americans
3rd Japanese
4th Italians
5th French, Norwegians and Swedes

4 Grammar

Complete.

> *get/have something done*
> It makes sense to get your eyes _____ .
> You have your car _____ before you go.
>
> *It's time (that)* + past simple
> It's _____ the British _____ up to reality.

5 Grammar Practice

Complete these sentences about Jens using the words in brackets.

1 He's at a photographer's. He's going to (have/a passport photo/take)
2 He's at a hairdresser's. He's (have/his hair/do)
3 He needs new glasses. He's going to (get/his eyes/test)
4 He's been to the dentist. He's just (have/a tooth/fill)
5 He's lost his front door key. He's going to (get/a new key/cut)
6 He's leaving a garage. He's just (have/his car/service).

6 Pronunciation

Listen and choose: strong or weak?

> **Strong and weak forms of *have***
> 1 They expect to have everything done for them.
> 2 What would you have done?
> 3 Are you going to have your eyes tested?
> 4 I'd like to have my hair cut.
> 5 I have had some photos taken.
> 6 It would have been fun.

7 Vocabulary

How many of these phrasal verbs can you find in this lesson? Match the verbs with their meanings a–g.

1 break into   a investigate
2 come in   b get into something by force
3 fill in   c understand and think about
4 give in   d finish
5 look into   e become
6 take in   f complete in writing
7 turn into   g accept you can't win

8 Speaking

Read and answer the questionnaire. Then compare your answers with two other students.

DO-IT-YOURSELF QUESTIONNAIRE

How much do you do yourself and how much do you get others to do for you?

1 If your one-year-old iPod stopped working, would you:
A try to repair it yourself?
B take it back to the shop and get it repaired?
C go back to the shop and get it exchanged for a new one?

2 If you and your friends felt like a pizza, would you:
A make one yourself?
B take one out of the freezer and defrost it?
C telephone and get one delivered?

3 If your bicycle had a puncture, would you:
A mend it yourself?
B go to the shop and buy a new tyre and tube?
C take the bike to the shop and get it mended?

4 If you'd spilt tea on a tablecloth, would you:
A wash it yourself?
B leave it for someone else to wash?
C get it dry-cleaned?

5 If you'd bought a pair of jeans but found the legs were too long, would you:
A turn them up yourself?
B ask your mother to turn them up?
C get them turned up in a shop?

6 If you'd bought some new software for your computer, would you:
A install it yourself?
B ask a friend to install it?
C pay to have it installed in a shop?

7 If you needed a new passport photo, would you:
A try to take one yourself?
B get one taken by a machine?
C have one taken by a photographer?

8 If you wanted to give flowers to a friend in hospital, would you:
A pick some in the garden and take them with you?
B buy some on the way to the hospital?
C have some sent from a flower shop?

9 Writing

Write a paragraph comparing your answers to the questionnaire with the answers of two other students.

I'd try to repair the iPod. But both Andreas and Kris would try to get it exchanged.

6 ON THE MOVE

4 Integrated Skills
Reporting and summarising what people said

TRAVELLING WITH PARENTS
Alison Cryan lives in west London

1 It was last summer: I went to the Philippines with my mum to visit her family. She's from Manila, and she's got lots of relatives there. I've been before, but not for several years, so it was almost like meeting them for the first time. I was quite worried about how I'd get on with all these new cousins and aunts and uncles, especially as they don't all speak English and I don't speak Tagalog, their language. But it was fine, although it was a bit embarrassing that I seemed so rich to them: they think because I live in London, I must be really well-off. And in Filipino terms I suppose I am, because the cost of living is much less there than in the UK.

2 We'd been talking about a trip to the Philippines for ages, so it wasn't really a big decision to go there. I've been emailing my cousins about it for years, so it was really exciting to be finally on the plane and on our way.

3 Often I just like lazing around: the year before last, we went to Portugal, and I liked swimming and reading and being on the beach. In the Philippines, it was different, because we were with people who lived there, so we did more normal things like shopping for groceries. But my mum and I did have a few days when we did tourist things: we climbed up some beautiful mountains, and we visited an aquarium and a lovely beach.

4 It took 22 hours to get to the Philippines, but I enjoyed being on the plane because we had games consoles. The most fun way of getting around once we arrived was in the jeepneys, a cross between a taxi and a bus – they're packed with people, and you just shout when you want to get off.

5 Don't wear a huge hat or a funny shirt – it's really embarrassing for us kids. And the other thing is to keep cultural visits short, especially if you get to a museum and you just know it's not going to be as interesting as you'd hoped. Parents always seem to want to spin these things out, even when it's obvious that no one is really enjoying themselves.

6 Back to the Philippines, this summer. We weren't planning to return so quickly, but after we left there was a devastating fire in the area of Manila where my mum's family live. No one died, but lots of people lost possessions and their homes. We've been raising money to help – I think we've got £7,000 so far – and are planning to go back in August to hand it over and see everyone again.

1 Opener
In this lesson, two teenagers talk about holidays with their parents. What are the advantages and disadvantages of holidays with parents?

Reading
2 Read *Travelling with parents* and match these questions with Alison's answers.

A What do you like doing most on holiday?
B Any tips for parents on holiday?
C Where was your best holiday?
D Where are you off to next?
E Do you have a say in where you go?
F What's your favourite way to travel?

🎧 Now listen and check.

3 Find words or phrases in the text which mean:
1 electronic equipment for playing computer games *n*
2 food and other household goods *n*
3 causing a lot of harm or damage *adj*
4 rich, or having enough money to live well *adj*
5 relaxing *v*
6 make something last longer than necessary *v*
7 very clear, easy to see or understand *adj*
8 members of a family *n*
9 something with the qualities of two different things *n*
10 extremely crowded *adj*

4 What do the words in *italics* refer to?

Paragraph
1 … it was almost like meeting *them* for the first time. And in Filipino terms I suppose *I am* …
2 I've been emailing my cousins about *it* for years …
4 … *they're* packed with people …
5 Parents always seem to want to spin *these things* out …
6 … go back in August to hand *it* over …

5 Listening

You are going to hear an interview with Ben Mackenzie, who lives in Bristol. First, look at the photos and try to predict some of his answers to the questions in exercise 2.

Now listen and see if you were right. Note down Ben's answers to the questions.

6 Speaking

Use your notes to tell each other what Ben said in the interview.

A He said his best holiday had been in Canada …
B … and they'd seen whales and dolphins.

Now ask another student the six questions from exercise 2 (in the right order). Note down the answers.

7 Writing

Write a report of your interview with the student in exercise 6. You can summarise the information – you don't need to include all the details.

I asked Hans where his best holiday had been, and he told me …

Learner Independence

8 Thinking skills: listening and note-taking

- Before you listen, try to predict some of the words and information you are going to hear. Think about the topic, look at pictures or charts, and read through comprehension questions.
- While listening, focus on key words – they're usually stressed – and don't try to understand every word.
- When taking notes, only write down the most important words. Ben gave examples of watersports he enjoyed – surfing, snorkelling, swimming, sailing – but the most important word was *watersports*.
- Remember that people often say the same thing twice in different ways, eg 'Parents are too bossy on holiday – they don't need to tell us what to do all the time.'

9 Word creation: add the prefix *well-* to these words to make adjectives, and complete the sentences.

> balanced behaved done
> dressed known off paid

1 She wears smart clothes and always looks ____.
2 He hasn't got a ____ job, so he can't afford to take a holiday.
3 If you want to be healthy, it's important to eat a ____ diet.
4 'How would you like your steak cooked?' '____, please.'
5 The children are usually polite and ____.
6 Unfortunately a lot of people aren't ____ when they retire.
7 Bill Bryson is a ____ author of books about travel.

10 Phrasebook

Find these useful expressions in Unit 6. Then listen and repeat.

> You'll never guess what!   I've changed my mind.
> It's out of the question.   You're welcome.
> It's time that people realised …   Where are you off to?
> Do you have a say?   And the other thing is …

Now write a five-line dialogue using three of the expressions.

Unit 6 Communication Activity
Student **A** page 108
Student **B** page 118

6 ON THE MOVE
Inspiration Extra!

PROJECT Ideal Holiday File

Make a file about the ideal holiday.

1 Work in a group and make a list of different kinds of holiday, for example: beach holidays, walking holidays, adventure holidays, safari holidays. Then choose one kind of holiday which you would all like to go on.

2 Find out as much as you can about your ideal kind of holiday from newspapers, magazines, travel brochures and the Internet. Where can you have this holiday? What time of the year is best for it? Do you need any special skills, preparation or equipment? What can you do to be a 'good' tourist? Are there any disadvantages, eg cost, location, timing? Is there anyone you can interview who has been on this holiday?

3 Work together and make an Ideal Holiday File. Read it carefully and correct any mistakes. Use photos from travel brochures, magazines or the Web to illustrate it. Show your Ideal Holiday File to the other groups.

GAMES Question Games

1 **Questions and answers**
- Form two teams. One student is the question master.
- The question master puts the answer to an imaginary question on the board. For example, *150* or *At home*.
- The teams have five minutes to write as many questions as possible which can go with the answer on the board. For example, *How old are you? What's 3 times 50? What's your house number?* or *Where's your book? Where did you sleep last night?*
- The winner is the team with the most questions.

2 **Only questions**
- Play in pairs. The aim is to have a conversation asking only questions.
- Student A asks a question, Student B replies with a question, Student A replies with another question and so on until one student makes a statement or repeats a question.
- Students lose a point if they make a statement or repeat a question. A student wins when the other student has lost three points.

SONG

Read and complete with these words.

> along call conversation door
> hall ignore sensation wrong

Hanging On The Telephone

I'm in the phone booth, it's the one across the __1__
If you don't answer, I'll just ring it off the wall
I know he's there, but I just had to __2__
Don't leave me hanging on the telephone
Don't leave me hanging on the telephone

I heard your mother, now she's going out the __3__
Did she go to work or just go to the store?
All those things she said, I told you to __4__
Oh why can't we talk again?
Oh why can't we talk again?
Oh why can't we talk again?
Don't leave me hanging on the telephone
Don't leave me hanging on the telephone

It's good to hear your voice, you know it's been so lo
If I don't get your calls then everything goes __5__
I want to tell you something you've known all __6__
Don't leave me hanging on the telephone
Don't leave me hanging on the telephone

I had to interrupt and stop this __7__
Your voice across the line gives me a strange __8__
I'd like to talk when I can show you my affection

Oh I can't control myself!
Oh I can't control myself!
Oh I can't control myself!
Don't leave me hanging on the telephone

Hang up and run to me! Oh!

🎧 Now listen and check.

UNIT 6

REVISION for more practice

LESSON 1

Look at Laura's email on page 68. Write questions beginning with *Who ...?* using these reporting verbs, and answer the questions.

> invite   reply   hope   refuse   explain   point out
> agree   promise   remind   warn   suggest

Who invited Laura to go to India with her?
Nisha did.

LESSON 2

Look at exercise 7 on page 71. Write five sentences, each using at least one of the words in the exercise.

The waitress brought me a napkin and some cutlery.

LESSON 3

Look at exercise 7 on page 73. Write sentences using five of the phrasal verbs.

The burglar broke into the house.

EXTENSION for language development

LESSON 1

Look at the *What do you say?* questionnaire on page 69. Write a similar questionnaire about five situations. Ask two other students the questions and write a paragraph reporting the answers using as many reporting verbs as possible.

LESSON 2

Look at exercise 9 on page 71. Write a report of the questions another student asked you and your answers.

Nabil asked me when I went on holiday last year.
I replied that I had gone on holiday in July.

LESSON 3

Look at exercise 1 on page 72 and the first paragraph of *The British – the world's worst tourists* in exercise 2 again. Now write a paragraph about the behaviour of foreign tourists in your country, commenting on the same topics.

YOUR CHOICE!

CONSTRUCTION   Reported speech

Complete with the correct form of these reporting verbs.

ask   offer   remind   refuse   reply   suggest   warn   wonder

1. Laura _____ Nisha what the weather in Kerala would be like.
2. Laura's mother _____ her to take a guidebook.
3. Laura's father _____ that she took a digital camera with her.
4. Laura's mother _____ her not to forget her passport.
5. Nisha's father _____ if Laura's parents had any questions.
6. Nisha's parents _____ to take any money for Laura's stay in Kerala.
7. Nisha _____ to teach Laura some words of Malayalam, the language of Kerala.
8. When Laura asked how many people spoke Malayalam, Nisha _____ that 38 million did.

INTERACTION   A collage of myself

- Work individually and then in a small group. A collage is a big piece of paper with cut-out pictures, drawings and words stuck to it.
- Make a collage which shows the person you are but don't put your name on it. You can use magazine pictures, your own photos of things which mean a lot to you, and words which are important to you.
- Show your collage to your group and answer questions about it.
- Show your group's collages to other students and see if they can identify whose they are.

REFLECTION   Reported speech

Match the examples a–j with language functions 1–8.

1 Advice   2 Command   3 Invitation   4 Offer
5 Question   6 Statement   7 Suggestion   8 Warning

a They wondered if there was anything they could do to help.
b Her father warned her not to eat unwashed salad.
c She suggested taking a big rucksack.
d The police officer told him to get out of the car.
e She invited her to stay the night.
f He explained that it was a 12-hour flight.
g She asked what the time difference was between Britain and Kerala.
h He replied that he didn't know.
i She wanted to know if it was safe to drink tap water.
j He advised her to look in the guidebook.

ACTION   Sense mimes

- Work in a small group.
- Each student mimes eating something, eg: spaghetti, a boiled egg, a hot Mexican dish, a melon, a fish with lots of bones. The other students try to guess what it is.
- You can also mime listening to something, eg: rock music, a boring lesson, someone using a mobile on a train, instructions on how to do something, a phone call with bad news.

REVIEW UNITS 5–6

Grammar

1 Read and complete. For each number 1–10, choose word or phrase A, B or C.

REINDEER MAN

Researcher Piers Vitebsky spends part of each year with the Eveny people. They live in the Verhoyansk Mountains of north-east Siberia, where winter temperatures fall to –71°C.

'I communicate mostly in Russian, but if I hadn't learnt Eveny I __1__ have been able to understand everything. The Eveny language has about 1,500 words to describe the appearance and behaviour of reindeer. I learnt Eveny because otherwise I __2__ have misunderstood exactly what people meant.

The Eveny move camp every few days. We're moving camp today, and I wake in a tent full of the smells of reindeer fur and wood smoke. One of us makes sweet tea. Another has already used his dog to help bring the herd of 2,000 reindeer back to the camp. Then we catch the reindeer. We __3__ catch all 2,000, just the ones we'll ride and use to carry our things.

Now it's time we __4__ our tents. I've calculated that the old lady in the family I'm with __5__ have packed and unpacked 1,500 times. When the Eveny leave a camp, they believe they __6__ look back or they will never return to the place. And they always leave wood and stones behind for the next year. Other people can use these, but they __7__ always replace them.

On the first morning in a new camp it's important to tell each other what you dreamt about in the night. These dreams show how successful the new camp will be. Last time we moved I told the herders that I __8__ about mountains, animals and running water. They asked me __9__ I dreamt about these things when I was back home in England. I replied that I only dreamt about reindeer when I was in the Verhoyansk Mountains.

I explained that soon I would have to return to Britain. As always I wished that I had had more time with the Eveny. There is never enough time to get everything __10__.'

1	A can't	B won't	C wouldn't
2	A can	B will	C might
3	A mustn't	B needn't	C didn't have to
4	A packed	B to pack	C are packing
5	A had to	B must	C will
6	A don't have to	B mustn't	C needn't
7	A must	B need	C had to
8	A am dreaming	B dream	C had dreamt
9	A if	B when	C where
10	A doing	B do	C done

2 Write sentences saying what would and wouldn't have happened if things had been different.

The Gunpowder Plot didn't succeed. The King didn't die.
If the Gunpowder Plot had succeeded, the King would have died.

1 Amelia Earhart was daring. She attempted to fly round the world.
2 Something strange happened. The plane didn't reach the island.
3 The boys didn't realise Maribel was a girl. They called her 'Mario'.
4 Maribel was a brilliant footballer at the age of 20. She played for Mexico.
5 FIFA said Maribel couldn't play for a men's club. She didn't play for Celaya.
6 Nisha invited her. Laura went to India for the holidays.
7 The restaurant looked friendly. Bill Bryson decided to have dinner there.
8 Alison didn't speak Tagalog. She was worried about meeting her relatives.

3 Nick planned to fly to Greece for a holiday, but everything went wrong. What does he regret? Write sentences beginning *I wish …* and *If only …* .

He decided to drive to the airport.
'I wish I hadn't decided to drive to the airport.'

1 He didn't take the train.
2 The traffic was heavy.
3 He didn't stop for petrol.
4 The car ran out of petrol.
5 He didn't get to the airport in time.
6 He missed his flight.
7 He didn't have a holiday.

4 Complete with *mustn't, need(s) to* or *needn't* and these verbs.

> book   forget   go   have   look   start   stay   stop

1 He _____ his eyes tested because reading gives him a headache.
2 We _____ a table – the restaurant is never full.
3 I _____ up too late – I've got an exam tomorrow.
4 She _____ taking malaria tablets before she goes to India.
5 There's plenty of food in the fridge, so you _____ to the supermarket.
6 I _____ at the road map because I know the way.
7 You _____ to lock the door when you leave.
8 We _____ at a garage before we run out of petrol.

5 You're waiting for a friend to join you at a gig, but she's very late. Talk about what could/might have happened to her.

get the date wrong
A She could have got the date wrong.
B Yes, she might have got the date wrong.

1 lose the address
2 forget about it
3 feel too tired
4 go to another gig
5 miss the bus
6 decide not to come

UNITS 5-6 REVIEW

6 Write the sentences in reported speech using the correct form of these verbs.

> complain explain invite offer
> refuse remind suggest warn

1. Paul: 'Sue, don't forget to phone me this evening.'
2. Sally: 'Tom, would you like to go to the cinema?'
3. Robert: 'You press the red button to turn on the DVD player.'
4. Marta: 'I'm not going to tidy my room.'
5. Dan: 'Emma, don't drive too fast.'
6. Doctor: 'Why don't you take a holiday, Mr Evans?'
7. Jenny: 'I can't concentrate with all this noise.'
8. Bill: 'I'll carry your suitcase, Mum.'

7 Marion is a tourist in the UK. Report her questions using the words in brackets.

1. 'When does the next train leave?' (want to know)
2. 'Do I have to change trains?' (wonder)
3. 'How long does the journey take?' (ask)
4. 'Is the hotel near the station?' (want to know)
5. 'How much does a single room cost?' (wonder)
6. 'Can I pay by credit card?' (ask)

8 Ask and answer questions about what Laura did before going to India.

have/her clothes/wash ✓
A Did she have her clothes washed?
B Yes, she did.

1. get/a new passport photo/take ✓
2. have/eyes/test ✗
3. have/her hair/cut ✗
4. get/her teeth/check ✓
5. have/nails/paint ✗
6. get/shoes/repair ✓

Now write sentences.

She had her clothes washed.

Vocabulary

9 Complete with correct form of these verbs.

> collapse install pick point out push off
> spill stick supervise tip warn

1. People shouldn't _____ the flowers in the park.
2. She _____ him that the dog was dangerous but he didn't listen.
3. The waitress was very helpful so we _____ her well.
4. It's not at all polite to tell someone to _____!
5. After the explosion a lot of buildings _____.
6. The instructor _____ us when we made our first dives.
7. Can you help me _____ this new software on my computer?
8. Her father _____ that the air ticket would be quite expensive.
9. My fingers _____ to the wet paint when I touched it.
10. The glass was too full and I _____ a lot of water.

10 Match these words with their definitions.

> abduct aisle blow up defrost mall
> massive puncture remote trace *n*

1. enormous
2. American English for *shopping centre*
3. raise the temperature of something frozen to over 0°C
4. kidnap
5. hole in a tyre which lets the air out
6. explode
7. sign
8. where you can walk between lines of seats
9. far away from everything

11 Match the verbs in list A with the words and phrases in list B.

	A	B
1	catch	a joke
2	fly	a goal
3	give	light to
4	remain	something over
5	score	solo
6	set	someone a chance
7	take	someone red-handed
8	talk	a mystery
9	tell	a tablet

12 Find the odd word.

1. bonfire ceiling cellar roof
2. break crack destroy repair
3. bored disappointed behaved shocked
4. injection illness spray tablet
5. napkin tray roll cutlery
6. dressing soup gravy ketchup
7. brave courageous dangerous daring

PROGRESS CHECK

Now you can …

1. Talk about unreal or imaginary past events
2. Express regret about the past
3. Express obligation and lack of obligation
4. Make deductions and speculate about the past
5. Report what people said
6. Report what people asked
7. Describe problems
8. Suggest solutions

Look back at Units 5 and 6 and write an example for 1–8.

1 What would have happened if the gunpowder had exploded?

How good are you? Tick a box.
★★★ Fine ☐   ★★ OK ☐   ★ Not sure ☐

Not sure about something? Ask another student.

7 GETTING THE MESSAGE ACROSS

1 Well done – keep it up!

Passive tenses
Describing changes and experiences

1 Opener

An idiom is an expression whose meaning isn't obvious from the words. For example, 'You're pulling my leg' means 'You're joking'. Do you remember these English idioms?

> in the red   down-to-earth
> touch wood   learn by heart
> be a guinea pig

2 Reading

🎧 Read and listen to *What does it mean?*

❶ Why do people say 'I've been given **the sack**' when they've lost their job? It's thought that the expression comes from the days when workers carried their tools in a sack. This was left with the employer until the job was finished. When the worker was no longer needed, he was given the sack back.

❷ If someone is doing well, for example at school or in a sport, we can say 'Well done – **keep it up!**' to encourage them to continue to do well. The phrase comes from the game of badminton or shuttlecock, where the shuttlecock is kept up in the air for as long as possible.

What does it mean?

Thousands of idioms have entered the English language throughout its history. Here are some common idiomatic words and phrases.

❸ If you **know the ropes**, you understand how a system works. This expression comes from the days of sailing ships, when sailors had to learn what to do with hundreds of different ropes. So when you start a new job or activity, someone with experience will explain what to do: you will be shown the ropes.

❹ When you're **under the weather**, you don't feel very well. This expression also has nautical roots. In the past, when a sailor was ill, he was sent down below the deck of the ship, away from the weather, to help him to recover.

❺ The word **jumbo** – meaning very large – came into English thanks to a very large elephant. The elephant was named Jumbo when he arrived at London Zoo in 1865. Jumbo became extremely popular and since then, unusually big things have been called *jumbo-sized* or *jumbo*, for example, the Boeing 747 jumbo jet.

❻ The English language is constantly changing, and new words and expressions are being added to dictionaries all the time. Meanings of words are being changed too. The adjective **wicked** means *very bad* or *evil*. But now *wicked* is being used by young people as slang for *very good* or *fantastic*: 'We had a wicked time!' Similarly, **cool** means the opposite of warm, but it is now being used, mainly by young people, to describe something very good – or wicked!

3 Comprehension

Answer the questions.

1. What does 'He's been given the sack' mean? Why?
2. Which two expressions are connected with sailing?
3. How can you describe a very large packet of crisps? Where does this word come from?
4. What can you say to encourage someone to continue working hard? Where does the expression come from?
5. What can you say if you're not feeling very well?
6. Which two words are slang for 'very good'?
7. How can you describe a person with a lot of experience in her job? Where does this expression come from?

4 Grammar

Complete.

Passive tenses
Past simple The elephant _____ _____ (name) Jumbo.
Present perfect I _____ _____ _____ (give) the sack.
Present simple The shuttlecock _____ _____ (keep) up in the air.
Present continuous New expressions _____ _____ _____ (add) all the time.
Future simple You _____ _____ _____ (show) the ropes.

We form the different passive tenses with the appropriate tense of _____ + past participle.

➡ Check the answers: Grammar Summary page 113

5 Grammar Practice

Write sentences using the correct passive form of the verbs.

1. Written messages (deliver) by post for a long time. *Present perfect*
2. Now millions of messages (send) by email. *Present simple*
3. How do you think messages (transmit) in 2050? *Future simple*
4. In the past, most holidays (arrange) by travel agents. *Past simple*
5. These days more and more tickets (bought) online. *Present continuous*
6. One day, holidays (take) in space. *Future simple*
7. Electrical appliances (use) for 100 years. *Present perfect*
8. More and more work (carry) out by machines. *Present continuous*
9. In future, housework (do) by robots. *Future simple*

6 Listening

🎧 *Changing Places* is a TV show, where a room is changed in three days. Look at the kitchen plan and listen to a phone conversation between the producer and kitchen designer on Day 2. For each item on the kitchen plan, write Y (yesterday), N (now) or T (tomorrow).

Now tell each other what was done yesterday, what is being done now, and what will be done tomorrow.

7 Pronunciation

🎧 Listen and repeat.

A	B
They've been made.	They're being made.
It's been bought.	It's being bought.
He's been asked.	He's being asked.
She's been phoned.	She's being phoned.

Now listen and decide: A or B?

8 Speaking

Ask two students the questions in the *What about you?* questionnaire and note down the answers. If they answer yes, ask for more information.

A Have you ever been injured playing sport?
B Yes, I have.
A What happened?
B I was injured playing football last year – I twisted my ankle. What about you?

Questionnaire What about you?

1. Have you ever been injured playing sport?
2. Have you ever been involved in a demonstration?
3. Are you given pocket money or paid for household tasks?
4. Have you ever been sent a chain email?
5. Are you allowed to wear whatever you like?
6. Have you ever been taken to hospital in an ambulance?
7. Have you ever been given a prize or award?
8. Are you often asked to do things you don't want to do?
9. Will you be taken on holiday this year?
10. Are you being taught to do something new?

9 Writing

Use your notes from the questionnaire to write a paragraph comparing the two students.

Sara hasn't been injured playing sport, but Stefan has. He was injured playing football last year, and he twisted his ankle.

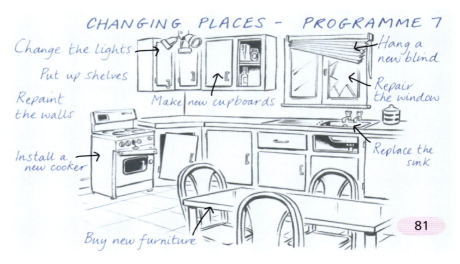

CHANGING PLACES – PROGRAMME 7
Change the lights
Put up shelves
Repaint the walls
Install a new cooker
Make new cupboards
Hang a new blind
Repair the window
Replace the sink
Buy new furniture

7 GETTING THE MESSAGE ACROSS

2 She deserves to be awarded a prize

Passive infinitive
either … or   both … and
Talking about what's right

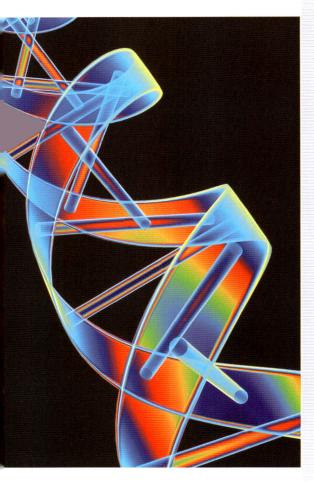

They Cracked The Code – Or Did They?

Francis Crick and James Watson solved the mystery of human DNA in 1953 and shared the Nobel Prize for Medicine in 1962. But was it all their own work, or did they steal someone else's?

Many believe that Crick and Watson's discovery was largely based on X-ray pictures of atoms taken by a woman scientist, Rosalind Franklin. In 1950 Franklin started taking photos of atoms at King's College London, believing that the structure of DNA could be discovered from them. In the race to describe DNA, either Franklin or Crick and Watson could have been the first to publish their results. But did the men win by cheating?

Franklin was accustomed to male prejudice against female scientists. Her father had refused to pay for her to study at Cambridge until he was persuaded to change his mind. And when she passed her exams, the university did not give her a full degree – only men could be given full degrees. At King's women couldn't be served in the same dining room as male scientists. What's more, her male colleague, Maurice Wilkins, treated her like an assistant; according to Watson, he believed that Franklin 'had to go or be put in her place'.

Yet it was Franklin's pictures, described as 'the most beautiful X-ray photographs of any substance ever taken', which provided the clue to the mystery of DNA. In 1953 Maurice Wilkins showed one of Franklin's X-rays (Photo 51) to Watson without telling her. Wilkins explained to Watson how the picture could be used to work out the structure of DNA. Both Crick and Watson clearly benefited from Franklin's work, but didn't acknowledge it at the time. Ironically, the cancer from which Franklin died five years later, at the age of 37, was probably caused by X-rays.

Many people think that Franklin deserves to be awarded a Nobel Prize now. However, Nobel prizes may only be given to the living, so Franklin can't be honoured in this way. But her life shouldn't be seen as a failure. She is beginning to be recognised as a brilliant scientist, and in 2002 the British government created the Franklin prize, worth £30,000, to be given each year to a woman scientist.

1 Opener

Look at the photo above. What structure does it show?

2 Reading

 Read and listen to the text.

3 Comprehension

Complete the questions with *How, What, When, Who* or *Why*.
Then match the questions with the answers.

1 _____ were both Crick and Watson given the Nobel Prize?
2 _____ was Crick and Watson's work largely based on?
3 _____ did Franklin start taking X-ray photos of atoms?
4 _____ could have been the first to publish a description of DNA?
5 _____ was Franklin not given a degree by Cambridge?
6 _____ did Wilkins treat Franklin?
7 _____ was Watson shown Photo 51 by Wilkins?
8 _____ could Photo 51 be used to do?
9 _____ did Franklin die?
10 _____ can't Franklin be given a Nobel Prize?

a In 1950.
b Work out the structure of DNA.
c In 1958.
d Only men could be given them.
e In 1953.
f X-ray pictures of atoms.
g It can't be given to the dead.
h Like an assistant.
i In 1962.
j Crick and Watson, or Franklin.

UNIT 7

4 Grammar

Complete.

Passive infinitive
Many people think that Franklin deserves _____ _____ _____ a Nobel Prize.
She is beginning _____ _____ _____ as a brilliant scientist.

After modal verbs
The picture could _____ _____ to work out the structure of DNA.
Women couldn't _____ _____ in the same dining room.
Nobel Prizes may only _____ _____ to the living.
Her life shouldn't _____ _____ as a failure.

either ... or   both ... and
_____ Crick _____ Watson clearly benefited from Franklin's work.
_____ Franklin _____ Crick and Watson could have been the first.

➡ Check the answers: Grammar Summary pages 113-114

5 Grammar Practice

Complete with the passive infinitive.

Women scientists who should __1__ (not forget)
In 1786 Caroline Herschel became the first woman to discover a comet. Her brother was the king's astronomer and she worked as his assistant. But scientists now think what she did deserves __2__ (give) more recognition.

Lise Meitner, who was described by Einstein as 'Germany's Marie Curie' for her work on nuclear fission, is someone else who people think should __3__ (award) a Nobel Prize now. However, like Franklin, she can't __4__ (honour) in this way because she died in 1968. The Nobel Prize for Chemistry was given to her male colleague, Otto Hahn, instead.

Jocelyn Bell Burnell was a Cambridge research student who discovered tiny stars called pulsars, and also deserved __5__ (give) an award. Her discovery led to a Nobel Prize in 1974 – for her male teacher.

Many people think the Nobel rules should __6__ (change) to allow prizes __7__ (award) after someone's death. The worth of some people's work may not __8__ (recognise) while they are alive. Or is the reason why scientists like Meitner, Franklin and Burnell don't get Nobel Prizes more to do with prejudice against women?

6 Grammar Practice

Complete with the passive infinitive of these verbs.

> allow   catch   do   forbid
> mark   teach   use write

Internet cheats

People say that Crick and Watson cheated and won a Nobel Prize. So what's wrong with a little Internet help with homework? Should students __1__ to download essays from the Internet if they like? Or should they __2__ to copy from the Web? Teachers argue that essays must __3__ by the students themselves or else they can't __4__ fairly. But students say that sometimes homework can't __5__ without a little help from the Web. Schools on the other hand believe that cheats must __6__ a lesson. But how can Internet cheats __7__? Anti-cheating software can __8__ to check essays, but in the end schools may just have to trust their students to be honest. After all, you can't copy something from the Web in an exam!

7 Role Play

Role play a discussion between a teacher and a student about copying homework from the Internet. Use ideas and language from the text in exercise 6.

8 Pronunciation

Mark the stress. Which words are stressed on the first syllable?

> accustomed   acknowledge   astronomer   benefit
> colleague   honour   ironically   persuade   prejudice
> recognise   substance

🎧 Now listen and check. Repeat the words.

9 Speaking

Make notes under these headings and compare them with another student.

How teenagers want to be treated
Three things that teenagers should be encouraged to do:

think for themselves

> We should be encouraged to think for ourselves.

Three things that teenagers deserve:

to be listened to

> We deserve to be listened to.

10 Writing

Write a paragraph comparing your notes from exercise 9 about how teenagers want to be treated with another student's ideas.

Both Richard and I think we should be encouraged to think for ourselves.

83

7 GETTING THE MESSAGE ACROSS

3 They couldn't ring up a doctor

Phrasal verbs
Using the phone

IT'S GOOD TO TALK

1 Opener

We all use phones to talk to friends and family. What else do we use phones for?

You are going to read about mobile phones in Africa. Which of these words and phrases do you expect to find in the text?

> bus conductor   business
> colleague   contact
> driving licence   ladder
> landline   parliament
> passport   signal   subscribers

2 Reading

Read and listen to *It's good to talk*.

3 Comprehension

True, false, or no information? Correct the false sentences.

1. Africa has more mobile phone users than Europe.
2. Very few Africans had phones at the beginning of the 21st century.
3. Nearly half the population of South Africa had mobiles in 2005.
4. The Japanese spend more time talking on their mobiles than the French.
5. People in Nigeria use mobiles more than people in South Africa.
6. Entrepreneurs in Ghana charge people to make calls from phone towers.
7. Only rich Africans can afford to buy mobiles.
8. The ITU predicts huge mobile phone sales for at least the next ten years.

The mobile phone explosion is transforming Africa. It has already become the first continent to have more mobile phone users than landline subscribers. The International Telecommunications Union (ITU) says Africa is the world's fastest-growing mobile phone market.

In 2001, only three per cent of Africans had telephones of any kind. Countless thousands of people died because they couldn't ring up a doctor. 'Now every bus conductor and street vendor has a mobile phone,' said Anthony Zwane, a sociologist at the University of Swaziland. 'They've become the people's way of communicating.'

In 1995 there were only four million landline telephones in South Africa. By 2005, 10 years after the country's first two mobile networks were switched on, there were 20 million mobile phone subscribers in a population of 42 million. It's predicted that there will be 30 million subscribers by the time the first match in the 2010 football World Cup kicks off in South Africa.

Traditional African culture, with its emphasis on oral story telling, encourages phone use as a means of social and family contact. The average Nigerian uses his or her mobile for 200 minutes a week, compared to 154 minutes per week in France, 149 minutes in Japan, 120 in Britain, and 88 in Germany.

Mobile transmission signals can be cut off by hills, but clever entrepreneurs in Ghana have found out how to solve this problem. They have put up tall towers with a platform on top where you can pick up a mobile phone signal. People pay a few pence, climb up a ladder and make a call. It's much easier than taking a bus to a place where there's a signal.

Phone companies had thought that only very rich Africans would buy mobiles. But it turned out that it was ordinary people who needed them most. People with mobiles no longer have to walk miles to talk to a friend or make a business deal. The pace of life in Africa is speeding up. And Africa's mobile phone revolution is likely to go on for many years – the ITU predicts 65% annual growth for at least another decade.

4 Grammar

Complete.

> **Phrasal verbs**
> **Verb + adverb**
> The pace of life in Africa is speeding _____.
> It is likely to go _____ for many years.
>
> **Verb + adverb with direct object**
> They have put _____ tall towers.
> OR They have put tall towers _____.
> The noun object can go before or after the adverb.
>
> They have put them _____.
> The pronoun object *must* go between the verb and the adverb.
>
> **Verb + preposition with direct object**
> People climb _____ a ladder.
> People climb _____ it.
> Noun *and* pronoun objects go at the end of the phrase.
>
> Words like *up* and *on* can be either adverbs or prepositions. They are usually stressed as adverbs, but not as prepositions.
>
> ➡ Check the answers: Grammar Summary page 114

5 Grammar Practice

Rewrite the sentences replacing the words in *italics* with pronouns.

1 She looked up *the phone number* in the directory.
2 He wrote down *the number* in his address book.
3 I want to talk to *my sister*.
4 Please switch off *your mobile phones*.
5 We're looking for *the Pizza Palace restaurant*.
6 Don't forget to ring up *your parents*.
7 It took an hour to climb up *the hill*.
8 Can you work out *the answer*?

6 Vocabulary

Rewrite the sentences replacing the words in *italics* with the correct form of these phrasal verbs.

> come down   cut off   find out   go on
> kick off   pick up   put up   ring up

1 Could you *telephone* the restaurant and book a table?
2 They plan to *build* a mobile phone mast near our school.
3 While we were talking on the phone, we were *disconnected*.
4 I *continued* speaking, but he couldn't hear me.
5 You can't *receive* a signal on your mobile in a tunnel.
6 The cost of mobile phone calls is *falling*.
7 Have you *discovered* what time the football match starts?

7 Listening

You are going to hear a phone conversation between a caller (C) and a company receptionist (R). Before you listen, look at sentences 1–8 and decide who says what.

1 Good morning, can I help you?
2 Can I speak to Carol Evans, please?
3 Hold on, I'll put you through.
4 Oh, sorry, the line's engaged.
5 Can I take a message?
6 Could you ask her to call me back?
7 Can I take your name and number?
8 I'll pass your message on as soon as possible.

🎧 Now listen and check. Then listen again and write down the message.

8 Pronunciation

🎧 Listen and repeat sentences 1–8 in exercise 7.

9 Role Play

A group of UK students are visiting your school.

Student A answers the school phone and notes down messages. Student B plays the roles of UK callers who want to contact the visitors. He/She invents the callers' names and messages, or can use some of these ideas:

> ring home tonight
> send the email address of the host family
> send a text with the host family's phone number
> invite the host family to come and stay in Britain
> take photos of the host family
> remember to buy the host family a present
> remember to bring home some souvenirs

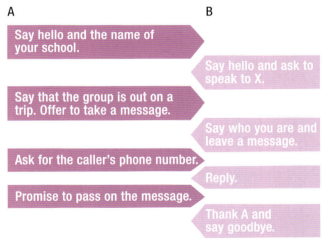

Now change roles.

10 Writing

Write out three of the messages from the phone conversations in exercise 9.

Message for Peter Preston
Your father called at 11.20 am. Your sister has had a baby girl. Both mother and child are fine. Can you call him back as soon as possible?

7 GETTING THE MESSAGE ACROSS

4 Integrated Skills
Discussing languages

1 Opener

How many languages are spoken in your country and by whom? Which languages are taught in school?

Reading

2 Read and complete the text with phrases a–h.

  a what they have left behind
  b like Chinese
  c The answer is yes
  d on radio and television
  e or a plant species
  f a bigger, more powerful language
  g and can't be recreated
  h that's 3,000 languages in 1,200 months

🎧 Now listen and check. Which words in the phrases helped you to complete the text?

3 Find words in the text which mean:

  1 people who study languages *n*
  2 in danger of something bad happening to it *v*
  3 events which cause a lot of damage, or kill or injure a lot of people *n*
  4 small number of people *n*
  5 varieties of a language which are only spoken by particular groups of people *n*
  6 recognised position *n*
  7 able to speak a language well *adj*

4 What do the words in *italics* refer to?

  Paragraph
  1 Of *these*, there are 51 languages …
  2 Should we be worried about *this*?
  3 … or man-made *ones* like war …
  4 … linguists say there are at least half a dozen *more*.
  5 Romansch Grishum, as *it* is now called …

5 The article says that there are at least half a dozen killer languages, apart from English. Which do you think they are?

6 Linking words: *not only … but also*

We can use *not only … but also* instead of *and* to add emphasis. Find two examples in the text.

7 Non-defining relative clauses

Non-defining relative clauses begin with *which, who* or *whose*. They give us more information about a noun and are separated from it by a comma. For example, *Take the case of Romansch, which is spoken in Switzerland*. Find two more examples in the text.

86

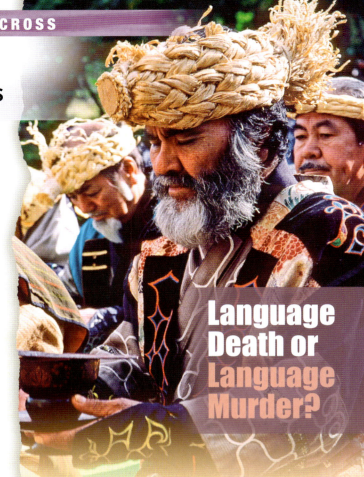

Language Death or Language Murder?

1 Linguists tell us that there are about 6,000 languages in the world. Of these, there are 51 languages with just one speaker left, nearly 500 languages with less than 100 speakers and 1,500 languages with less than 1,000 speakers. About half the world's languages are going to die out during the next century: __1__.

2 Should we be worried about this? Yes, in the same way that we ought to be concerned when an animal __2__ is threatened with extinction. When people die, archaeologists can investigate __3__. But when a spoken language dies it leaves nothing behind it __4__.

3 Why are languages dying? Language death may be caused not only by natural disasters like earthquakes, or man-made ones like war, but also by 'language murder'. This term is used to explain what happens when speakers of a minority language stop using it in favour of a 'killer language', __5__.

4 English is often called the world's most dangerous killer language, but linguists say there are at least half a dozen more. These killers are not only European languages, like French, but also Asian ones, __6__.

5 Can anything be done? __7__. Take the case of Romansch, which is spoken in Switzerland. In the 1980s Romansch, whose five very different dialects were used by fewer and fewer people, was facing a difficult situation. The solution was the creation of a written language for all these dialects. Romansch Grishum, as it is now called, has official status in parts of Switzerland and is increasingly used in its spoken form __8__.

6 The Maori language has been kept alive in New Zealand through lessons where under-five-year-olds are taught the language. And in Japan new government policies brought the Ainu language, which only had eight fluent speakers left, back from the edge of extinction.

8 Listening

Listen to the debate. What is the result? Then listen again and complete the speakers' notes and the details of the voting.

Introduction

CHAIR Hello, my name's Anna and I'm chairing this debate. The motion today is: 'The growth of English is killing other languages. Other foreign languages should be studied at school instead'. Susy is proposing the motion and Peter is opposing it.

Susy's notes for the start of her speech

What I'm going to argue is that we need to be able to speak lots of languages. Firstly, because knowing a language helps us __1__ the people who speak it better. Secondly, because the growth of English all around the world makes everywhere seem __2__. And thirdly, because people like to buy and sell in their own language. Being able to speak someone else's language is good for __3__.

Peter's notes for the end of his speech

What I've argued is this. Firstly, the world has a __4__ language already – and that's English. Secondly, it's better to be able to speak one language really __5__ than lots of languages badly. And thirdly, who is going to __6__ which languages are taught?

Conclusion

CHAIR Now you have one sentence each to sum up your argument before we have a vote.
SUSY The more languages the better – not just one.
PETER We can't survive without English.
CHAIR And now raise your hands to vote. Those in favour of the motion? Thank you. And those against? Thank you. The result is __7__ votes for the motion and __8__ votes against.

9 Speaking

Have a class or group debate. Choose a chair and two speakers. Look at exercise 8 again and use the structure for a debate in exercise 7 on page 51.

Choose your own topic or one of these:
- What's the point of saving disappearing languages? Hardly anyone speaks them.
- English isn't a killer language, it's what the world communicates in.
- What's the point of learning other languages? Everyone speaks English.

10 Writing

Write two paragraphs giving the arguments for and against the topic of your debate.

Learner Independence

11 Thinking skills: a revision diary

Reflecting on the way you revise can make you a better learner.
- Keep a diary showing your revision plan and details of what you've revised each week.
- Say how you feel about different revision techniques. Which ones work best for you?
- Review your plan and set a new target for this week.

12 Word creation: add the prefix *re-* to these verbs and complete the sentences.

appear   build   create   discover
paint   place   play   tell   write

1 The students _____ the project after they had corrected the mistakes in the text.
2 After the earthquake everyone worked to _____ the houses.
3 Please _____ the books on the table after you have looked at them.
4 A 'lost' Picasso was _____ in a house near Barcelona last week.
5 When she _____ she had changed into dry clothes.
6 I don't like the colour of the door, so I'm going to _____ it.
7 You can't _____ a spoken language when it is dead.
8 He _____ the recording several times but still couldn't hear the message.
9 When she _____ the story to the police, some of the details had changed.

13 Phrasebook

Find these useful expressions in Unit 7. Then listen and repeat.

Well done.   Keep it up.   know the ropes
under the weather   Wicked!
Hold on.   I'll put you through.
Can I take a message?
Can anything be done?   The more ... the better.

Which expression means ...?

a Cool.
b not feeling very well
c Wait a moment.
d understand how a system works

Unit 7 Communication Activity
Student **A** page 108
Student **B** page 118

7 GETTING THE MESSAGE ACROSS
Inspiration Extra!

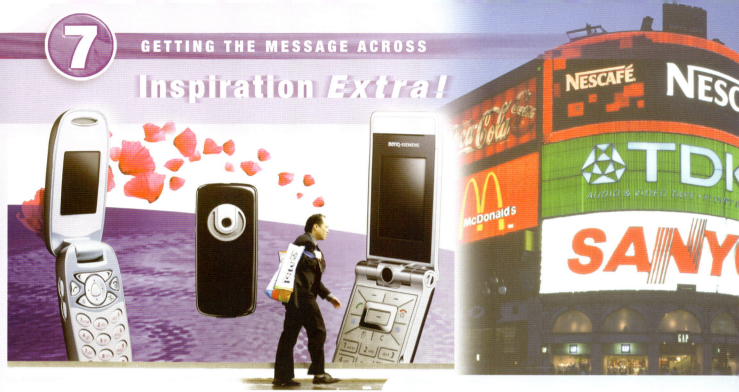

PROJECT Advertising File

Make a file about advertisements.

1. Work in a group and make a list of different kinds of advertisements and the kinds of products they advertise. For example, posters, TV commercials, web pop-ups, junk mail. What are your most favourite and least favourite adverts? Why do you like or dislike them? What do the adverts use to get their message across – colour, surprise, humour, music, attractive models, famous people?

2. Collect examples of advertisements (in English or your own language) from newspapers and magazines, and write descriptions of other adverts. Choose up to five adverts and write a paragraph about each, describing how they work and your reaction to them.

3. Work together and make an Advertising File, using the adverts and your paragraphs. Read it carefully and correct any mistakes. Draw pictures or use photographs to illustrate it. Show your Advertising File to the other groups.

GAME Call my bluff

- Work in groups of three, each group with a dictionary.
- Each group chooses a word from the dictionary which they think the other students don't know. They write out the definition of the word and then make up two more wrong definitions.
- When all groups have chosen a word and have three definitions of it, only one of which is correct, the game begins.
- Each group reads out their word and the three definitions. Without using the dictionary, the other students decide which is the correct definition. If they are right, they get a point; if they are wrong, the group giving the definitions gets a point.

SKETCH Find A Friend

🎧 Read and listen.

SARAH Find A Friend, Sarah speaking. Can I help you?
KEVIN Yes, I hope so. I'm looking for a friend.
SARAH OK, let me take down your personal details. Can I have your name?
KEVIN My name is Kevin Morgan.
SARAH How old are you, Kevin?
KEVIN I'm 24.
SARAH Right, and what colour are your hair and eyes?
KEVIN I've got dark hair and blue eyes. But I …
SARAH And what are your hobbies?
KEVIN I don't understand – why are you asking me all these questions?
SARAH I need to find out your personal details.
KEVIN But don't you want to know about my friend?
SARAH We'll talk about the kind of person we're looking for in a minute.
KEVIN Can we talk about her now, please? Her name is Maggie and she's 22.
SARAH How do you know?
KEVIN Well, we've been going out together for three months!
SARAH I'm sorry, Kevin. I'm afraid you've got the wrong end of the stick.
KEVIN Stick, what stick? What do you mean?
SARAH You've misunderstood – we find girlfriends or boyfriends for people.
KEVIN That's fine – Maggie is my girlfriend. But she didn't turn up for our date last night. And her mobile is switched off.
SARAH I'm sorry, but we don't look for missing people.
KEVIN Don't you?
SARAH No – this is a dating agency. If you think your girlfriend is missing, you should call the police.
KEVIN Well, actually, I think she's found another boyfriend. So I'd like you to find me another girlfriend, please!

Now act out the sketch in pairs.

UNIT 7

REVISION for more practice

LESSON 1

Look at exercise 6 on page 81. Write sentences saying what has been done, what is being done and what will be done.

The window has been repaired. The new cupboards are being ....

LESSON 2

Look at exercise 3 on page 82. Write five more questions beginning with *How, What, When, Who* or *Why* and answer them.

When did Crick and Watson solve the mystery of human DNA?
In 1953.

LESSON 3

Look at the list of phrasal verbs in exercise 6 on page 85 and write sentences using five of them.

EXTENSION for language development

LESSON 1

Look at the questionnaire in exercise 8 on page 81. Write answers to the questions for yourself.

LESSON 2

Look at exercise 7 on page 83. Write the conversation between a teacher and a student that you role-played.

LESSON 3

Look at exercise 7 on page 85. Write a phone conversation between a receptionist and a caller who wants to speak to someone who is not there.

YOUR CHOICE!

CONSTRUCTION The passive

Complete with the correct form of the verbs: present continuous, past simple or future simple.

'English is not enough' is true not only for native speakers but also for second language speakers of English. A language other than English __1__ (speak) at home by 1 in 10 children in the UK. Although language exams at UK schools __2__ (take) by fewer and fewer students, more than 60 languages __3__ (teach) in ethnic communities. For example, in 2005 in Birmingham, French __4__ (study) by 20% fewer students, and classes in languages like German and Spanish __5__ (chose) by up to 50% fewer students. However, over the same period, numbers studying Arabic __6__ (see) to rise by 40%. In a recent report it is estimated that 160,000 speakers of foreign languages other than English __7__ (need) in the next five years in India, but that only 40,000 __8__ (produce) by the educational system.

ACTION It could be used for …

- Work in groups of four. Each group is given a small everyday object, eg a hat, a pen, a paper clip, cutlery, a wire coathanger, an elastic band, a plastic bag, a sock.
- Groups work together for five minutes to think of as many uses as possible for their object.
- One student from each group takes the object to another group and mimes the uses that have been thought of. The group try and guess what the uses are.
- Then a different student takes the object to another group.

REFLECTION The passive

Match the beginnings with the endings.

1 The present simple passive is formed with the present simple of *be*
2 We can use the passive with a modal verb. The form is: modal verb
3 The present perfect passive is formed with
4 Negatives and questions in the passive are formed
5 The passive is often used
6 When we want to focus on the 'do-er' of the action we use

a in writing to describe processes.
b *by* + agent.
c + *be* + past participle.
d in the same way as in active sentences.
e the present perfect of *be* + past participle.
f + past participle.

INTERACTION The other me

- **Work in a small group.**
- **Imagine you are another person: the person you have always wanted to be, the person of your dreams.**
- **Take turns to interview each other: you are the 'other you' and the rest of the group are reporters. The reporters ask questions:**

Tell us a few things about yourself now and in the past.
What are you most proud of now?
What was your greatest success?
What do you do best?
What do you think the future will bring?

… and follow-up questions:

Really?   For example?   Why is that?
Can you say a bit more about …?

89

Culture

STUDENT LIFE

How much do you know about student life in Britain? Try our quiz!

1 What percentage of young people go to university?

- A 10%
- B 20%
- C 30%
- D 40%

2 How old are most students when they start university?

- A 16
- B 18
- C 20
- D 22

3 What percentage of undergraduates are female?

- A 35%
- B 45%
- C 55%
- D 65%

4 Where do most students go to university?

- A In their own town.
- B In a nearby town.
- C Somewhere else in the country.
- D Abroad.

5 What do students usually have to pay for?

- A Teaching.
- B Food.
- C Accommodation.
- D All the above.

6 How long does it usually take to get a university degree?

- A Two years.
- B Three years.
- C Four years.
- D Five years.

What are the answers to the quiz for your country?

I think the worst moment was when I first walked into my room. There were just bare walls, a bed, a table, and a wardrobe. It was pouring with rain, and I felt like going straight back home. But I unpacked my stuff and put up some posters and I suppose the room doesn't look so awful now. Things started looking up this evening when I met my flatmates, and we all decided to go to the bar in the students' union. We've been chatting to loads of people and everyone is really friendly. I've just rung up my parents to tell them I'm actually quite happy!

Lizzie
University of Portsmouth
Media Studies

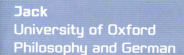

TAKE FOUR STUDENT

I've got my final exams in a couple of months so I'm trying to revise and cut down on late nights. That's quite hard – part of the problem is sharing a flat with five lively people! But you have to learn to work on your own – we're constantly told that we're here to learn and not to be taught. If you miss a lecture, no one is going to tell you off.

Jack
University of Oxford
Philosophy and German

I'm looking forward to it, but I'm also terrified. Will I make friends? Will I be able to cope with the work? Will I feel homesick? I'll be staying in a hall of residence on the campus so I guess that's a good place to meet people. I'm not too worried about money – I worked during my gap year so I've saved up some cash. I'll live on that and my student loan to start with, but eventually I'll have to find a part-time job to make ends meet. I really don't want to end up with thousands of pounds of debt.

Rachel
University of Manchester
Computer science

I can't believe how much I've changed during the last year – I've got much more independent and confident in all sorts of ways. But it took me a few weeks to settle down. At first I was terribly shy, and everyone else seemed to know the ropes. But now I realise that most of the other freshers were as nervous as I was. In a way I wish I didn't have to live with my parents, because I miss out on some of the social life. But student accommodation is hugely expensive and I simply can't afford it.

Alex
University of Edinburgh
Biology

1 Reading

Read *Take four students* and find out which student:
– is about to go to university.
– has just arrived at university.
– is at the end of the first year.
– is going to leave university soon.

2 Vocabulary

Find words and phrases that match these definitions.
1 uncovered, empty
2 university building for social activities
3 talk given to a group of students about a particular subject
4 criticise you for doing something wrong
5 manage to do something difficult
6 miserable because you are away from home
7 university accommodation with lots of rooms
8 have enough money to live on
9 money that you owe
10 first-year students

3 Comprehension

Answer the questions. Some questions have more than one answer.

Who …
1 is sharing a flat?
2 is living at home?
3 is living in the university grounds?
4 is short of money?
5 has borrowed money?
6 has regrets about something?
7 was miserable at first?
8 didn't go to university immediately after leaving school?
9 has often stayed up late?

4 Speaking

Look at the quiz and *Take four students* again. Discuss the similarities and differences between student life in Britain and your country.

5 Writing

Imagine you are going to study in Britain for a short period. What things are you looking forward to? What things are you worried about? Make two lists and discuss them with another student. Then write two paragraphs.

91

8 MAKING THE GRADE

1 He wasn't able to get a job

could(n't), was(n't) able to, managed to
in order to   so that
Talking about past ability
Expressing purpose

Success Stories

1 Opener

Look at the photos of four famous people. What do you know about them? What are they famous for?

2 Reading

🎧 Read and listen to *Success Stories*.

3 Comprehension

Choose the best answer.

1 Beethoven's music teacher thought he
  A could compose music.
  B was no good at composing.
  C hoped to be a composer.

2 Towards the end of his life, Beethoven couldn't
  A hear.
  B see.
  C work.

3 Zephaniah was taken out of school because he
  A asked too many questions.
  B couldn't read or write.
  C was a problem student.

4 JK Rowling moved to Edinburgh in order to
  A write her first Harry Potter book.
  B be unemployed.
  C live near her sister.

5 While she was writing the first Harry Potter book, she was
  A very short of money.
  B living in an unheated flat.
  C working in a café.

6 Einstein wasn't able to
  A read when he was seven.
  B study in Switzerland.
  C work in a Swiss university.

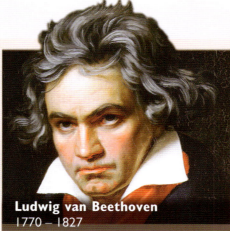

Ludwig van Beethoven
1770 – 1827

Ludwig van Beethoven's music teacher once said that he was hopeless as a composer. But Beethoven became one of the most important classical composers of all time. Although he was often ill and finally became totally deaf, he managed to produce an extraordinary quantity of work, including concertos, symphonies and operas. It has often been said: 'Though Beethoven wasn't able to hear, he was able to listen.'

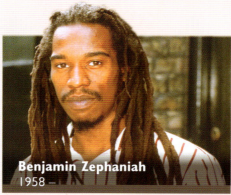

Benjamin Zephaniah
1958 –

Millions of people around the world have heard the voice of Benjamin Zephaniah, Britain's best-known rap poet. But Zephaniah was told by his teacher that he was 'a born failure', and he was taken out of school at the age of 12 because he couldn't behave. 'I was one of those kids that kept asking Why?' He was sent to an approved school (a kind of youth prison) and then twice to prison. But while in prison he decided to become a poet and was able to educate himself. 'I wasn't really able to read and write until I was in my 20s,' Zephaniah says. He started performing with bands so that his poems could reach people who didn't read books. Today his books of poetry are best-sellers and one of his most famous fans is Nelson Mandela.

J K Rowling
1965 –

JK Rowling started writing her first Harry Potter novel while she was teaching English in Portugal. In December 1994 she moved to a tiny flat in Edinburgh so that she could be near her sister. At that time she was unemployed and broke, and there was a rumour that she wrote in local cafés in order to escape from her freezing flat. But she later denied that she couldn't afford to heat her home. Amazingly, *Harry Potter and the Philosopher's Stone* was rejected by several publishers – when it was finally published in 1997 it was an instant best-seller. Rowling later became the richest woman in Britain and one of the most successful authors in the world.

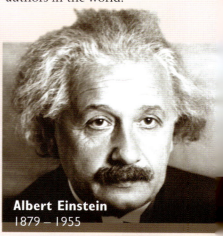

Albert Einstein
1879 – 1955

Nobel prize-winner Albert Einstein didn't speak until he was four, and couldn't read until he was seven. One of his teachers called him 'mentally slow'. After failing the entrance examination once, he managed to get a place at the Swiss Institute of Technology in Zurich in 1896. Although he did fairly well as a student in Zurich, he wasn't able to get a job at a Swiss university because he was thought to be extremely lazy. But in 1905, at the age of 26, Einstein published his Special Theory of Relativity, which led to the most famous equation in physics: $E=mc^2$.

4 Grammar

Complete.

> **Past ability: could(n't), was(n't) able to, managed to**
> **could and couldn't**
> She moved to Edinburgh so that she _____ be near her sister.
> Einstein _____ read until he was seven.
>
> **was/wasn't able to**
> Though Beethoven _____ _____ _____ hear, he _____ _____ _____ listen.
> Einstein _____ _____ _____ get a job at a Swiss university.
>
> We don't use *could* to talk about past ability on a particular occasion. Instead we use *was able to* or *managed to*.
> Zephaniah was able to educate himself in prison.
> NOT He could educate himself in prison
> Einstein managed to get a place at SIT.
> NOT He could get a place at SIT
>
> **Expressing purpose: in order to and so that**
> She wrote in cafés **in order to** escape from her flat.
> = She wrote in cafés **so that** she could escape from her flat.
>
> ➡ Check the answers: Grammar Summary page 114

5 Grammar Practice

Rewrite the sentences using the verb in brackets.

1. Steven Spielberg couldn't get into film school because his grades weren't good enough. (be able)
2. Maria Sharapova succeeded in winning Wimbledon at the age of 17. (manage)
3. Pope John Paul II could speak eight languages. (be able)
4. Olympic triathlete Michelle Dillon wasn't able to swim until she was 23. (could)
5. At first, Michael Jordan couldn't play for his school basketball team because he was too short. (be able)
6. Mozart was able to play the piano at the age of four. (could)
7. Ming Kipa Sherpa, a 15-year-old girl, managed to climb Mount Everest in 2003. (be able)
8. Harry Houdini was able to escape from a locked prison cell in two minutes in 1902. (manage)

6 Grammar Practice

Join the sentences with *in order to* where possible. Otherwise use *so that*.

1. The students read through all their notes. They wanted to pass the exam.
2. My parents gave me a camera. I could take photos at the party.
3. The police locked the cell. The thief couldn't escape.
4. They're visiting the UK. They want to learn English.
5. We left home early. We wanted to get to the gig on time.
6. He gave me his number. I could phone if I got lost.
7. Can you buy some eggs? I want to make a cake.
8. She goes to the gym every day. She wants to keep fit.

7 Pronunciation

Mark the stressed syllable.

> behave   classical   educate   examination
> institute   philosopher   poetry   publisher
> relativity   technology   unemployed

 Now listen and check. Repeat the words.

8 Speaking

 Read and listen to the poem by Benjamin Zephaniah.

Confessions of a Runner

On my first day at school
   My sister cried and cried
On my first day at school
   I could have died and died
On my first day at school
   My twin embarrassed me
On my first day at school
   I learnt schoolology.

On my second day at school
   My sister wouldn't come
On my second day at school
   She was dragged there by my Mom
On my second day at school
   I came dressed in pink
On my second day at school
   I was made to think.

On my third day at school
   I explored everywhere
On my third day at school
   I fell offa chair
On my third day at school
   We all went for a swim
On my third day at school
   I cried just like my twin.

On my fourth day at school
   They made me run in shorts
On my fourth day at school
   I discovered sports
On my fourth day at school
   I ran fast and far
On my fourth day at school
   I earned myself a star.

On my fifth day at school
   We had tomato crumble
On my fifth day at school
   I began to grumble
On my fifth day at school
   My teacher got stuck in red tape
On my fifth day at school
   Me and my twin escaped.

Now discuss these questions with other students.

- Why is the poem called *Confessions of a Runner*?
- Which day at school did the child enjoy most/least?
- Zephaniah has invented the word 'schoolology'. What do you think it means?
- Which two words has he put together to make one word?
- Can you remember your first day at school? What happened, and how did you feel?

Do you like this poem?

9 Writing

Work in groups of five if possible. Following the pattern of the poem, each group member writes a verse for a different day beginning:
On my … day at school.

Put your verses together to make your own group poem. Choose a title for your poem.

8 MAKING THE GRADE

2 She needn't have worried

Modal expressions in the past and future
Expressing obligation and ability

1 Opener

Look at the pictures of schools in the past. What do you think school life was like then? What subjects did they study? What differences are there between school then and now?

2 Reading

Read and listen to the text.

School in the Past and in the Future

In Britain in the early and mid-nineteenth century, children didn't have to go to school at all. There were schools, of course, but you had to pay to go to them, and often parents couldn't afford the fees. Many people also believed that girls didn't need to go to school, as their future was to get married and have children. Although from 1870 the law said that all children aged 5 to 10 had to go to school, many poor families weren't able to pay. The children of these families needed to have a job in order to pay the fees, and school timetables were organised to make this possible. It wasn't until 1918 that children had to be at least 12 years old to work for a living.

Schools 100 years ago were certainly very different from those today. But what about the future? A national newspaper recently organised a competition for schools called *The School I'd Like*. 'I'm concerned that the pressures of the national curriculum will mean that there won't be time for a project like this,' a reporter said. She needn't have worried, as there were over 15,000 entries full of ideas!

And what great ideas: a school in a giant submarine with waterproof maps of the underwater world, private helicopters to fly students to France for French lessons, and rockets to take children to distant planets to study the solar system. There are also some down-to-earth suggestions: clean toilets with locks that work so that students won't have to wait until they get home, no uniforms so that students will be able to choose what to wear, chill-out rooms to relax in, and enough computers so that students won't need to queue for them. Safety and comfort are clearly important: one student suggests an anti-bullying alarm, and another writes 'We don't want interactive whiteboards, we want comfortable chairs!'

3 Comprehension

Match the beginnings with the endings. There are two extra endings.

1 In the nineteenth century parents often
2 A hundred years ago many people thought that girls
3 In Britain until 1870 children
4 Children of poor families needed to work so that they
5 After 1918 if you wanted to work you
6 There were 15,000 entries for competition so the reporter
7 One idea is for schools to have rockets so that students
8 Another idea is a school without uniforms where students
9 More computers are recommended so that students
10 An anti-bullying alarm is also suggested so that students and teachers

a won't all have to wear the same clothes.
b were able to pay school fees.
c didn't have to go to school.
d will be able to study the stars and planets.
e needn't have gone to school until they were ten years old.
f had to be twelve years old.
g won't need to wait to use one.
h will need to study more and more subjects.
i needn't have worried.
j will be able to take action before it starts.
k weren't able to pay school fees.
l didn't need to be educated.

4 Grammar

Complete.

> **Modal expressions in the past:** *had to, didn't have to, was(n't) able to, were(n't) able to, needed to/didn't need to, needn't have*
>
> You _____ _____ pay to go to them.
> Children _____ _____ _____ go to school at all.
> Many poor families _____ _____ _____ pay.
> People believed that girls _____ _____ _____ go to school.
> She _____ _____ worried.
>
> ***didn't need to*** refers to something which wasn't done because it wasn't necessary.
> ***needn't have*** refers to something which was done but was unnecessary.
>
> **Modal expressions in the future:** *will/won't have to, will/won't be able to, will/won't need to*
>
> Students _____ _____ _____ wait until they get home.
> Students _____ _____ _____ _____ choose what to wear.
> Students _____ _____ _____ queue.

➡ Check the answers: Grammar Summary page 114

5 Grammar Practice

Complete with the correct form of the verb.

In the nineteenth century rich families __1__ (need to) worry about paying school fees. In fact many rich children __2__ (have to) go to school at all – they had teachers at home until they were seven or eight. Then the boys were sent away to schools like Eton where they __3__ (have to) study Latin and Greek. However, girls from rich families __4__ (be able to) stay at home and study subjects like French, music and sewing. Rich or poor, nineteenth century schoolchildren __5__ (have to) obey their teachers and show respect for them at all times. The word 'respect' is also used a lot in *The School I'd Like* competition. 'Of course there __6__ (have to) be rules,' someone wrote, 'and students __7__ (be able to) do whatever they like. But in the future teachers and students will respect each other so teachers __8__ (need to) shout so much, and __9__ (be able to) get on with their teaching. And students __10__ (have to) respect their teachers too!' So people who were worried that students would want to get rid of teachers __11__ (need not be) concerned.

6 Pronunciation

 Listen and decide if the speaker is stating a fact (F) or is very surprised (S).

1. Students will have to stay at school until they're 21.
2. They'll also need to study more subjects.
3. They'll be able to do all their classwork on computer.

Now say these. Then listen and check.

4. They won't need to go to school every day. (F)
5. They'll be able to study online at home. (S)
6. They won't have to take any examinations. (S)

7 Listening

Read the questionnaire. Then listen to Mary's answers and decide: true or false? Correct the false answers.

THEN AND NOW QUESTIONNAIRE

Tell me about something which you:
1. can do now which you weren't able to do a year ago.
2. had to do in the past but don't have to do now.
3. didn't have to do which you have to do now.
4. you needn't have worried about.
5. need to do now, but hope you won't need to do in the future.
6. can't do now, but will be able to do.
7. don't have to do now, but will have to do.
8. can do now, but won't be able to do.

Mary
1. Swim on my back.
2. Get help with spreadsheets.
3. Work hard in science classes.
4. Making friends.
5. Go to bed really early.
6. Drive a car.
7. Ironing.
8. Beat my sister at tennis.

Now listen to Matt's answers and correct the false ones.

Matt
1. Ride a bicycle.
2. Collect my brother from school.
3. Work in a bookshop on Saturdays.
4. Exams.
5. Think before I speak in Spanish.
6. Vote.
7. Clean my own room.
8. Get into this shirt.

8 Speaking

Do the *Then and Now Questionnaire* with two other students and note down their answers.

9 Writing

Write two paragraphs comparing the students' answers to the *Then and Now Questionnaire*.

Both Alicia and Magda weren't able to use PowerPoint a year ago, but they can now.

8 MAKING THE GRADE

3 Let your colours shine out bright!

make and *let*
Talking about obligation, permission and prohibition

1 Opener

You are going to read an interview with an award-winning singer/songwriter, who answered questions from the public on a BBC website. Which of these words do you expect to find in the text?

chords   chorus   confidence   equation   inspiration
inventor   lyrics   perform   practise   uniform   verse

2 Reading

Read Sarah Bennett's answers and match them with questions A–H. Then listen and check.

A Who is your favourite musician of all time?
B How did you start performing?
C When did you know you wanted to be a singer?
D What are your top tips for young budding musicians?
E How hard is it to write songs?
F Where do you get the inspiration for your lyrics from?
G What would be your dream project?
H Can you remember the first song you ever wrote?

Sarah Bennett – singer/songwriter

1 It was when I took part in the Prince's Trust *Sound Live Workshop*. It gave me the experience of loads of different music styles which I'd never had the chance to explore before. And I was made to understand how hard I had to work to make it as a singer. I decided then I was going to give it 110% and I would practise until my fingers bled.

2 I would say the hardest part is the life you've had to live to get the inspiration for your songs. I play some chords, which make me think of a time in my life, and I go into a kind of daydream and let the words flow out.

3 I started off doing the *Big Note* event – where anyone can sing – in Covent Garden. The guy who runs it let me do one song, which went down really well. So I started going every week and I got more and more material together. I was then allowed to do my first 30-minute set.

4 Yes, it was called *Inspiration*. It only had one verse and one chorus. I just wanted to reach out to other people who shared my dream but didn't have the confidence to get up there and perform. That was my inspiration for the song.

5 Some of it comes from when I was younger. I used to read a lot of books and poetry. I've learnt different ways to be descriptive and say things symbolically. All my friends are quite poetic and they don't even realise it. You can get inspiration from anything.

6 That's hard. I would say Tracy Chapman and Tina Turner. They are really strong role models and they show that it doesn't matter how bad things get, you can pull through. Both those women had really difficult lives and managed to succeed.

7 To be able to get together with Bob Geldof and put together something like another *Live Aid*. I would like to do some good in the world with my gift for music. I think something like that would be amazing. I hope that if I keep practising one day I will be good enough to work on a project like that.

8 Practise, practise a lot. Follow your own gut instincts. Don't get upset if you're not ready to progress as quickly as other people. It will happen when it's right for you. That's all that matters – YOU! And remember to let your colours shine out bright!

3 Comprehension

Answer the questions.

1. What did Sarah have the chance to explore at the *Sound Live Workshop*?
2. When she writes songs, what comes first: the words or the music?
3. What was the reaction when she first sang at the *Big Note* event?
4. How long was the first song she wrote?
5. What is it that her friends don't realise?
6. Why does she think her favourite musicians are strong role models?
7. What kind of project would she like to work on?
8. Which expression means: 'Do what you feel is right'?

4 Grammar

Complete.

> **make and let**
> I play some chords, which _____ me think of a time in my life.
> I was _____ to understand how hard I had to work.
> The guy who runs it _____ me do one song.
>
> **Active:** *make* and *let* are both followed by object + infinitive without *to*.
>
> **Passive:** *make* is followed by object + infinitive with *to*. The verb *let* has no passive form. Instead we use *allowed to*.
> I was then _____ _____ do my first 30-minute set.

➡ Check the answers: Grammar Summary page 115

5 Grammar Practice

Complete the sentences with the correct form of *make*, *let* or *be allowed to*.

1. Steel bands _____ me think of carnival.
2. Can you _____ me know when the gig starts?
3. You (not) _____ talk during this exam.
4. Performing _____ lots of musicians feel nervous.
5. The students _____ stay late at school yesterday.
6. People _____ drive when they pass their driving test.
7. Do your parents _____ you wear torn jeans?
8. Professional footballers _____ train hard.

6 Listening

 Listen to Luke, who is 16, talking about his parents. Note down what they make him do, what they let him do, and what they don't let him do.

Obligation
They make him …   *turn his music down*

Permission
They let him …

Prohibition
They don't let him …

Now tell each other what Luke is made to do and what he is/isn't allowed to do.

> He's made to turn his music down.

7 Speaking

Ask three students these questions and compare their answers.

- What do your parents make you do?
- What do they let you do?
- What don't they let you do?

Do you think your parents are strict or not?

8 Vocabulary

Make a word map for music. Use words from this lesson, and add other words you know.

- PEOPLE – songwriter
- STYLES – classical
- MUSIC
- INSTRUMENTS
- SONGS – lyrics

9 Pronunciation

Write the words in the correct column.

> longer   singer   single   strong   stronger
> strongly   young   younger   wrong

/ŋ/ long	/ŋg/ finger

🎧 Now listen and check. Repeat the words.

10 Writing

Complete these questions with your own words. Then exchange questions with another student and write your answers to your partner's questions.

Who is your favourite … of all time?
How did you start …?
When did you know you wanted to …?
What are your top tips for …?
How hard is it to …?
Can you remember the first … you ever …?
Where do you get the inspiration for … from?
What would be your dream …?

8 MAKING THE GRADE

4 Integrated Skills
Making an application

1 Opener
Have you ever thought about doing voluntary work, or do you know someone who has done it? What kinds of voluntary work can people do?

Reading
2 Read Tiffany's letter and match these topics with sections of the letter 1–10.

> **Topics**
> Her personal reasons for choosing a particular expedition
> Ending the letter   Her address
> Personal details   Date
> Why she is writing   Money
> Address of the person she is writing to
> Why she would be a good volunteer
> Starting the letter

3 ReefAid asked Tiffany to fill in a form. Complete using the information in her letter.

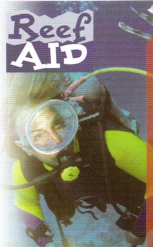

VOLUNTEER WITH US AND HELP SAVE THE PLANET

- Expeditions to endangered coral reefs.
- Work with local people to protect the environment.

NO MONEY? We'll show you how to fundraise to pay for your trip.
NO TIME? You can join our expeditions for only four weeks.
NO SKILLS? We'll teach you what you need, including scuba diving.

> click here to find out more

① 53 Mill Lane
   London AW7 8QQ

② 26th May

③ Janet Rawlings
   ReefAid
   12 Water Crescent
   Manchester OC3 4QA

④ Dear Ms Rawlings

⑤ I have read about ReefAid on your website and I would like to apply to join a coral reef expedition.

⑥ I am 17 and I am still at school. I am taking my A level examinations next year in history, art and English. My mother tongue is English and I also speak good Spanish. I like to keep fit and I go dancing a lot. I am very interested in politics, but not in politicians! One of my main interests is conservation.

⑦ I believe that I would be a good team member because I enjoy working as a volunteer at our local nature reserve. I get on well with most people and enjoy making new friends.

⑧ I would like to join an expedition to Honduras because I speak Spanish, and also because I have always wanted to go to Central America. I am a good swimmer and the chance to learn scuba diving is a great opportunity for me.

⑨ I understand that I will have to pay for my flights and accommodation myself, as well as making a contribution to the cost of the conservation project. I am confident that I will be able to raise the money.

⑩ I look forward to getting more information from you, and to hearing if my application has been successful.

Yours sincerely

Tiffany Bell

Tiffany Bell

APPLICATION FORM
(please complete in black ink)

Family name: _____
Other names: _____
      Age: ___ Male/female Married/(single)
Nationality: British
Address: _____
(Block capitals) _____
Telephone no: 02970602721
Mobile: 07334380268
Email address: tiffany4@i-net.co.uk
Occupation: Student
Languages: (fluent/good/basic) _____
Interests: _____

Give two reasons why we should select you as a volunteer.
_____
_____

Circle the expedition you would you like to join and say why.
Fiji   Honduras   Indonesia   Malaysia
_____

Now please turn over and complete the medical details.

98

4 Listening

Listen to extracts from four telephone interviews with Janet Rawlings of ReefAid and match the applicants with four of the problems 1–8.

Ann   Jake   Carol   Steve

1. Sent in the application too late.
2. Wants to be with their boy/girlfriend.
3. Not free at time of expedition.
4. Wouldn't say why they wanted to join.
5. Has already been on an expedition.
6. Has wrong scuba diving certificate.
7. Didn't fill in all the form.
8. Not old enough.

One of the applicants rings back and is offered a place on an expedition. Discuss which applicant you think it will be and why. Then listen and check.

5 Speaking

Complete the ReefAid application form for yourself or an imaginary person. Listen to the telephone interviews in exercise 4 again. Then use the completed form to role-play a telephone interview between an applicant and a worker at ReefAid.

6 Writing

Write a letter of application to one of these volunteer organisations. Structure your letter like the one in exercise 2. You can write as yourself or as an imaginary person.

Make a difference
Short-term aid projects in developing countries.
Contact: VolAid

WATER IS LIFE
Help bring clean water to the poor in the Third World.
Write to us at WatAid

THINK GLOBAL VOLUNTEER LOCAL
Volunteer work in your local environment: nature reserves, cleaning up the countryside and much more. Contact EcolVol

Learner Independence

7 Thinking skills: visualising exam success

- Top sports men and women always visualise before a competition, closing their eyes and going through the event in their minds until they win. You can do the same with your exam revision.
- Look at or smell something which you are going to take into the exam with you, like a pencil case, or perfume/after-shave on a tissue. Close your eyes and imagine the exam itself. Think about yourself doing really well and getting great marks.
- When you go into the exam look at the pencil case, or smell the tissue, and you will get the feeling of success that you visualised and be really confident.

8 Word creation: add the suffix -ness to these adjectives to make nouns and complete the sentences.

> careless   clever   fit   happy   ill   polite
> sad   thoughtful   useful   weightless

1. He was famous for his _____ – he always said 'please' and 'thank you'.
2. We share your _____ at the loss of your pet.
3. _____ is always a problem for astronauts.
4. Oh no! You've broken another glass! I'm fed up with your _____.
5. It's terrible. He's never well and gets one _____ after another.
6. Many thanks for your _____ – you always think about other people.
7. It's very easy for footballers who are injured to lose their _____.
8. Everyone knows about her _____ – she always finishes the crossword first.
9. I'm not complaining about the new computer's _____, just about its cost.
10. _____ is the one thing money can't buy.

9 Phrasebook

Find these useful expressions in Unit 8. Then listen and repeat.

> His grades weren't good enough.   I'm concerned that …
> She needn't have worried.
> Who's your favourite … of all time?
> What are your top tips for …?
> How hard is it to …?   give it 110%
> That's hard.   That's all that matters.

Which expression:
a states how difficult something is?
b means to do the best you can?
c requests advice?
d says that only one thing is important?

Unit 8 Communication Activity
Student **A** page 108
Student **B** page 118

8 MAKING THE GRADE
Inspiration *Extra!*

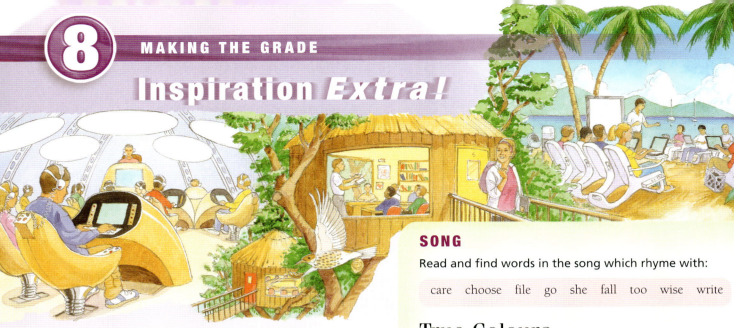

PROJECT *Ideal School File*

Make a file about your ideal school.

1. Work in a group and look back at Lesson 2. Then discuss your ideal school in broad terms, eg, Where will it be? How big will it be? Will it be quite strict or quite liberal?

2. Make notes to answer these questions about your ideal school:

   What will the buildings and the classrooms be like?
   What subjects will students be able to study?
   What sports will be taught?
   How much homework will students have to do?
   What about exams?
   How long will the terms be?   What about holidays?
   What school rules will there be?
   What will the teachers be like?

3. Work together and make an Ideal School File. Read it carefully and correct any mistakes. Draw pictures or use photographs from magazines to illustrate your school. Show your Ideal School File to the other groups. Finally, have a class vote on the best ideal school.

GAME *Puzzle Words*

- Work in pairs.
- Each of the boxes contains a nine-letter word. All the consecutive letters of the words touch each another. Find the three words as quickly as possible.

T	N	W
E	I	E
R	V	I

E	C	A
D	U	T
N	O	I

A	T	N
R	L	U
Y	O	V

- Now make your own puzzle words: copy the grid, choose a nine-letter word from *Inspiration 4* and arrange it in the squares so that all the letters touch.
- Exchange your puzzle with another pair and try to find their puzzle word.

SONG
Read and find words in the song which rhyme with:

care   choose   file   go   she   fall   too   wise   write

True Colours
Tom Kelly & Billy Steinberg

You with the sad eyes
Don't be discouraged
Oh I realise
It's hard to take courage
In a world full of people
You can lose sight of it all
And the darkness inside you
Can make you feel so small

Chorus 1
But I see your true colours
Shining through
I see your true colours
And that's why I love you
So don't be afraid to let them show
Your true colours
True colours are beautiful,
Like a rainbow

Show me a smile then,
And don't be unhappy, can't remember when
I last saw you laughing
If this world makes you crazy
And you've taken all you can bear
You call me up
Because you know I'll be there

Chorus 2
And I see your true colours
Shining through
I see your true colours
And that's why I love you
So don't be afraid to let them show
Your true colours
True colours are beautiful,
Like a rainbow

Oh I can't remember
When I last saw you laugh
If this world makes you crazy
And you've taken all you can bear
You call me up
Because you know I'll be there

Repeat Chorus 2

🎧 Now listen and check.

UNIT 8

REVISION for more practice

LESSON 1

Look at the text on page 92. Write five questions beginning with *What*, *When*, *Where*, *Who* and *Why*, and answer them.

What kind of music did Beethoven compose?
Classical music, including concertos, symphonies and operas.

LESSON 2

Look at the *Then and Now Questionnaire* on page 95. Write *your* answers to the questions.

LESSON 3

Look at exercise 7 on page 97. Write about two things your mother or father makes you do, two things they let you do, and two things they don't let you do.

My mother makes me have a shower every day.

EXTENSION for language development

LESSON 1

Think about situations in the past when you finally managed to do something that you couldn't do before. Think about sport, music, school subjects, life skills, etc. Write about three situations.

I learnt to swim when I was seven, but I couldn't dive. I kept trying, and I finally managed to dive into the swimming pool when I was ten.

LESSON 2

Look at exercise 4 on page 95 again and write two paragraphs using modal expressions from the Grammar box.

Paragraph 1: write about your time at primary school.
Paragraph 2: write about what will happen after you leave school.

LESSON 3

Think about the rules of football or another sport. Write sentences saying what you are and are not allowed to do.

YOUR CHOICE!

CONSTRUCTION Modal expressions

Rewrite the sentences using the correct form of the verb in brackets.

1. Thank you! But it wasn't necessary to buy me a present. (need)
2. He got up early because he needed to finish his homework. (have)
3. Are you allowed to wear what you like at school? (let)
4. We have to do a maths test every week. (make)
5. It's OK – you won't have to pay for your ticket. (need)
6. I wasn't able to work out the answer. (could)
7. Will you manage to attend an interview next week? (be able)
8. They don't let us wear jewellery at school. (allow)

REFLECTION Modal expressions

Match the examples a–h with language functions 1–6.

1 Ability 2 Obligation 3 Permission 4 Possibility
5 Prohibition 6 Request

a The students were made to learn 50 words a week.
b Could you write down your phone number, please?
c You aren't allowed to send text messages during lessons.
d I don't know how old he is – he could be 21.
e Could you read when you were five years old?
f Our teacher said we could go home early.
g My parents let me stay up late at weekends.
h He'd lost his key, but he managed to get in through a window.

ACTION Hot-air balloon

- Work in a small group. Imagine you are in a hot-air balloon.
- Each group member chooses a different role: eg, doctor, teacher, engineer, musician, single parent with four children. Alternatively, you can choose to be famous people.
- The balloon is losing height, and one person will have to jump out. Take turns to explain to the rest of the group why you should stay in the balloon.
  Parent: My children won't be able to manage without me …
- Finally everyone votes for the person they think should jump.

INTERACTION Goodbye presents

- Look at the list of personality adjectives below. Can you think of positive words to add to the list?
- Imagine that you are going to give one of the words as a goodbye present to another student. Which word would you like to give? Which word would you like to receive and why?
- Write a short note to the student to whom you are giving the word explaining why you have chosen it.

Personality adjectives

enthusiastic friendly funny happy helpful imaginative inspiring intelligent kind polite popular reliable responsible strong successful

REVIEW UNITS 7-8

Grammar

1 Read and complete. For each number 1–15, choose word or phrase A, B or C.

The medium and the message

People have always been able to send messages over short distances. Before message-sending machines __1__, information __2__ transmitted in all kinds of ways, for example by drums, fires, bells, or flashing mirrors. But with the invention of __3__ the electric telegraph and Morse code in the 19th century, people __4__ to send messages over much greater distances. (The word *telegraph* comes from Greek words for *distant* and *write*.)

It wasn't long before people who were far apart __5__ actually speak to each other on the telephone (*distant + sound*). But until quite recently, long-distance phone calls were extremely expensive and callers usually __6__ speak very loudly __7__ be heard. Sometimes they __8__ hear each other at all. Nowadays international calls __9__ transmitted via satellites in space __10__ messages can travel much further and more clearly. Communication has __11__ even easier by the development of mobile phones, which __12__ people contact each other almost anywhere.

And in the future? Some people think that one day we __13__ use phones at all – messages __14__ via telepathy (*distant + feeling*), so we __15__ to communicate directly with each other's minds!

	A	B	C
1	are invented	were invented	had invented
2	has	was	were
3	each	either	both
4	were able	were allowed	could
5	were able	managed	could
6	have to	had to	needed
7	in order to	so that	to make
8	can't	couldn't	weren't able
9	are	have	have been
10	because	in order to	so that
11	made	been made	been making
12	let	make	allow
13	needn't	won't need to	needn't have
14	are sent	are being sent	will be sent
15	can	could	will be able

2 Complete with the correct passive form of the verbs: past simple, present perfect, present simple, present continuous or future simple.

A 44-year-old man __1__ (send) to prison after walking in the Scottish Highlands wearing only a hat, socks and walking boots.

Stephen Gough __2__ (arrest) several times over the last six months. He is coming to the end of a 900-mile trek from Land's End in south-west England to John O'Groats in Scotland. On 29 November, the police __3__ (call) by someone who had seen a naked man walking through a village. Eventually Gough __4__ (find) and __5__ (take) to a police station.

Gough argues that going naked __6__ (permit) by the Human Rights Act as freedom of expression, and it is wrong that he __7__ (treat) like a criminal. Since he started his trek he __8__ (ask) by dozens of people to have their pictures taken with him.

Now Gough __9__ (hold) in a local prison, but it is likely that he __10__ (release) in a few days. He has 100 miles to go to complete his journey.

3 Complete with the passive infinitive of these verbs.

> allow   encourage   give   hear
> pay   see   tell   treat

1 Women deserve _____ the same as men for doing the same job.
2 If you don't speak up, your voice won't _____.
3 Do you think people should _____ to smoke in public places?
4 We don't have _____ what to do all the time.
5 Students need _____ the chance to express themselves.
6 Young people must _____ to take more exercise.
7 Teenagers want their ideas _____ with respect.
8 People no longer believe that 'children should _____ and not heard'.

4 Complete the sentences with these phrasal verbs.

> cut off   fill in   pass on   put up
> switch off   take in   turn up   work out

1 Would you _____ *the sound on the radio* so I can hear the news.
2 Tiffany was asked to _____ *an application form*.
3 It's hard to _____ *difficult mathematical equations*.
4 Don't forget to _____ *the lights* when you leave.
5 She looks very different – she's _____ *all her hair!*
6 Could you help me _____ *some shelves*.
7 It's hard to _____ *so much new information*.
8 Please don't forget to _____ *the message*.

Now rewrite the sentences replacing the words in *italics* with pronouns.

UNITS 7-8 REVIEW

5 Complete with *could(n't)*, *was(n't) able* or *managed to*.

When Thomas Edison was a boy, his teacher told him he __1__ learn anything because he was too stupid. He once said: 'I __2__ to get along at school – I was always at the bottom of my class.' But Edison __3__ become one of the most famous inventors in history. One of his first inventions was the phonograph (1877), a machine which __4__ record sounds and play them back. Later Edison and other inventors improved its design so that it __5__ to record music. Edison also __6__ invent a practical light bulb. He didn't invent the first light bulb, but after eighteen months of hard work, he __7__ to produce a reliable, long-lasting bulb in 1879. He said: 'Genius is one per cent inspiration and 99 per cent perspiration.'

6 Complete with *didn't need to* or *needn't have* and the correct form of the verb.

1. I knew we had plenty of time, so we _____ (hurry).
2. You _____ (cook) all this food – there's only two of us.
3. He _____ (worry) about his exam results – he got top marks.
4. They _____ (buy) tickets in advance – they paid at the door.
5. I _____ (wait) long for a train – one came almost immediately.
6. She _____ (be) so upset about losing her watch – it wasn't valuable.

7 Rewrite the sentences using the correct form of the verbs in brackets.

1. You can't park your car here during the day. (allow)
2. The thief forced me to give him my mobile. (make)
3. Did your teacher allow you to go home early? (let)
4. The hot sun caused the ice to melt. (make)
5. I won't allow you to talk like that. (let)
6. We had to work 12 hours a day. (make)
7. They don't let you carry weapons on planes. (allow)
8. I know a joke which will cause everyone to laugh. (make)

Vocabulary

8 Complete with these words.

> cash   cupboard   dialect   earthquake   fan
> fees   instinct   platform   prejudice   volunteer

1. The train to Brussels will depart from _____ two.
2. 'Hip-hop English' is a kind of _____ spoken by young people.
3. She's a big _____ of Johnny Depp and has seen all his movies.
4. I need to go to the bank to get some _____.
5. There's still a lot of _____ against women in politics.
6. Most people have to pay _____ to study at UK universities.
7. I don't know why, but I had an _____ that something was wrong.
8. You don't earn money if you work as a _____.
9. The plates are on the bottom shelf of the _____.
10. Many houses had to be rebuilt after the _____.

9 Match these words with their definitions.

> annual   appliance   chorus   colleague   decade
> emphasis   entrepreneur   loan   lyrics   solar

1. money that is lent to you n
2. period of ten years n
3. to do with the sun adj
4. person who works with you in an organisation n
5. household machine, eg fridge, coffee maker n
6. words of a song n
7. special importance given to a particular thing n
8. person who uses money to start a business n
9. happening once a year adj
10. part of a song that is repeated several times n

10 Match the verbs in list A with the phrases in list B. Then write eight sentences using the expressions.

	A	B
1	award	a cooker
2	book	a problem
3	change	a table
4	climb	an examination
5	fail	homesick
6	feel	a prize
7	install	the walls
8	repaint	up a ladder
9	solve	your mind

11 Find the odd word.

1. education   examination   curriculum   timetable
2. astronomer   composer   cooker   producer
3. confess   deny   disagree   refuse
4. landline   network   signal   subscriber
5. regret   replay   retell   rewrite
6. concerto   opera   poem   symphony
7. download   software   spreadsheet   waterproof
8. advice   rumour   tip   warning

PROGRESS CHECK

Now you can …

1. Describe changes and experiences
2. Talk about what's right
3. Use the phone
4. Talk about past ability
5. Express purpose
6. Expressing obligation and ability
7. Talk about obligation, permission and prohibition

Look back at Units 7 and 8 and write an example for 1–7.

1 He's been given the sack.

How good are you? Tick a box.

★★★ Fine ☐   ★★ OK ☐   ★ Not sure ☐

Not sure about something? Have a look at the Grammar Summary.

CONGRATULATIONS!

You've finished *Inspiration 4*. Well done! Now take some time to reflect on what you've achieved.

★ Grammar

You've revised and extended the grammar which you already knew and you've met and practised new grammar points. Turn to the Grammar Summary on page 109 and see how much you've covered.

★ Vocabulary

The Word List on page 120 lists all the new words in *Inspiration 4* as well as groups of words by topic. On the Contents pages you can find all the vocabulary areas you have covered. Choose some of the areas (eg Travel, Science) and write a list of all the words you can remember for each one.

But you've learnt more than grammar and vocabulary. In *Inspiration 4* you've also developed your communication skills.

★ Communication

You can …
Exchange information about what you eat and drink
Describe something and say what it's used for
Discuss health and medicine
Express your views on works of art
Talk about things which have happened recently
Describe a series of past events
Discuss the value of education
Explain why things happen
Talk about and predict future events
Discuss future possibilities
Talk about wishes
Take part in a debate
Say what would have happened if things had been different
Talk about what people are and aren't obliged to do
Consider past possibilities and probabilities
Discuss equal opportunities
Use appropriate language in tourist situations
Report and summarise what people said and asked
Describe how things were, are and will be done
Discuss how you want to be treated
Make phone calls and take phone messages
Describe what people could or were able to do
Talk about past and future obligation and ability

What else can you do?

You've also developed other language skills.

★ Writing

You can write …
A recipe
An account of arguments for and against an issue
A comparison of hopes and ambitions
A short biography
A folk tale
The results of a survey
An evaluation of the life of an important person
Predictions about your life in the future
A statement of your wishes for the future
A job description
A description of a mysterious event
A situational dialogue
A report of an interview
Messages from phone calls
A poem
A letter of application

What else can you write?

★ Reading

You can read …
An article about food and drink myths
A description of useful gadgets
An article about alternative medicine
An interview about attitudes to East and West
An article about the work of modern artists
A web forum
A biography of a writer
A folk tale
An article about the origin of the Earth and universe
An interview about space tourism
Life stories of significant people
Predictions about life in the future
An interview about an ideal holiday
An article about direct action
A description of unusual jobs
A questionnaire
An email to a friend
An extract from a travel book
An article about idioms
An article about scientific discovery
An account of mobile phone use
An article about the death of languages
A quiz on education
Personal accounts of student life
A poem
An article about schools in the past and future
An interview with a musician
A letter of application and an application form

What else can you read?

★ Listening

You can listen to and understand …
A discussion of popular beliefs
The life story of a writer
A story
A song
A description of space records
A tour schedule
An account of an important discovery
A radio phone-in
A debate
An interview with a lottery winner
A radio programme about jobs
Tourist conversations in a bank, hostel and station
An interview with a writer
An interview about a holiday
A business phone conversation
Answers to a questionnaire
Phone conversations about an application

What else can you listen to and understand?

You've also developed another very important skill.

★ Learner Independence

You have learnt …
A variety of thinking skills
Ways to create words using prefixes and suffixes
How to create a chart recording the week's learning
How to learn abstract nouns
How to revise groups of words or phrases
Listening and note-taking skills
How to plan revision and keep a revision diary
How to visualise exam success
How to assess your own progress

How do you feel?

Have a class discussion about your English lessons and *Inspiration 4*.

Talk about
- Three things you liked about the lessons
- Three things you liked about the Student's Book and the Workbook
- Three things that you learnt (apart from English!)
- Activities and exercises you would like to do more or less often
- The topics which you enjoyed most and least
- Whether you have become a better language learner
- How you can keep your English up during the holidays
- What you would like to do in your English lessons next year

Now write a letter to your teacher giving your opinions.

COMMUNICATION ACTIVITIES
STUDENT A

UNIT 1

You have half a recipe for Spaghetti Bolognese and Student B has the other half. The sentences are not in the right order. Work with Student B to put the recipe in the right order. Don't look at Student B's sentences. You have the first sentence and Student B has the last one.

Spaghetti Bolognese

Serves 6

Ingredients: 450g spaghetti, 900g minced beef, 50g bacon, 1 medium onion, 1 carrot, 2 cloves of garlic, 100ml olive oil, 100ml red wine, 1 tin of chopped tomatoes, 75g grated Parmesan cheese, salt and pepper

- When the spaghetti is cooked, drain it. Spoon the sauce over the spaghetti.
- After adding the beef to the vegetables, pour the red wine into the frying pan and turn up the heat.
- Put the frying pan back on the heat, add the rest of the oil and fry the minced beef until it is brown.
- After frying the vegetables, add the chopped tomatoes. Stir and cook for a few minutes.
- When the sauce has cooked for two hours, boil 3–4 litres of water in a saucepan.
- First, chop the onion, garlic, carrot and bacon into small pieces.

UNIT 2

Read the text. Then ask Student B questions to complete it. Answer Student B's questions.

Where did Kam live?

A Korean folk tale

Long ago a hard-working farmer called Kam lived ___1___ (where?) deep in the Korean countryside. He'd always dreamt of visiting the capital city, Seoul. Then one day he decided ___2___ (what?).

Kam enjoyed his visit to the city and bought presents for all his family. Then in one shop he found ___3___ (what?). It was a round shining piece of metal. In it a man was ___4___ (what/do?). Not only that, but the man copied everything that Kam did. Kam had never seen ___5___ (what?) before and bought it to take home.

When he got home Kam's family were delighted with their presents. It was his daughter who found ___6___ (what?) in his bag when Kam wasn't in the room. She cried 'Look! Father's been hiding something. He's brought a pretty young girl back with him and by magic put her into this metal.'

Kam's wife heard and ran into the room. Seeing ___7___ (who?) in the mirror, she shouted 'My husband has brought a woman back from the city to take my place. And she looks very angry!'

Then ___8___ (who?) appeared. His father took the mirror and shouted at Kam 'Why have you brought this ugly old man back with you?'

Kam took ___9___ (who?) to see the village chief. 'Let me see this magic metal,' said the chief, who knew Seoul well. 'You are all wrong,' he went on. 'All I can see is the face of a wise old man.' Then he explained ___10___ (what?). 'And remember,' he said, 'a mirror doesn't always tell you the whole truth.'

STUDENT A

UNIT 3

You've written this from notes you took from a TV programme. But you're not sure about some parts so you have underlined them. You phone Student B, a schoolfriend who also watched the programme. Ask Student B questions to check the underlined parts. Then answer Student B's questions.

> When did twelve astronauts walk on the Moon?

Living on the Moon

Twelve astronauts walked on the Moon <u>between 1969 and 1982</u> and now we're going back! The technology will soon exist for people to live on the Moon. We are going to build a Moon Station in the next 20 years. <u>Hundreds</u> of astronauts are going to live and work in the Station, which will take <u>ten</u> years to build.

A robot spaceship which takes off in two months' time is flying to the Moon to <u>test equipment</u>. The journey to the Moon will take three days at a speed of <u>11 kms per minute</u>. When the robot arrives on the Moon it will search for water and oxygen on the surface. The spaceship returns to Earth <u>once a week</u> with the results of its trip.

'In some ways living on the Moon will be easier than living on a space station,' an astronaut said. 'In space you're weightless but on the Moon we will have <u>one-tenth</u> of the Earth's gravity. And it will certainly be cheaper as we won't have to bring everything up by rocket. There are going to be <u>farms using animals</u> we know are there.'

So what problems are the first people on the Moon going to face? 'They're going to feel lonely,' another astronaut said. 'It'll be a bit like sleeping on a nuclear submarine, except that on the Moon every time you wake up you'll see how far you are from Earth.'

Living on the Moon is clearly going to be a huge adventure but it will only be the start. We'll use the <u>knowledge</u> we get from living there to plan expeditions to Mercury and Pluto.

UNIT 4

Here are some predictions about life in 2020, in 2060 and in 3000, which may or may not be true. Ask Student B questions to complete the chart.

A Will we still be driving cars by 2020?
B Yes, we will.
A Will we have used up all the oil by 3000?
B Yes, we will.

	2020	2060	3000
still drive cars		✓	✗
use up all the oil	✗	✗	
live until we are 150			✗
make the perfect robot		✗	
discover life on another planet	✗	✗	
still watch TV	✓		
enjoy Moon holidays every summer	✗		✓
kill the last whale	✗		

Now look at the chart and answer Student B's questions.

B Will we be living until we're 150 by 3000?
A No, we won't.
B Will we have made the perfect robot by 2060?
A No, we won't.

UNIT 5

Last summer, six students went on holiday. They all went to different Mediterranean countries:

Egypt   France   Greece   Italy   Spain   Turkey

and they all did different activities on holiday.

horse riding   paragliding   rock climbing
sailing   scuba diving   windsurfing

Look at the clues below. Student B also has five clues. Take turns to read out your clues and work together to complete the chart.

	Country	Activity
Alice		
Bob		
Cathy		
Dave		
Ellen		
Fred		

Clues
Alice doesn't enjoy watersports.
Bob spoke Arabic on holiday.
Cathy didn't go to Spain or Italy.
One of the boys went sailing in Greece.
The climber went to Spain.

> Alice can't have been sailing, scuba diving or windsurfing.

> Bob must have gone to Egypt.

STUDENT A

UNIT 6

What did these people actually say? Ask Student B and complete the speech bubbles.

A What did Laura say?
B She reminded …

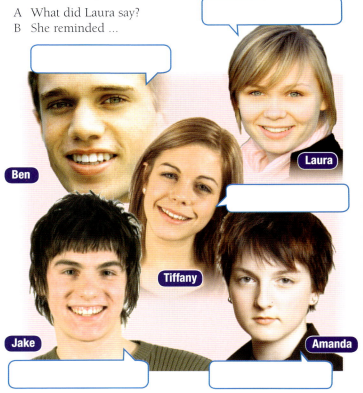

Now tell Student B what these people said. Use reported speech.

B What did Andy say?
A He explained …

I can't paint at night because I need plenty of light. (Andy)

I'm studying medicine in Manchester. (Mustafa)

Winning the lottery has changed my life. (Sally)

Will any of my friends be at the party? (Rachel)

Why didn't I get the text message? (Luke)

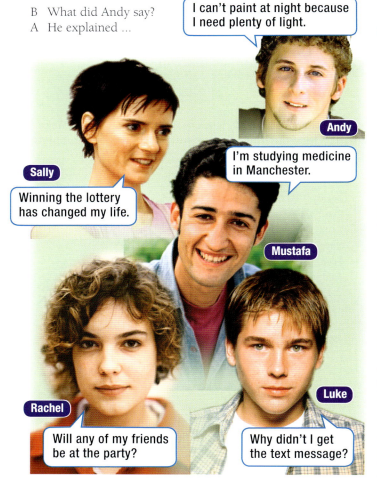

UNIT 7

You have one half of 11 separate sentences about languages. Student B has the other half of the sentences. One of you reads out a sentence beginning; the other finds and reads its ending, and then follows the arrow to read the next sentence beginning. You start by reading the first sentence beginning.

Ending	Beginning
	START! When Julius Caesar landed in Britain over 2,000 years ago,
that begins and ends with the letters 'und'.	The word 'hotel' was originally French,
but 50% of the global population speak one of the top 12 languages.	In 1945, the United Nations charter was signed by 50 countries
which is spoken by about 200,000 people.	The word 'queue' is the only word in the English language
(meaning 'in the end') has been voted the most annoying phrase in the English language.	The 'sh' sound can be spelt in over a dozen different ways in English:
and it wasn't spoken outside Britain.	Around 8,000 years ago, the Indo-European tribe were speaking a language

UNIT 8

Student B has the missing words from this crossword. You have Student B's missing words. Don't say the words! Take turns to ask each other for clues and try to complete the crossword.

A What's 1 across?
B It's someone who writes music.

B What's 1 down?
A It's a kind of material. It's grown in India and Egypt.

	1	2		3		4		5
	C		P		S		R		S
	O		U		T		E		P
6	T		N		7 R		P		Y
	T		C		I		A		
	O		T		8 K	N	I	F	9 E
10	N			U		E		R	
				R					
11				E			12		
13	N	O	V	E	L		14 D	I	E	T

GRAMMAR SUMMARY

Verbs not usually used in continuous forms
UNIT 1 LESSON 1

- The following verbs are not usually used in continuous forms. Many of these verbs refer to states (including mental states, eg *think*) rather than actions, or to the senses (eg *taste*):
  agree/disagree appear believe consist contain depend feel hear include know lack like/dislike love matter mean need prefer promise realise recognise remember see seem smell taste suppose sound think understand want
  Fruit juice contains sugar.
  It often seems that this is true.
  It doesn't matter whether they are fresh, frozen, ...
  People suppose that they are OK.
  They think that bottled water tastes better.
- Modal verbs (eg *must*) do not have continuous forms.

Gerund
UNIT 1 LESSON 2

- A gerund (*-ing* form) is a noun formed from a verb. It can be the subject of a sentence:
  Keeping in touch is easy.
  Walking 10,000 steps a day is great fun.
- We can also use a gerund after prepositions.
  We can use *by* + gerund to say how to do something:
  You can get more power by plugging the charger into your phone.
- We can use *for* + gerund to describe the function or purpose of something:
  It's a clever gadget for opening bottles.

after/before + participle clause
UNIT 1 LESSON 2

- We can use the present participle (*-ing* form) in time clauses introduced by the conjunctions *after* and *before*:
  She came up with the idea after struggling to get up in the morning.
  You are fully awake before turning it off.
- We can also use *when*, *while* and *since* to introduce participle time clauses:
  The media often exaggerate when reporting scientific research.

Spelling: *-ing* form
UNIT 1 LESSON 2

- Most verbs add *-ing*:
  keep – keep**ing**   walk – walk**ing**
- Verbs ending in *-e* drop the *-e* and add *-ing*:
  hid**e** – hid**ing**   mak**e** – mak**ing**
  But we don't make a change after *be* or *-ee*:
  be – be**ing**   see – see**ing**
- One-syllable verbs ending in a consonant after a single vowel double the last letter and add *-ing*:
  chop – cho**pp**ing   get – ge**tt**ing   plug – plu**gg**ing
  put – pu**tt**ing   run – ru**nn**ing   swim – swi**mm**ing
  Other verbs:
  begin – begi**nn**ing   travel – trave**ll**ing

Verb + gerund or infinitive
UNIT 1 LESSON 3

- We can use the gerund after these verbs:
  avoid enjoy go (+ activity) hate can't help keep like love mind risk can't stand start stop suggest
  I didn't exactly enjoy having acupuncture.
  Acupuncture keeps growing in popularity.
  Acupuncture stopped the woman feeling pain.
- We can use the infinitive after these verbs:
  agree appear ask choose continue dare decide expect hope learn manage prepare pretend promise refuse seem want
  When people expect to get better, they often do.
  I pretended to be calm.
- Some verbs can be followed by either the gerund or the infinitive.
- *try* + gerund = do something to see what happens:
  Patients who tried having acupuncture had fewer headaches.
  try + infinitive = attempt something difficult:
  He tried to stop smoking last year.
- *remember/forget* + gerund refers to an action in the past:
  I remember going to the doctor.
  I'll never forget meeting Nelson Mandela.
  remember/forget + infinitive refers to a necessary action – something that should be done – and looks ahead:
  He didn't remember to take it every day.
  We mustn't forget to lock the door.
- *stop* is usually followed by the gerund, but it can also be followed by the infinitive of purpose:
  The walkers stopped (walking) to have a rest.

109

GRAMMAR SUMMARY

Present perfect continuous
UNIT 2 LESSON 1

- We can use the present perfect continuous with *for* and *since* to talk about a continuous or repeated activity which started in the past and continues up to now:
  Since 1992 I've been making a series of drawings and prints of birds.
  For many years, Chris Ofili has been using elephant dung in his paintings.
  How long has Andy Goldsworthy been working with natural materials?
- We can also use this tense to talk about recently completed continuous actions which have present results:
  I can tell she's been crying. (Her eyes are red.)
- We form the present perfect continuous with *have/has been* + present participle.
- See also Unit 1 Lesson 1 and Unit 2 Lesson 2.

Present perfect simple and continuous
UNIT 2 LESSON 2

- We can use the present perfect simple to talk about a recent completed action or series of actions:
  Some of the work has been quite badly paid.
  I've only had two jobs so far.
- We can use the present perfect continuous to talk about a recent action or a repeated series of actions which continues up to now. The activity may still be continuing and is often temporary:
  I've been working on the new Bond movie.
  I've been calling the agencies every morning.
  They've been trying to get the lighting right.
- We use the present perfect simple to focus on *how much/many*:
  How much work have you had this year?
  I've had plenty of offers.
- We use the present perfect continuous to focus on *how long*:
  My phone has been ringing all week.
- See also Unit 1 Lesson 1 and Unit 2 Lesson 1.

Past perfect simple and continuous
UNIT 2 LESSON 3

```
              Past perfect simple   Past simple    NOW
                     ↓                  ↓
  Past perfect continuous  - - - - - →
```

- We use the past perfect simple to describe the earlier of two past events, to make the order of events clear. We use the past simple for the more recent event:
  Before I was 11 I had been to eight different schools.
  It was much harder than I'd expected.
  TV hadn't reached Australia yet.
  I had never known comics before.

- If the order of events is clear, we don't need to use the past perfect for the earlier event:
  Pullman started writing his first novel the day after he (had) finished his final exams.
  But compare these sentences:
  The train left when I reached the station.
  (I saw the train.)
  The train had left when I reached the station.
  (I didn't see the train.)
- We use the past perfect continuous to talk about a continuous or repeated earlier activity:
  I'd been reading books for a long time.
  Before he became a full-time writer, Pullman had been teaching for many years.
- We form the past perfect simple with *had* + past participle.
- We form the past perfect continuous with *had been* + present participle.
- See also Unit 1 Lesson 1.

Comparison of adverbs
UNIT 3 LESSON 1

- Adverbs ending in *-ly* take *more/most*:
  Lightning travels more slowly than light.
  Where does the Earth rotate most quickly?
- Adverbs with the same form as adjectives add *-er/-est*:
  fast   faster   (the) fastest
  hard   harder   (the) hardest
  high   higher   (the) highest
  late   later   (the) latest
  long   longer   (the) longest
  Which travels faster?
  Which began later: life on land or in the sea?
  Russian astronauts have been in space longest.
- Irregular forms:
  well   better   (the) best
  badly   worse   (the) worst
  far   further   (the) furthest
- We often use *the* before superlative adverbs when making comparisons with other things:
  Of all the planets, Jupiter rotates the most quickly.
  BUT *The Earth rotates most quickly at the Equator.*
  (The Earth isn't compared with anything else.)

Adverbs of degree
UNIT 3 LESSON 1

- These adverbs are followed by another adverb or by an adjective:
  quite really extremely incredibly very
  The universe has been expanding extremely rapidly.
  Lightning also travels really quickly.
  Our universe is incredibly large.

GRAMMAR SUMMARY

Position and order of adverbial phrases
UNIT 3 LESSON 1

- Adverbial phrases usually follow the verb in this order:
  Manner → *Place* → *Time*
  Life began suddenly in the sea after that.
  Apes started to walk on two feet millions of years ago.
  The Earth rotates most quickly at the Equator.

Making exclamations
UNIT 3 LESSON 2

- We can use *What (a/an)* + (adjective) + noun to express surprise and make exclamations:
  What fun!
  What a discovery!
  What a fantastic sight!
- We can also use *so* + (adjective/adverb) and *such(a/an)* + (adjective) + noun to make exclamations:
  It's so unexpected!
  The three of us are having such an amazing time.

Result clauses: *so/such … that*
UNIT 3 LESSON 2

- We can use these structures to express consequence or result:
  so + (adjective/adverb) + *that*
  It was so deep that they didn't expect to see any life.
  such (a/an) + (adjective) + noun + *that*
  It's been such an exciting dive that I haven't noticed the time.
- We often leave out *that*, especially in spoken English:
  It was so dark (that) I couldn't see anything.

Order of adjectives
UNIT 3 LESSON 2

- Adjectives usually precede the noun in this order:
  Opinion → *Size* → *Age* → *Shape* → *Colour* → *Origin*
  I've just seen a beautiful small flat blue fish.
  We're diving in a comfortable, spacious, modern Russian submersible.

The future
UNIT 3 LESSON 3 AND UNIT 4 LESSON 1

- We use the future simple (*will/won't*) to give information about future events and to make predictions:
  Every passenger will have a spectacular view.
  I'm sure the cost of space flights will come down.
  It won't be cheap.
  Will the dream ever become reality?
- We use the present simple to talk about schedules and timetables:
  The tour starts at 9.45am.
- We use the present continuous to talk about fixed future arrangements:
  I'm visiting the Kennedy Space Center tomorrow.
- We use *going to* to talk about plans and intentions:
  Branson is going to travel on the first flight.
  I'm going to book a ticket!
- We use the future continuous to talk about events that will be in progress at a particular time in the future:
  In 2020 …
  They'll be working longer.
  Doctors won't be treating diseases any longer.
  Will we all be living longer?
  We can also use the future continuous to talk about future arrangements:
  I'll be seeing Jenny later, so I can give her your message.
- We use the future perfect to talk about something which will/won't have finished by a certain time in the future:
  Scientists will have invented earrings which take our pulses.
  We won't have got rid of cars.
  Will we have created a bright new future?
- See also Unit 4 Lesson 2.

First conditional
UNIT 4 LESSON 2

- We use the first conditional to talk about the possible future when discussing the consequences of actions or events. First conditional sentences have this structure:
  if/unless + present simple, future simple:
  If we don't travel so far, we'll reduce carbon emissions.
  Unless we take action now, we won't reduce the impact …
- The conditional clause can follow the main clause:
  It will be OK for me to fly if I plant enough trees.
  The situation won't improve unless we all work together.
- *unless = if not*

Future time clauses
UNIT 4 LESSON 2

- *when/as soon as/until* + present simple, future simple
  In the future when we fly, we'll pay a compulsory carbon tax.
  As soon as carbon emissions decrease, air pollution will decrease.
- The time clause can follow the main clause:
  We won't halt global warming until we stop flying.
- *as soon as = immediately after something happens*
  until = up to the time when something happens

GRAMMAR SUMMARY

Second conditional
UNIT 4 LESSON 3

- We use the second conditional to talk about imaginary present or unlikely future situations. Second conditional sentences have this structure:
  If + past simple, would(n't) …
    If I had enough time, I'd travel overland.
    If I were in Nepal for a short time, I wouldn't leave Kathmandu.
    If you could choose, where would you stay?
- In the conditional clause we can use either *were* or *was* after I/he/she/it: *was* is informal:
    If I was in Nepal for a short time, I wouldn't leave Kathmandu.
- We can use *If I were you, I'd/I wouldn't* … to give advice and warnings:
    If I were you, I'd stay in a guesthouse.
- The conditional clause can follow the main clause:
    I'd stay in a guesthouse if I were you.

wish/if only
UNIT 4 LESSON 3 AND UNIT 5 LESSON 1

- We can use *wish* or *if only* + past simple to express a hope or desire for something in the present to be different:
    I wish I could take all my friends!
    He wishes he had more time.
    If only people were like that in London.
    I wish I were/was in Kathmandu.
- We can use *wish* or *if only* + past perfect to express regret about the past:
    I wish I had succeeded.
    Some people still wish he had got away with it.
    If only they hadn't caught me!

Third conditional
UNIT 5 LESSON 1

- We use the third conditional to talk about unreal or imaginary past events. Third conditional sentences have this structure:
  If + past perfect, would(n't) have …
    If the plot had succeeded, the king would have died.
    If the gunpowder had exploded, he wouldn't have survived.
- The conditional clause can follow the main clause:
    What would have happened if the gunpowder had exploded?

must, have to and need to
don't have to, don't need to and needn't
UNIT 5 LESSON 2

- We use *must, have to* and *need to* to express present and future obligation:
  You must/You have to = It's obligatory.
  You need to = It's necessary.
    Why must Jo be very careful?
    You have to watch their swim patterns.
    The team needs to clean the tank walls regularly.
- We use *mustn't* to say that something is not allowed or that it is wrong:
    She mustn't use a very hot hairdryer.
- The past tense of both *must* and *have to* is *had to*:
    I had to tell myself to stay calm.
- The past tense of *need to* is *needed to*:
    We needed to be careful.
- We use *don't have to, don't need to* and *needn't* to express lack of obligation:
    Why doesn't Mark have to heat the oil himself?
    You don't need to worry about me.
    You needn't worry about me.
  The past forms are *didn't have to* and *didn't need to*.
- *needn't* (= *don't need to*) is a modal auxiliary verb. We can't use *need* as a modal auxiliary in affirmative statements; instead we use *need to*. But note that *need* can also be a main verb with an object:
    The elaborate hairstyles need work.
- See also Unit 8 Lesson 2.

must have and can't have
could/may/might have
UNIT 5 LESSON 3

- We use *must have* and *can't have* + past participle to make deductions about the past. We use *must have* when we are sure something happened:
    The plane must have run out of fuel.
  We use *can't have* when we are sure something didn't happen:
    It can't have blown up in mid-air.
- We use *could/may/might have* + past participle to speculate about the past and to talk about what possibly happened:
    What could have happened to them?
    They could have ended up on a desert island.
    Earhart and Noonan may have been US spies.
    Aliens might have abducted them. (Less likely)

GRAMMAR SUMMARY

Reported speech
UNIT 6 LESSONS 1 AND 2

- **Reported speech with various reporting verbs**
- Verb + infinitive:
  agree   ask   hope   offer   promise   refuse
  They agreed to let me go.
  I promised to send loads of emails.
- Verb + object + infinitive:
  advise   ask   invite   promise   tell   warn
  She invited me to go with her.
  Dad told me to keep in touch.
- Verb + (that) clause:
  agree   explain   complain   hope   point out   promise   reply   say   suggest   warn
  Mum pointed out that I didn't like Indian food.
  You complained it was too spicy.
- Verb + object + (that) clause
  promise   remind   tell   warn:
  Mum reminded me that I had to have injections.
- suggest + -ing:
  Mum suggested inviting Nisha and her parents for supper.
- **Reported questions**
  Reported Yes/No questions: we use *if* before the reported question.
  Reported Wh- questions: we use the question word before the reported question.
  'Is everything all right?'
  → She asked if everything was all right.
  'Can I get you anything else?'
  → She wanted to know if she could get him anything else.
  'Would you like some ketchup?'
  → She wondered if he would like some ketchup.
  'What do you want to drink?
  → She asked what he wanted to drink.
  In reported questions, the subject–verb order is the same as in statements. We don't use a question mark after reported questions.
- In reported speech, verbs in the present usually change into the past, and verbs in the past usually change into the past perfect:

Direct speech	→	Reported speech
Present simple	→	Past simple
Present continuous	→	Past continuous
Past simple	→	Past perfect
Present perfect	→	Past perfect
am/is/are going to	→	was/were going to
must	→	had to
can	→	could
will	→	would

  Note: Modal verbs *could, should, would, might* do not change.

- Time phrases and other reference words also usually change in reported speech:

Direct speech		Reported speech
today	→	that day
tonight	→	that night
tomorrow	→	the next/following day
yesterday	→	the day before
now	→	then
here	→	there
this	→	that/the

get/have something done
UNIT 6 LESSON 3

- We use *get/have something done* when we ask or arrange for someone to do something for us:
  It makes sense to get your eyes tested.
  You have your car serviced before you go.

It's time (that) + past simple
UNIT 6 LESSON 3

- We use *It's time (that)* + past simple to say that something should happen now. We often use this construction to criticise behaviour:
  It's time the British woke up to reality.
  It's time that people realised that their behaviour abroad is important.

The passive
UNIT 7 LESSONS 1 AND 2

- We form the different passive tenses with the appropriate tense of *be* + past participle:
  Past simple: *The elephant was named Jumbo.*
  Present perfect: *I have been given the sack.*
  Present simple: *The shuttlecock is kept up in the air.*
  Present continuous: *New expressions are being added all the time.*
  Future simple: *You will be shown the ropes.*
- We form the passive infinitive with *to be* + past participle:
  Many people think that Franklin deserves to be awarded a Nobel Prize.
  She is beginning to be recognised as a brilliant scientist.
- After modal verbs we use the infinitive without *to*:
  The picture could be used to work out the structure of DNA.
  Women couldn't be served in the same dining room.
  Nobel Prizes may only be given to the living.
  Her life shouldn't be seen as a failure.
- We use the passive to focus on the action rather than the agent (the person or thing that performs the action). When we want to refer to the agent, we use *by* + noun:
  Now 'wicked' is being used by young people as slang for 'very good'.

113

GRAMMAR SUMMARY

either ... or and both ... and
UNIT 7 LESSON 2

- We can use **either ... or**, meaning *one or the other*, to talk about two alternative possibilities:
  Either Franklin or Crick and Watson could have been the first.
- We can use **both ... and**, meaning *the two together*, for emphasis:
  Both Crick and Watson clearly benefited from Franklin's work.

Phrasal verbs
UNIT 7 LESSON 3

- Phrasal verbs are very common in English and there are three main structures:
- Verb + adverb with no object:
  The pace of life in Africa is speeding up.
  It is likely to go on for many years.
  Sometimes the meaning of a phrasal verb is clear, eg *speed up*, but phrasal verbs are idiomatic and their meaning isn't always obvious.
- Verb + adverb with direct object:
  The noun object can go before or after the adverb:
  They have put up tall towers.
  OR *They have put tall towers up.*
  The pronoun object **must** go between the verb and the adverb:
  They have put them up.
- Verb + preposition with direct object:
  Noun **and** pronoun objects go at the end of the phrase:
  People climb up a ladder.
  People climb up it.
- Words like *up* and *on* can be either adverbs or prepositions. They are usually stressed as adverbs, but not as prepositions.
- We often use phrasal verbs instead of single-word verbs:
  It is likely to go on (= continue) for many years.
  They have found out (= discovered) how to solve this problem.
- Phrasal verbs often have several different meanings:
  I need to turn up (= shorten) my jeans.
  He turned up (= arrived) with a couple of friends.
  Could you turn up (= increase the temperature) the heating?

could(n't), was(n't) able to, managed to
UNIT 8 LESSON 1

- We can use *could/couldn't* and *was/wasn't able to* to talk about ability in the past.
  could and *couldn't*:
  JK Rowling moved to Edinburgh so that she could be near her sister.
  Einstein couldn't read until he was seven.
  was/wasn't able to:
  Though Beethoven wasn't able to hear, he was able to listen.
  Einstein wasn't able to get a job at a Swiss university.
- BUT we don't use *could* in the affirmative to talk about achieving something on a particular occasion. Instead we use *was able to* or *managed to*:
  He was able to educate himself in prison.
  NOT *He could educate himself in prison.*
  Einstein managed to get a place at SIT.
  NOT *He could get a place at SIT.*
- See also Unit 5 Lesson 2 and Unit 8 Lesson 2.

in order to and so that
UNIT 8 LESSON 1

- We can use *in order to* and *so that* to express purpose.
- We can use either form when the subject is the same:
  She wrote in cafés in order to escape from her flat.
  = She wrote in cafés so that she could escape from her flat.
- When the subject is different we use *so that*:
  He started performing with bands so that his poems could reach people who didn't read books.
- We often leave out *that*, especially in spoken English:
  She moved to Edinburgh so (that) she could be near her sister.

Modal expressions in the past and future
UNIT 8 LESSON 2

- Modal expressions for obligation, ability and necessity in the past: *had to, didn't have to, was(n't) able to, were(n't) able to, needed to/didn't need to, needn't have*:
  You had to pay to go to them.
  Children didn't have to go to school at all.
  Many poor families weren't able to pay.
  Girls didn't need to go to school.
  She needn't have worried.
  didn't need to refers to something which wasn't done because it wasn't necessary.
  needn't have refers to something which was done but was unnecessary.
- Modal expressions for obligation, ability and necessity in the future: *will/won't have to, will/won't be able to, will/won't need to*:
  Students won't have to wait until they get home.
  Students will be able choose what to wear.
  Students won't need to queue.
- See also Unit 5 Lesson 2 and Unit 8 Lesson 1.

GRAMMAR SUMMARY

make and let
UNIT 8 LESSON 3

- Active: *make* and *let* are both followed by object + infinitive without *to*:
  I play some chords, which make me think of a time in my life.
  The guy who runs it let me do one song.
- Passive: *make* is followed by object + infinitive with *to*:
  I was made to understand how hard I had to work.
  The verb *let* has no passive form. Instead we use *allowed to*:
  I was then allowed to do my first 30-minute set.

Linking words

- We use these conjunctions to introduce participle time clauses:
  after   before   when   while   since
  She came up with the idea after struggling to get up in the morning.
  You are fully awake before turning it off.
  The media often exaggerate when reporting scientific research.
- **unless** means *if not*:
  The situation won't improve unless we all work together.
- **as soon as** means *immediately after something happens*:
  As soon as carbon emissions decrease, air pollution will decrease.
- **until** means *up to the time when something happens*:
  Fry the minced beef until it is brown.
- We use these phrases to express reason or cause:
  as a result of ...   because (of) ...   thanks to ...
- We use these words and phrases to express consequence or result:
  as a result   consequently   so   so ... that   such ... that   therefore
- We can use **in order to** and **so that** to express purpose:
  She wrote in cafés in order to escape from her flat.
  He started performing with bands so that his poems could reach people who didn't read books.
- We use these words and phrases to add information:
  also   in addition   what is more
  in addition and *what is more* usually come at the start of a sentence.
- We use these phrases to give examples:
  for example   for instance   such as
  such as can't come at the start of a sentence.
- We use **whereas** and **while** to contrast two facts or ideas:
  Maribel got £600 a month, whereas a top male player got £60,000.
  The women's team reached the quarter-finals, while the men's team were knocked out in the first round.
- **either ... or** means *one or the other*:
  Either Franklin or Crick and Watson could have been the first.
- **neither ... nor** means *not one or the other*:
  You've studied neither geography nor history!
- **both ... and** means *the two together*:
  Both Crick and Watson clearly benefited from Franklin's work.
- We can use **not only ... but also** instead of *and* to add emphasis:
  These killers are not only European languages but also Asian ones.
- We use **which**, **who** and **whose** to introduce non-defining relative clauses, which give us more information about a noun:
  Take the case of Romansch, which is spoken in Switzerland.
  Sir Richard Branson, who is the Virgin boss, is going to travel on the first flight.

COMMUNICATION ACTIVITIES
STUDENT B

UNIT 1

You have half a recipe for Spaghetti Bolognese and Student A has the other half. The sentences are not in the right order. Work with Student A to put the recipe in the right order. Don't look at Student A's sentences. Student A has the first sentence and you have the last one.

Spaghetti Bolognese

Serves 6

Ingredients: 450g spaghetti, 900g minced beef, 50g bacon, 1 medium onion, 1 carrot, 2 cloves of garlic, 100ml olive oil, 100ml red wine, 1 tin of chopped tomatoes, 75g grated Parmesan cheese, salt and pepper

- Sprinkle with Parmesan cheese and serve immediately.
- When the wine has come to the boil, put the beef and vegetable mixture back into the frying pan, and add a litre of water. Cook the sauce very slowly for two hours, stirring from time to time.
- Then add the cooked beef to the tomatoes and vegetables. Season with pepper and salt.
- Now take the cooked vegetables and tomatoes out of the frying pan and put on one side.
- Put the spaghetti in the boiling water, add salt and stir for a few seconds.
- Then heat half the oil in a frying pan and fry the bacon for a minute. Add the chopped onion, garlic and carrot, and fry until they are soft.

UNIT 2

Read the text. Then ask Student A questions to complete it. Answer Student A's questions.

> What had Kam always dreamed of doing?

A Korean folk tale

Long ago a hard-working farmer called Kam lived in a small village deep in the Korean countryside. He'd always dreamt of __1__ (what/do?). Then one day he decided to make the journey.

Kam enjoyed his visit to the city and bought presents for __2__ (who?). Then in one shop he found the strangest thing he'd ever seen. It was a __3__ (what shape?) shining piece of metal. In it a man was staring in amazement at Kam. Not only that, but the man __4__ (what/do?). Kam had never seen a mirror before and bought it to take home.

When he got home __5__ (who?) were delighted with their presents. It was his daughter who found the mirror in his bag when Kam wasn't in the room. She cried 'Look! Father's been hiding something. He's brought __6__ (who?) back with him and by magic put her into this metal.'

Kam's wife heard and ran into the room. Seeing the face of a woman in the mirror, she shouted 'My husband has brought a woman back from the city to take my place. And she looks __7__ (how?)!'

Then Kam and his father appeared. His father __8__ (what/do?) and shouted at Kam 'Why have you brought this ugly old man back with you?'

Kam took his family to see the village chief. 'Let me see this magic metal,' said the chief, who knew __9__ (what?) well. 'You are all wrong,' he went on. 'All I can see is the face of a wise old man.' Then he explained what a mirror was. 'And remember,' he said, __10__ (what/say?).

STUDENT B

UNIT 3

You've written this from notes you took from a TV programme. But you're not sure about some parts so you have underlined them. Student A, a schoolfriend who also watched the programme, phones you. Answer Student A's questions. Then ask Student A questions to check the underlined parts you're not sure about.

> When are we going to build a Moon Station by?

Living on the Moon

Twelve astronauts walked on the Moon between 1969 and 1972 and now we're going back! The technology will soon exist for people to live on the Moon. We are going to build a Moon Station <u>by 2020</u>. Dozens of astronauts are going to live and work in the Station, which will take years to build.

A robot spaceship which takes off in <u>six</u> months' time is flying to the Moon to start research. The journey to the Moon will take <u>five</u> days at a speed of 11 kms per second. When the robot arrives on the Moon it will search for water and oxygen <u>in the atmosphere</u>. The spaceship returns to Earth after a week with the results of its trip.

'In some ways living on the Moon <u>won't</u> be easier than living on a space station,' an astronaut said. 'In space you're weightless but on the Moon we will have one-sixth of the Earth's gravity. And it will certainly be <u>more expensive</u> as we won't have to bring everything up by rocket. There are going to be factories using the minerals we know are there.'

So what problems are the first people on the Moon going to face? 'They're going to feel <u>happy</u>,' another astronaut said. 'It'll be a bit like living on a nuclear submarine, except that on the Moon every time you wake up you'll see how <u>close</u> you are to Earth.'

Living on the Moon is clearly going to be a <u>difficult project</u> but it will only be the start. We'll use the experience we get from living there to plan expeditions to <u>Mars</u> and Pluto.

UNIT 4

Here are some predictions about life in 2020, in 2060 and in 3000, which may or may not be true. Look at the chart and answer Student A's questions.

A Will we still be driving cars by 2020?
B Yes, we will.
A Will we have used up all the oil by 3000?
B Yes, we will.

	2020	2060	3000
still drive cars	✓		
use up all the oil			✓
live until we are 150	✗	✗	
make the perfect robot	✗		✓
discover life on another planet			✗
still watch TV		✓	✗
enjoy Moon holidays every summer		✗	
kill the last whale		✗	✓

Now ask Student A questions to complete the chart.

B Will we be living until we're 150 by 3000?
A No, we won't.
B Will we have made the perfect robot by 2060?
A No, we won't.

UNIT 5

Last summer, six students went on holiday. They all went to different Mediterranean countries:

Egypt   France   Greece   Italy   Spain   Turkey

and they all did different activities on holiday.

horse riding   paragliding   rock climbing
sailing   scuba diving   windsurfing

Look at the clues below. Student A also has five clues. Take turns to read out your clues and work together to complete the chart.

	Country	Activity
Alice		
Bob		
Cathy		
Dave		
Ellen		
Fred		

Clues
Dave spent his holiday in the French Alps.
Bob is afraid of heights.
Ellen didn't go climbing.
One of the girls went riding in Turkey.
The windsurfer went to Italy.

> Dave must have gone to France.

> Fred can't have been paragliding or climbing.

STUDENT B

UNIT 6

Tell Student A what these people said. Use reported speech.

A What did Laura say?
B She reminded …

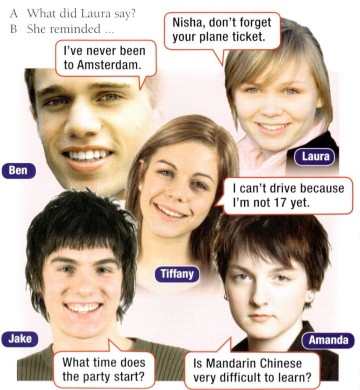

What did these people actually say? Ask Student A and complete the speech bubbles.

B What did Andy say?
A He explained …

UNIT 7

You have one half of 11 separate sentences about languages. Student A has the other half of the sentences. One of you reads out a sentence beginning; the other finds and reads its ending, and then follows the arrow to read the next sentence beginning. Student A starts by reading the first sentence beginning.

Ending	Beginning
that is still pronounced the same when the last four letters have been removed.	'Underground' is the only word in the English language
which generated many of the languages used in the world today.	There are about 6,000 languages spoken in the world today,
but it was first used to mean 'a place to stay the night' in America.	The expression 'at the end of the day'
the English language did not exist.	Four hundred years ago, English was used by 5–7 million people
and its text was in five languages: Chinese, English, French, Russian and Spanish.	The smallest national language is Icelandic,
FINISH! ocean, population, Russian, champagne, sugar, luxury etc.	

UNIT 8

Student A has the missing words from this crossword. You have Student A's missing words. Don't say the words! Take turns to ask each other for clues and try to complete the crossword.

A What's 1 across?
B It's someone who writes music.

B What's 1 down?
A It's a kind of material. It's grown in India and Egypt.

¹C	O	²M	³P	O	S	⁴E	R	⁵
⁶T	W	I	N		⁷R	E	P	L	Y
					⁸			⁹E
¹⁰N	A	T	U	R	E			X
								P
¹¹F	R	E	E	D	O	¹²M		E
						A		R
¹³						¹⁴D		T

Culture Saying the right thing
Shopping Skills questionnaire
Answers

1 C is the best answer. Both A and B sound rude.

2 B is the best answer. 'Try on' means 'put them on to see if they fit and take them off again'; 'wear' and 'put on' mean 'put them on and keep them on.'

3 A is the best answer. B is wrong because 'jeans' is a plural noun, and C is wrong because bigger jeans are needed, not smaller.

4 A is the best answer: 'It doesn't suit me' means 'I don't look good in it'. B is wrong because 'fit' is about size, and C is wrong because 'match' is used to say how one colour goes with another.

5 B is the best answer. A is wrong because 'more' is used to compare two things. C is quite rude – 'knock off' is slang and it isn't usual to bargain in shops in the UK.

6 C is the best answer. A is too informal for a polite request, and 'fiver' is slang. B is wrong because the speaker means 'lend me' and not 'borrow'.

WORD LIST

(adj) = adjective
(adv) = adverb
(conj) = conjunction
(n) = noun
(prep) = preposition
(v) = verb
(AmE) = American English
(TS) = tapescript

Unit 1

advertising (n)	/ˈædvəˌtaɪzɪŋ/
astronaut (n)	/ˈæstrəˌnɔːt/
at best	/ət ˈbest/
at least (adv)	/ət ˈliːst/
at worst	/ət ˈwɜːst/
back (n)	/bæk/
beep (n)	/biːp/
belief (n)	/brˈliːf/
bottled (adj)	/ˈbɒtld/
brain scan (n)	/ˈbreɪn ˌskæn/
break down	/ˌbreɪk ˈdaʊn/
calm (adj)	/kɑːm/
chest (n)	/tʃest/
choice (n)	/tʃɔɪs/
claim (v)	/kleɪm/
clever (adj)	/ˈklevə/
clip (v)	/klɪp/
clockwise (adv)	/ˈklɒkˌwaɪz/
consist (v)	/kənˈsɪst/
count (as) (v)	/kaʊnt/
current (adj)	/ˈkʌrənt/
daily (adv) (TS)	/ˈdeɪli/
damage (v)	/ˈdæmɪdʒ/
dead (= dead people) (n)	/ded/
decay (n)	/dɪˈkeɪ/
delicious (adj)	/dɪˈlɪʃəs/
digest (v)	/daɪˈdʒest/
drawer (n)	/drɔː/
emphasise (v)	/ˈemfəˌsaɪz/
equally (adv)	/ˈiːkwəli/
estimated (adj)	/ˈestɪˌmeɪtəd/
exaggerate (v)	/ɪɡˈzædʒəˌreɪt/
experiment (n)	/ɪkˈsperɪmənt/
expert (n)	/ˈekspɜːt/
fake (adj)	/feɪk/
fault (n)	/fɔːlt/
fiction (n)	/ˈfɪkʃ(ə)n/
fine (= delicate) (adj)	/faɪn/
form (of transport) (n)	/fɔːm/
furry (adj)	/ˈfɜːri/
gadget (n)	/ˈɡædʒɪt/
gene (n)	/dʒiːn/
go off (alarm)	/ˌɡəʊ ˈɒf/
hip (n)	/hɪp/
human (n)	/ˈhjuːmən/
improve (v)	/ɪmˈpruːv/
in reality	/ɪn riˈæləti/
indicate (v)	/ˈɪndɪˌkeɪt/
individual (n)	/ˌɪndɪˈvɪdʒuəl/
insert (v)	/ɪnˈsɜːt/
key ring (n)	/ˈkiː ˌrɪŋ/
label (n)	/ˈleɪb(ə)l/
lack (v)	/læk/
landmark (n)	/ˈlændmɑːk/
learning (n)	/ˈlɜːnɪŋ/
lightning conductor (n)	/ˈlaɪtnɪŋ kənˌdʌktə/
link (v)	/lɪŋk/
logic (n)	/ˈlɒdʒɪk/
man-made (adj)	/ˈmænˌmeɪd/
maximise (v)	/ˈmæksɪˌmaɪz/
meditation (n)	/ˌmedɪˈteɪʃ(ə)n/
medium (adj)	/ˈmiːdiəm/
mind's eye (n)	/ˈmaɪndz ˌaɪ/
muscle (n)	/ˈmʌs(ə)l/
myth (n)	/mɪθ/
neither ... nor (conj)	/ˈnaɪðə ... ˌnɔː/
nightmare (n)	/ˈnaɪtˌmeə/
obviously (adv)	/ˈɒbviəsli/
occasionally (adv)	/əˈkeɪʒ(ə)li/
on the contrary	/ˌɒn ðə ˈkɒntrəri/
on the other hand	/ˌɒn ði ˈʌðə ˌhænd/
option (n)	/ˈɒpʃ(ə)n/
orbit (n)	/ˈɔːbɪt/
particularly (adv)	/pəˈtɪkjʊləli/
pedometer (n)	/peˈdɒmɪtə/
phone charger (n)	/ˈfəʊn ˌtʃɑːdʒə/
plug in	/ˌplʌɡ ˈɪn/
point (= position) (n)	/pɔɪnt/
point of view (n)	/ˌpɔɪnt əv ˈvjuː/
portion (n)	/ˈpɔːʃ(ə)n/
positive (adj)	/ˈpɒzətɪv/
prepared (adj)	/prɪˈpeəd/
pure (adj)	/pjʊə/
raindrop (n)	/ˈreɪnˌdrɒp/
reaction (n)	/riˈækʃ(ə)n/
recognise (v)	/ˈrekəɡˌnaɪz/
recommend (v)	/ˌrekəˈmend/
reflect (v)	/rɪˈflekt/
regularly (adv)	/ˈreɡjʊləli/
research (n)	/rɪˈsɜːtʃ, ˈriːsɜːtʃ/
scientific (adj)	/ˌsaɪənˈtɪfɪk/
selected (adj)	/sɪˈlektəd/
sensible (adj)	/ˈsensəb(ə)l/
session (n)	/ˈseʃ(ə)n/
set (alarm clock) (v)	/set/
simply (adv)	/ˈsɪmpli/
snooze button (n)	/ˈsnuːz ˌbʌt(ə)n/
so-called (adj)	/ˌsəʊˈkɔːld/
source (n)	/sɔːs/
statistics (n pl)	/stəˈtɪstɪks/
strength (n)	/streŋθ/
strike (v)	/straɪk/
struggle (v)	/ˈstrʌɡ(ə)l/
suppose (v)	/səˈpəʊz/
swallow (v)	/ˈswɒləʊ/
synthetic (adj)	/sɪnˈθetɪk/
technique (n)	/tekˈniːk/
therefore (adv)	/ˈðeəfɔː/
treat (v)	/triːt/
trial (n)	/traɪəl/
type (n)	/taɪp/
unfortunately (adv)	/ʌnˈfɔːtʃ(ə)nətli/
unhealthy (adj)	/ʌnˈhelθi/
wind (= wind up) (n)	/waɪnd/
wind up (clock)	/ˌwaɪnd ˈʌp/

FOOD and DRINK

add (v)	/æd/
balanced (diet) (adj)	/ˈbælənst/
beat (v)	/biːt/
boil (v)	/bɔɪl/
cereal (n)	/ˈsɪəriəl/
chop (v)	/tʃɒp/
cream (n)	/kriːm/
dish (n)	/dɪʃ/
drain (v)	/dreɪn/
dried fruit (n)	/ˌdraɪd ˈfruːt/
fat (n)	/fæt/
fry (v)	/fraɪ/
grate (v)	/ɡreɪt/
heat (n & v)	/hiːt/
ingredient (n)	/ɪnˈɡriːdiənt/
junk food (n)	/ˈdʒʌŋk ˌfuːd/
margarine (n)	/ˌmɑːdʒəˈriːn/
mineral (n)	/ˈmɪn(ə)rəl/
mixture (n)	/ˈmɪkstʃə/
olive oil (n)	/ˌɒlɪv ˈɔɪl/
protein (n)	/ˈprəʊtiːn/
recipe (n)	/ˈresəpi/
serve (v)	/sɜːv/
slice (v)	/slaɪs/
soft drink (n)	/ˌsɒft ˈdrɪŋk/
sprinkle (v)	/ˈsprɪŋk(ə)l/
stir (in) (v)	/stɜː (ˈɪn)/
tap water (n)	/ˈtæp ˌwɔːtə/
tinned food (adj)	/ˌtɪnd ˈfuːd/
toast (n)	/təʊst/
vitamin (n)	/ˈvɪtəmɪn/

KITCHEN EQUIPMENT

bottle opener (n)	/ˈbɒt(ə)l ˌəʊp(ə)nə/
bowl (n)	/bəʊl/
bread knife (n)	/ˈbred ˌnaɪf/
cheese grater (n)	/ˈtʃiːz ˌɡreɪtə/
coffee maker (n)	/ˈkɒfi ˌmeɪkə/
corkscrew (n)	/ˈkɔːkskruː/
frying pan (n)	/ˈfraɪɪŋ ˌpæn/
kettle (n)	/ˈket(ə)l/
sandwich toaster (n)	/ˈsæn(d)wɪdʒ ˌtəʊstə/
saucepan (n)	/ˈsɔːspən/
tin opener (n)	/ˈtɪn ˌəʊp(ə)nə/
toaster (n)	/ˈtəʊstə/

MEDICINE (1)

acupuncture (n)	/ˈækjʊˌpʌŋktʃə/
alternative medicine (n)	/ɔːlˌtɜːnətɪv ˈmed(ə)s(ə)n/
aspirin (n)	/ˈæsprɪn/
drug (n)	/drʌɡ/
general anaesthetic (n)	/ˌdʒenrəl ænəsˈθetɪk/
healing (n)	/ˈhiːlɪŋ/
herbal (adj)	/ˈhɜːb(ə)l/
herbalist (n)	/ˈhɜːbəlɪst/
hospital (n)	/ˈhɒspɪt(ə)l/
medical student (n)	/ˈmedɪk(ə)l ˌstjuːdnt/
open-heart surgery (n)	/ˌəʊpənˌhɑːt ˈsɜːdʒəri/
operating table (n)	/ˈɒpəreɪtɪŋ ˌteɪb(ə)l/
operating theatre (n)	/ˈɒpəreɪtɪŋ ˌθɪətə/
operation (n)	/ˌɒpəˈreɪʃ(ə)n/
pain (n)	/peɪn/
patient (n)	/ˈpeɪʃ(ə)nt/
pill (n)	/pɪl/
placebo effect (n)	/pləˈsiːbəʊ ɪˌfekt/
remedy (n)	/ˈremədi/
surgeon (n)	/ˈsɜːdʒ(ə)n/

NOUNS and ADJECTIVES

acid, acidic	/ˈæsɪd/ /əˈsɪdɪk/
danger, dangerous	/ˈdeɪndʒə/ /ˈdeɪndʒərəs/
harm, harmless	/hɑːm/ /ˈhɑːmləs/
health, healthy	/helθ/ /ˈhelθi/
herb, herbal	/hɜːb/ /ˈhɜːb(ə)l/
illness, ill	/ˈɪlnəs/ /ɪl/
importance, important	/ɪmˈpɔːtns/ /ɪmˈpɔːtnt/
reality, real	/riˈæləti/ /rɪəl/
risk, risky	/rɪsk/ /ˈrɪski/
sense, sensible	/sens/ /ˈsensəb(ə)l/
strength, strong	/streŋθ/ /strɒŋ/
thirst, thirsty	/θɜːst/ /ˈθɜːsti/
truth, true	/truːθ/ /truː/

CULTURE East and West

allow (v)	/əˈlaʊ/
against (prep)	/əˈɡenst/
basically (adv)	/ˈbeɪsɪkli/

WORD LIST

capitalism (n)	/ˈkæpɪtəˌlɪz(ə)m/
chase (v)	/tʃeɪs/
conservative (adj)	/kənˈsɜːvətɪv/
consumption (n)	/kənˈsʌmpʃ(ə)n/
essentially (n)	/ɪˈsenʃ(ə)li/
freedom (n)	/ˈfriːdəm/
generous (adj)	/ˈdʒenərəs/
independent (adj)	/ˌɪndɪˈpendənt/
military (adj)	/ˈmɪlɪt(ə)ri/
place (v)	/pleɪs/
possession (n)	/pəˈzeʃ(ə)n/
principal (adj)	/ˈprɪnsəp(ə)l/
principally (adv)	/ˈprɪnsəp(ə)li/
racism (n)	/ˈreɪˌsɪz(ə)m/
society (n)	/səˈsaɪəti/
stereotype (n)	/ˈsteriəˌtaɪp/

RELIGION

Buddhist (n)	/ˈbʊdɪst/
Christianity (n)	/ˌkrɪstiˈænəti/
Hindu (n)	/ˈhɪnduː/
Islam (n)	/ˈɪzlɑːm/
Muslim (n)	/ˈmʊzləm/

Unit 2

abroad (adv)	/əˈbrɔːd/
adventure (n)	/ədˈventʃə/
agency (n)	/ˈeɪdʒənsi/
alibi (n)	/ˈælɪbaɪ/
arch (n)	/ɑːtʃ/
art gallery (n)	/ˈɑːt ˌɡæləri/
award-winning (adj)	/əˈwɔːd ˌwɪnɪŋ/
bank (n)	/bæŋk/
bare (adj)	/beə/
best-selling (adj)	/ˌbestˈselɪŋ/
brightly-coloured (adj)	/ˌbraɪtliˈkʌləd/
cast (n & v)	/kɑːst/
catch sight of	/ˌkætʃ ˈsaɪt əv/
charge (v)	/tʃɑːdʒ/
childhood (n)	/ˈtʃaɪldˌhʊd/
collapse (v)	/kəˈlæps/
comic (n)	/ˈkɒmɪk/
crash-land (v)	/ˈkræʃlænd/
cupboard (n)	/ˈkʌbəd/
define (v)	/dɪˈfaɪn/
delighted (adj)	/dɪˈlaɪtɪd/
directly (adv)	/dɪˈrektli, daɪˈrektli/
discovery (n)	/dɪˈskʌv(ə)ri/
domestic (adj)	/dəˈmestɪk/
entertain (v)	/ˌentəˈteɪn/
ever since (adv)	/ˌevə ˈsɪns/
everyday (adj)	/ˈevrɪdeɪ/
ex- (prefix)	/eks/
excuse (n)	/ɪkˈskjuːs/
experience (n)	/ɪkˈspɪəriəns/
explore (v)	/ɪkˈsplɔː/
ferryman (n)	/ˈferimən/
fighter pilot (n)	/ˈfaɪtə ˌpaɪlət/
final (adj)	/ˈfaɪn(ə)l/
focus (n)	/ˈfəʊkəs/
folk tale (n)	/ˈfəʊk ˌteɪl/
free of charge (adj)	/ˌfriː əv ˈtʃɑːdʒ/
full-time (adj)	/ˈfʊltaɪm/
gang (n)	/ɡæŋ/
gangster (n)	/ˈɡæŋstə/
gradually (adv)	/ˈɡrædʒuəli/
growth (n)	/ɡrəʊθ/
grumble (v)	/ˈɡrʌmb(ə)l/
hang about	/ˌhæŋ əˈbaʊt/
hardly (adv)	/ˈhɑːdli/
heritage (n)	/ˈherɪtɪdʒ/
hut (n)	/hʌt/
in detail (adv)	/ɪn ˈdiːteɪl/
injure (v)	/ˈɪndʒə/
innocence (n)	/ˈɪnəs(ə)ns/
innocent (adj)	/ˈɪnəs(ə)nt/
inside (n)	/ɪnˈsaɪd/
item (n)	/ˈaɪtəm/
knowledge (n)	/ˈnɒlɪdʒ/
make up (= invent)	/ˌmeɪk ˈʌp/
murder (v)	/ˈmɜːdə/
Norwegian	/nɔːˈwiːdʒən/
odd (= strange) (adj)	/ɒd/
offer (n)	/ˈɒfə/
over and over (adv)	/ˌəʊvə ən(d) ˈəʊvə/
pole (n)	/pəʊl/
print (n)	/prɪnt/
prize-winning (adj)	/ˈpraɪzˌwɪnɪŋ/
profession (n)	/prəˈfeʃn/
progress (n)	/ˈprəʊɡres/
proud (of)	/ˈpraʊd (əv)/
racist (adj)	/ˈreɪsɪst/
reappear (v)	/ˌriːəˈpɪə/
represent	/ˌreprɪˈzent/
row (v)	/rəʊ/
Royal Air Force	/ˌrɔɪəl ˈeə ˌfɔːs/
rush about	/ˌrʌʃ əˈbaʊt/
sculpture (n)	/ˈskʌlptʃə/
separate (adj)	/ˈsep(ə)rət/
sequence (n)	/ˈsiːkwəns/
serial (n)	/ˈsɪəriəl/
series (n pl)	/ˈsɪəriːz/
shiny (adj)	/ˈʃaɪni/
staircase (n)	/ˈsteəˌkeɪs/
stand still (v)	/ˌstænd ˈstɪl/
statue (n)	/ˈstætʃuː/
stepfather (n)	/ˈstepˌfɑːðə/
storyteller (n)	/ˈstɔːriˌtelə/
striking (adj)	/ˈstraɪkɪŋ/
suspect (n)	/ˈsʌspekt/
symbol (n)	/ˈsɪmb(ə)l/
Syria	/ˈsɪriə/
take over	/ˌteɪk ˈəʊvə/
temporary (adj)	/ˈtemp(ə)rəri/
terraced house (n)	/ˈterəst ˌhaʊs/
theme (n)	/θiːm/
thunder (n) (TS)	/ˈθʌndə/
title (n)	/ˈtaɪt(ə)l/
tribute (n)	/ˈtrɪbjuːt/
trilogy (n)	/ˈtrɪlədʒi/
unique (adj)	/juˈniːk/
voyage (n)	/ˈvɔɪɪdʒ/
well-dressed (adj)	/ˌwelˈdrest/
well-polished (adj)	/ˌwelˈpɒlɪʃt/
wise (adj)	/waɪz/

FILM-MAKING

double (v)	/ˈdʌb(ə)l/
extra (n)	/ˈekstrə/
feature film (n)	/ˈfiːtʃə ˌfɪlm/
on location	/ɒn ləʊˈkeɪʃ(ə)n/
on screen	/ɒn ˈskriːn/
scene (n)	/siːn/
on set (n)	/ɒn ˈset/
studio (n)	/ˈstjuːdiəʊ/
take (n)	/teɪk/

MATERIALS

bronze (n & adj)	/brɒnz/
cardboard (n)	/ˈkɑːdˌbɔːd/
concrete (n & adj)	/ˈkɒŋˌkriːt/
dung (n)	/dʌŋ/
gold (n & adj)	/ɡəʊld/
ice (n)	/aɪs/
polystyrene (n & adj)	/ˌpɒliˈstaɪriːn/
plaster (n)	/ˈplɑːstə/
plastic (n & adj)	/ˈplæstɪk/
rubber	/ˈrʌbə/
sand (n)	/sænd/
snow (n)	/snəʊ/
stone (n)	/stəʊn/
wood (n)	/wʊd/

NOUN SUFFIX -MENT

advertisement	/ədˈvɜːtɪsmənt/
amazement	/əˈmeɪzmənt/
argument	/ˈɑːɡjomənt/
arrangement	/əˈreɪndʒmənt/
equipment	/ɪˈkwɪpmənt/
movement	/ˈmuːvmənt/
payment	/ˈpeɪmənt/
treatment	/ˈtriːtmənt/

REVIEW UNITS 1–2

bunch (of grapes) (n)	/ˌbʌntʃ (əv ˈɡreɪps)/
display (v)	/dɪˈspleɪ/
fool (v)	/fuːl/
horsewoman (n)	/ˈhɔːˌswʊmən/
hugely (adv)	/ˈhjuːdʒli/
impatient (adj)	/ɪmˈpeɪʃ(ə)nt/
misunderstand (v)	/ˌmɪsʌndəˈstænd/
rider (n)	/ˈraɪdə/
smash (v)	/smæʃ/
substance (n)	/ˈsʌbstəns/
true to life (adj)	/ˌtruː tə ˈlaɪf/
unhurt (adj)	/ʌnˈhɜːt/
vase (n)	/vɑːz/

Unit 3

accurate (adj)	/ˈækjʊrət/
accurately (adv)	/ˈækjʊrətli/
achievement (n)	/əˈtʃiːvmənt/
among (prep)	/əˈmʌŋ/
approximate (adj)	/əˈprɒksɪmət/
as a result (adv)	/ˌəz ə rɪˈzʌlt/
astonishing (adj)	/əˈstɒnɪʃɪŋ/
base (n)	/beɪs/
being (n)	/ˈbiːɪŋ/
blog (n)	/blɒɡ/
bottom (n)	/ˈbɒtəm/
calculate (v)	/ˈkælkjʊˌleɪt/
chain (of life) (n)	/ˌtʃeɪn (əv ˈlaɪf)/
chemical (n)	/ˈkemɪk(ə)l/
chimney (n)	/ˈtʃɪmni/
commercial (adj)	/kəˈmɜːʃ(ə)l/
consequently (adv)	/ˈkɒnsɪkwəntli/
controversial (adj)	/ˌkɒntrəˈvɜːʃ(ə)l/
cool (v)	/kuːl/
crack (n)	/kræk/
curve (n)	/kɜːv/
depart (v)	/dɪˈpɑːt/
descend (v)	/dɪˈsend/
destructive (adj)	/dɪˈstrʌktɪv/
development (n)	/dɪˈveləpmənt/
disturb (v)	/dɪˈstɜːb/
due (adj)	/djuː/
elevator (n) (Am E)	/ˈeləveɪtə/
evaporate (v)	/ɪˈvæpəˌreɪt/
expand (v)	/ɪkˈspænd/
expedition (n)	/ˌekspəˈdɪʃ(ə)n/
far (adv)	/fɑː/
fare (n)	/feə/
further (comp. adv)	/ˈfɜːðə/
furthest (superl. adv)	/ˈfɜːðɪst/
grandchild (pl -children) (n)	/ˈɡræn(d)ˌtʃaɪld/
Greetings	/ˈɡriːtɪŋz/
impact (n)	/ˈɪmpækt/
initially (adv)	/ɪˈnɪʃ(ə)li/
keep time	/ˌkiːp ˈtaɪm/
lead (v)	/liːd/
liquid (n)	/ˈlɪkwɪd/
luxurious (adj)	/lʌɡˈzjʊəriəs/
manned (adj)	/mænd/
massive (adj)	/ˈmæsɪv/
mining (n)	/ˈmaɪnɪŋ/
molten (adj)	/ˈməʊltən/
movement (environmental movement) (n)	/ˈmuːvmənt/
Newfoundland	/ˈnjuːfəndlənd/

WORD LIST

observer (n) /əbˈzɜːvə/
organism (n) /ˈɔːgəˌnɪzəm/
origin (n) /ˈɒrɪdʒɪn/
oxygen (n) /ˈɒksɪdʒən/
peer (v) /pɪə/
pesticide (n) /ˈpestɪˌsaɪd/
pioneering (adj) /ˌpaɪəˈnɪərɪŋ/
plant (n) /plɑːnt/
prevent (v) /prɪˈvent/
protest (n) /ˈprəʊtest/
rainbow (n) /ˈreɪnbəʊ/
rapidly (adv) /ˈræpɪdli/
rotate (v) /rəʊˈteɪt/
rumour (n) /ˈruːmə/
set (a record) (v) /set (ə ˈrekɔːd)/
sour (adj) /saʊə/
spacious (adj) /ˈspeɪʃəs/
successfully (adv) /səkˈsesf(ə)li/
take action /teɪk ˈækʃ(ə)n/
thanks to /ˈθæŋks tʊ/
theory (n) /ˈθɪəri/
transatlantic (adj) /ˌtrænzətˈlæntɪk/
trench (n) /trentʃ/
trillion (n) /ˈtrɪljən/
turn (= become) (v) /tɜːn/
unexpected (adj) /ˌʌnɪkˈspektɪd/
weak (adj) /wiːk/

COMMUNICATIONS (1)
broadband (n) /ˈbrɔːdˌbænd/
broadcasting (n) /ˈbrɔːdˌkɑːstɪŋ/
communications satellite (n) /kəˌmjuːnɪˈkeɪʃ(ə)nz ˌsætəlaɪt/
radar (n) /ˈreɪdɑː/
radio wave (n) /ˈreɪdiəʊ ˌweɪv/
signal (n & v) /ˈsɪgn(ə)l/
SOS /ˌes əʊ ˈes/
transmission (n) /trænzˈmɪʃ(ə)n/
transmit (v) /trænzˈmɪt/
transmitter (n) /trænzˈmɪtə/

EARTH and SPACE
Big Bang (n) /ˌbɪg ˈbæŋ/
Equator (n) /ɪˈkweɪtə/
extra-terrestrial (adj) /ˌekstrətəˈrestriəl/
latitude (n) /ˈlætɪtjuːd/
lift-off (n) /ˈlɪft ˌɒf/
light year (n) /ˈlaɪt ˌjɪə/
longitude (n) /ˈlɒŋgɪtjuːd/
mission (n) /ˈmɪʃ(ə)n/
moonwalk (n) /ˈmuːnˌwɔːk/
orbit (v) /ˈɔːbɪt/
pre-flight (adj) /priːflaɪt/
spacecraft (n) /ˈspeɪsˌkrɑːft/
spaceport (n) /ˈspeɪsˌpɔːt/
spacewalk (n) /ˈspeɪsˌwɔːk/
universe (n) /ˈjuːnɪˌvɜːs/
Venus /ˈviːnəs/
weightlessness (n) /ˈweɪtləsnəs/

MEDICINE (2)
bacteria (n pl) /bækˈtɪəriə/
disease (n) /dɪˈziːz/
germ (n) /dʒɜːm/
infectious (adj) /ɪnˈfekʃəs/
inject (v) /ɪnˈdʒekt/
medical (adj) /ˈmedɪk(ə)l/
pasteurisation (n) /ˌpɑːstʃərəˈreɪz(ə)n/
pasteurised (adj) /ˈpɑːstʃəˌraɪzd/
illness (n) /ˈɪlnəs/
vaccination (n) /ˌvæksɪˈneɪʃ(ə)n/

OCCUPATIONS (1)
biologist (n) /baɪˈɒlədʒɪst/
chemist (n) /ˈkemɪst/
engineer (n) /ˌendʒɪˈnɪə/
physicist (n) /ˈfɪzɪsɪst/

THE SEA
crab (n) /kræb/
depth (n) /depθ/
hydrothermal vent (n) /ˌhaɪdrəθɜːm(ə)l ˈvent/
mussel (n) /ˈmʌs(ə)l/
navy (n) /ˈneɪvi/
port (n) /pɔːt/
salty (adj) /ˈsɔːlti/
sea bed (n) /ˈsiː ˌbed/
shrimp (n) /ʃrɪmp/
submersible (n) /səbˈmɜːsəbl/
underwater (adj) /ˌʌndəˈwɔːtə/

PHRASAL VERBS
come down /ˌkʌm ˈdaʊn/
count down /ˌkaʊnt ˈdaʊn/
hang on /ˌhæŋ ˈɒn/
put down /ˌpʊt ˈdaʊn/
take off /ˌteɪk ˈɒf/
write down /ˌraɪt ˈdaʊn/

NOUN SUFFIXES -SION and -TION
accommodation (n) /əˌkɒməˈdeɪʃ(ə)n/
action /ˈækʃ(ə)n/
creation /kriˈeɪʃ(ə)n/
decision /dɪˈsɪʒ(ə)n/
discussion /dɪˈskʌʃ(ə)n/
evolution /ˌiːvəˈluːʃ(ə)n/
exploration /ˌekspləˈreɪʃ(ə)n/
pasteurisation /ˌpɑːstʃərəˈreɪʃ(ə)n/
permission /pəˈmɪʃ(ə)n/
pollution /pəˈluːʃ(ə)n/
possession /pəˈzeʃ(ə)n/
production /prəˈdʌkʃ(ə)n/
revision /rɪˈvɪʒ(ə)n/
solution /səˈluːʃ(ə)n/
transmission /trænzˈmɪʃ(ə)n/
vaccination /ˌvæksɪˈneɪʃ(ə)n/

CULTURE Your Culture
aim (n) /eɪm/
appearance (n) /əˈpɪərəns/
block (v) /blɒk/
brainstorm (v) /ˈbreɪnˌstɔːm/
category (n) /ˈkætəg(ə)ri/
combination (n) /ˌkɒmbɪˈneɪʃ(ə)n/
creative (adj) /kriˈeɪtɪv/
creativity (n) /ˌkriːeɪˈtɪvəti/
criticism (n) /ˈkrɪtɪsɪz(ə)m/
defensive (adj) /dɪˈfensɪv/
dialogue (n) /ˈdaɪəˌlɒg/
distinctive (adj) /dɪˈstɪŋktɪv/
evaluation (n) /ɪˌvæljuˈeɪʃ(ə)n/
explosion (n) /ɪkˈspləʊʒ(ə)n/
fill in /ˈfɪl ˌɪn/
generate (v) /ˈdʒenəˌreɪt/
jot down /ˌdʒɒt ˈdaʊn/
message board (n) /ˈmesɪdʒ ˌbɔːd/
mix and match /ˌmɪks ən ˈmætʃ/
note down /ˌnəʊt ˈdaʊn/
personally (adv) /ˈpɜːs(ə)nəli/
post (on message board) (v) /pəʊst/
re-arrange (v) /ˌriːəˈreɪndʒ/
reflect (v) /rɪˈflekt/
softly lit (adj) /ˌsɒf(t)li ˈlɪt/
stuck (adj) /stʌk/
take care /ˌteɪk ˈkeə/
take notes /ˌteɪk ˈnəʊts/
thought (n) /θɔːt/
untidy (adj) /ʌnˈtaɪdi/
value (n) /ˈvæljuː/
well lit (adj) /ˌwel ˈlɪt/

Unit 4

advance (n) /ədˈvɑːns/
as soon as (conj) /əz ˈsuːn əz/
aware (of) (adj) /əˈweə(r) (əv)/
balance (n & v) /ˈbæləns/
big business (n) /ˌbɪg ˈbɪznəs/
cause (v) /kɔːz/
chat (n) /tʃæt/
clash (v) /klæʃ/
compulsory (adj) /kəmˈpʌlsəri/
course (of study) (n) (TS) /kɔːs/
crucial (adj) /ˈkruːʃ(ə)l/
cruelty (n) /ˈkruːəlti/
decrease (n) /ˈdiːkriːs/
decrease (v) /dɪˈkriːs/
democracy (n) /dɪˈmɒkrəsi/
demonstration (n) /ˌdemənˈstreɪʃ(ə)n/
direct action (n) /dɪˌrekt, daɪˌrekt ˈækʃ(ə)n/
elect (v) /ɪˈlekt/
evidence (n) /ˈevɪdəns/
executive (n) /ɪgˈzekjʊtɪv/
feel strongly (about) /ˌfiːl ˈstrɒŋli (əˌbaʊt)/
for instance /fə(r) ˈɪnstəns/
free (v) /friː/
function (n) /ˈfʌŋkʃ(ə)n/
fund (v) /fʌnd/
get rid of /ˌget ˈrɪd əv/
glow (v) /gləʊ/
go trekking /ˌgəʊ ˈtrekɪŋ/
guesthouse (n) /ˈgestˌhaʊs/
halt (v) /hɔːlt/
hand-carved (adj) /ˌhændˈkɑːvd/
harmful (adj) (TS) /ˈhɑːmf(ə)l/
hijack (v) /ˈhaɪdʒæk/
hippy (n) /ˈhɪpi/
hoax (n) /həʊks/
household (n) /ˈhaʊsˌhəʊld/
human race (n) /ˌhjuːmən ˈreɪs/
hunger strike (n) /ˈhʌŋgə ˌstraɪk/
import (v) /ɪmˈpɔːt/
in addition /ɪn əˈdɪʃ(ə)n/
in harmony /ɪn ˈhɑːməni/
in theory /ɪn ˈθɪəri/
increase (n) /ˈɪnkriːs/
indication (n) /ˌɪndɪˈkeɪʃ(ə)n/
involve (v) /ɪnˈvɒlv/
issue (n) /ˈɪʃuː, ˈɪsjuː/
keyless (adj) /ˈkiːləs/
largely (adv) /ˈlɑːdʒli/
life expectancy (n) /ˌlaɪf ɪkˈspektənsi/
log on /ˌlɒg ˈɒn/
mad (adj) /mæd/
magical (adj) /ˈmædʒɪk(ə)l/
make a case /ˌmeɪk ə ˈkeɪs/
march (n) /mɑːtʃ/
method (n) /ˈmeθəd/
microchip (n) /ˈmaɪkrəʊˌtʃɪp/
moral (adj) /ˈmɒrəl/
MP3 player (n) /ˌempiːˈθriː ˌpleɪə/
multi-national (adj) (TS) /ˌmʌltɪˈnæʃn(ə)l/
Nepal /nəˈpɔːl(i)/
no longer (adv) /nəʊ ˈlɒŋə/
nuclear energy (n) /ˌnjuːkliə ˈenədʒi/
obtainable (adj) /əbˈteɪnəb(ə)l/
offset (v) /ˈɒfˌset/
order (= request) (v) /ˈɔːdə/
organisation (n) /ˌɔːgənaɪˈzeɪʃ(ə)n/
overland (adv) /ˈəʊvəˌlænd/
pace (of life) (n) /ˈpeɪs (əv ˈlaɪf)/
partly (adv) /ˈpɑːtli/
password (n) /ˈpɑːswɜːd/
perfectly (= completely) (adv) /ˈpɜːfɪktli/
permit (n) /ˈpɜːmɪt/
permit (v) /pəˈmɪt/
plant (v) /plɑːnt/
point (the whole point) (n) /pɔɪnt (ðə ˌhəʊl ˈpɔɪnt)/

WORD LIST

political (adj)	/pəˈlɪtɪk(ə)l/
produce (v)	/prəˈdjuːs/
protection (n) (TS)	/prəˈtekʃ(ə)n/
protestor (n)	/prəˈtestə/
publicity (n)	/pʌbˈlɪsəti/
pulse rate (n)	/ˈpʌls ˌreɪt/
racial segregation (n)	/ˌreɪʃ(ə)l ˌsegrɪˈgeɪʃ(ə)n/
representative (n)	/ˌreprɪˈzentətɪv/
researcher (n)	/rɪˈsɜːtʃə/
retire (v)	/rɪˈtaɪə/
retirement (n)	/rɪˈtaɪəmənt/
return flight (n)	/rɪˌtɜːn ˈflaɪt/
sit-in (n)	/ˈsɪtɪn/
slight (adj)	/slaɪt/
such as	/ˌsʌtʃ ˈæz/
suspect (v)	/səˈspekt/
take a decision	/ˌteɪk ə dɪˈsɪʒ(ə)n/
take seriously	/ˌteɪk ˈsɪərɪəsli/
tax (n)	/tæks/
threat (n)	/θret/
unless (conj)	/ənˈles/
use-by date (n)	/ˈjuːzbaɪ ˌdeɪt/
vaccine (n)	/ˈvæksiːn/
view (= opinion) (n)	/vjuː/
violence (n)	/ˈvaɪələns/
whaling ship (n)	/ˈweɪlɪŋ ˌʃɪp/
what's more (adv)	/ˌwɒts ˈmɔː/
whenever (conj)	/wenˈevə/
wireless technology (n)	/ˌwaɪələs tekˌnɒlədʒi/
wristwatch (n)	/ˈrɪstˌwɒtʃ/

CLIMATE CHANGE

atmosphere (n)	/ˈætməsˌfɪə/
carbon dioxide (CO_2) (n)	/ˌkɑːbən daɪˈɒksaɪd/
carbon emission (n)	/ˌkɑːbən ɪˈmɪʃ(ə)n/
carbon-offset project (n)	/ˌkɑːbənˌɒfset ˈprɒdʒekt/
drought (n)	/draʊt/
energy crisis (n)	/ˈenədʒi ˌkraɪsɪs/
flood (n)	/flʌd/
global warming (n)	/ˌgləʊb(ə)l ˈwɔːmɪŋ/
greenhouse gas (n)	/ˈgriːnhaʊs ˌgæs/
polar ice cap (n)	/ˌpəʊlə(r) ˈaɪs ˌkæp/

DEBATE

argument (n)	/ˈɑːgjʊmənt/
chair (n & v)	/tʃeə/
debate (n)	/dɪˈbeɪt/
firstly (adv)	/ˈfɜːs(t)li/
for and against	/ˌfɔː ən əˈgenst/
in favour (of)	/ɪn ˈfeɪvə/
motion (n)	/ˈməʊʃ(ə)n/
point (third point) (n) (TS)	/pɔɪnt/
propose (v)	/prəˈpəʊz/
opponent (n)	/əˈpəʊnənt/
oppose (v)	/əˈpəʊz/
secondly (adv)	/ˈsekən(d)li/
sum up	/ˌsʌm ˈʌp/
thirdly (adv)	/ˈθɜːdli/
vote (n & v)	/vəʊt/

PHRASAL VERBS WITH OUT

carry out	/ˌkæri ˈaʊt/
miss out on	/ˌmɪs ˈaʊt ɒn/
point out	/ˌpɔɪnt ˈaʊt/
wipe out	/ˌwaɪp ˈaʊt/
work out	/ˌwɜːk ˈaʊt/

PREFIXES ANTI- and NON-

non-fiction	/ˌnɒnˈfɪkʃ(ə)n/
non-iron	/ˌnɒnˈaɪən/
non-violent	/ˌnɒnˈvaɪələnt/
non-violence (n)	/ˌnɒnˈvaɪələns/
anti-globalisation	/ˌæntɪˌgləʊbələˈzeɪʃ(ə)n/
anti-GM (genetically modified) food	/ˌæntɪˌdʒiːem ˈfuːd/
anti-spam	/ˌæntɪˈspæm/
anti-terrorism	/ˌæntɪˈterəˌrɪz(ə)m/
anti-war	/ˌæntɪˈwɔː/

REVIEW UNITS 3–4

additive (n)	/ˈædətɪv/
countryside (n)	/ˈkʌntriˌsaɪd/
housing (n)	/ˈhaʊzɪŋ/
in order to	/ɪn ˈɔːdə tʊ/
inform (v)	/ɪnˈfɔːm/
poor (= low quality) (adj)	/pɔː/
predict (v)	/prɪˈdɪkt/
slum (n)	/slʌm/

Unit 5

accustomed (adj)	/əˈkʌstəmd/
alien (n)	/ˈeɪliən/
announce (v)	/əˈnaʊns/
attempt (v)	/əˈtempt/
barrel (n)	/ˈbærəl/
be sick	/bi ˈsɪk/
bishop (n)	/ˈbɪʃəp/
Briton (n)	/ˈbrɪt(ə)n/
burglar (n)	/ˈbɜːglə/
cannonball (n)	/ˈkænənˌbɔːl/
Catholic	/ˈkæθ(ə)lɪk/
ceiling (n)	/ˈsiːlɪŋ/
cellar (n)	/ˈselə/
character (= personality) (n)	/ˈkærɪktə/
circus (n) (TS)	/ˈsɜːkəs/
confess (v)	/kənˈfes/
crack (v)	/kræk/
crew (n)	/kruː/
daring (adj)	/ˈdeərɪŋ/
degree (university) (n)	/dɪˈgriː/
destruction (n)	/dɪˈstrʌkʃ(ə)n/
disappearance (n)	/ˌdɪsəˈpɪərəns/
driving licence (n)	/ˈdraɪvɪŋ ˌlaɪsns/
earn a living	/ˌɜːn ə ˈlɪvɪŋ/
elaborate (adj)	/ɪˈlæb(ə)rət/
end up	/ˌend ˈʌp/
farmhouse (n)	/ˈfɑːmhaʊs/
farmyard (n)	/ˈfɑːmjɑːd/
female (adj)	/ˈfiːmeɪl/
file (n)	/faɪl/
firmly (adv)	/ˈfɜːmli/
fit (adj)	/fɪt/
flatten (v)	/ˈflæt(ə)n/
get to know	/ˌget tə ˈnəʊ/
grin (v)	/grɪn/
guidelines (n pl)	/ˈgaɪdˌlaɪnz/
hairstyle (n)	/ˈheəstaɪl/
height (n)	/haɪt/
Houses of Parliament (n pl)	/ˌhaʊzɪz əv ˈpɑːləmənt/
junior (adj)	/ˈdʒuːnɪə/
lately (adv)	/ˈleɪtli/
look on	/ˌlʊk ˈɒn/
lottery (n)	/ˈlɒtəri/
male (adj)	/meɪl/
measurement (n)	/ˈmeʒəmənt/
MP (Member of Parliament) (n)	/ˌemˈpiː/
neither (pron)	/ˈnaɪðə/
New Guinea	/ˌnjuː ˈgɪni/
noble (adj)	/ˈnəʊb(ə)l/
pattern (n)	/ˈpæt(ə)n/
persecute (v)	/ˈpɜːsɪˌkjuːt/
petrol (n)	/ˈpetrəl/
physically (adv)	/ˈfɪzɪkli/
pioneer (n)	/ˌpaɪəˈnɪə/
pretty (= fairly/very) (adv)	/ˈprɪti/
previous (adj)	/ˈpriːviəs/
qualification (n)	/ˌkwɒlɪfɪˈkeɪʃ(ə)n/
raise (chickens) (v)	/reɪz/
record-breaking (adj)	/ˈrekɔːdˌbreɪkɪŋ/
refer (v)	/rɪˈfɜː/
reference (n)	/ˈref(ə)rəns/
regret (v)	/rɪˈgret/
release (v)	/rɪˈliːs/
row (in a row) (n) (TS)	/rəʊ/
run out (of)	/ˌrʌn ˈaʊt əv/
saying (n)	/ˈseɪɪŋ/
search operation (n)	/ˈsɜːtʃ ɒpəˌreɪʃ(ə)n/
sensitive (adj)	/ˈsensətɪv/
separation (n)	/ˌsepəˈreɪʃ(ə)n/
set light to	/ˌset ˈlaɪt tʊ/
short-haired (adj)	/ˌʃɔːtˈheəd/
sink (n)	/sɪŋk/
snowstorm (n)	/ˈsnəʊˌstɔːm/
speculation (n)	/ˌspekjʊˈleɪʃ(ə)n/
stand-by (adj)	/ˈstændbaɪ/
stick (v)	/stɪk/
strict (adj)	/strɪkt/
supervise (v)	/ˈsuːpəˌvaɪz/
surprisingly (adv)	/səˈpraɪzɪŋli/
take up (= start)	/ˌteɪk ˈʌp/
tank (n)	/tæŋk/
trace (n)	/treɪs/
trick (v)	/trɪk/
undamaged (adj)	/ʌnˈdæmɪdʒd/
use up	/ˌjuːz ˈʌp/
wasteland (n)	/ˈweɪs(t)lænd/
wax (n)	/wæks/
well-fed (adj)	/welˈfed/
whereas (conj)	/weərˈæz/
while (= whereas) (conj)	/waɪl/
willing (adj)	/ˈwɪlɪŋ/
yacht (n)	/jɒt/

CRIME and PUNISHMENT

abduct (v)	/æbˈdʌkt/
arrest (n)	/əˈrest/
blow up	/ˌbləʊ ˈʌp/
conspirator (n)	/kənˈspɪrətə/
execute (v)	/ˈeksɪˌkjuːt/
explosive (n)	/ɪkˈspləʊsɪv/
get away with	/ˌget əˈweɪ ˌwɪð/
gunpowder (n)	/ˈgʌnˌpaʊdə/
plot (n)	/plɒt/
red-handed (adj)	/ˌredˈhændɪd/
shoot down	/ˌʃuːt ˈdaʊn/
spy (n)	/spaɪ/
terrorist (n)	/ˈterərɪst/

FLIGHT

air traffic control (n)	/ˈeə ˌtræfɪk kənˈtrəʊl/
crossing (n)	/ˈkrɒsɪŋ/
emergency landing (n)	/ɪˈmɜːdʒənsi ˈlændɪŋ/
flight attendant (n)	/ˈflaɪt əˌtendənt/
fuel (n)	/ˈfjuːəl/
mid-air (n)	/ˌmɪdˈeə/
navigator (n)	/ˈnævɪˌgeɪtə/
solo (adj & adv)	/ˈsəʊləʊ/

SPORT

centre forward (n)	/ˌsentə ˈfɔːwəd/
club (football club) (n)	/klʌb/
division (second division) (n)	/dɪˈvɪʒ(ə)n/
goal (n)	/gəʊl/
knock out	/ˌnɒk ˈaʊt/
match (n)	/mætʃ/
professional (n)	/prəˈfeʃ(ə)nəl/
quarter-finals (n pl)	/ˈkwɔːtəˌfaɪnəlz/
round (first round) (n)	/raʊnd/
score (v)	/skɔː/

ADJECTIVE SUFFIX -OUS

courageous	/kəˈreɪdʒəs/
dangerous	/ˈdeɪndʒərəs/
infectious	/ɪnˈfekʃəs/
luxurious	/lʌgˈzjʊəriəs/
nervous	/ˈnɜːvəs/
poisonous	/ˈpɔɪzənəs/

123

WORD LIST

spacious	/ˈspeɪʃəs/
superstitious	/ˌsuːpəˈstɪʃəs/

CULTURE Saying the right thing

brush up	/ˈbrʌʃ ʌp/
fiver (n)	/ˈfaɪvə/
knock off	/ˈnɒk ɒf/
latest (superl. adj)	/ˈleɪtɪst/
Not at all.	/ˌnɒt ət ˈɔːl/
pale (adj)	/peɪl/
possibly (adv)	/ˈpɒsəbli/
Would you mind …?	/wʊd jʊ ˈmaɪnd/

SHOPPING

fit (v)	/fɪt/
match (v)	/mætʃ/
try on (clothes)	/traɪ ˈɒn/
tight (adj)	/taɪt/
lime green (adj)	/ˌlaɪm ˈgriːn/
suit (v)	/suːt/
change (= money) (n)	/tʃeɪndʒ (ˈmʌni)/

BANK

bank clerk (n)	/ˈbæŋk ˌklɑːk/
change (money) (v)	/tʃeɪndʒ (ˈmʌni)/
exchange (n)	/ɪksˈtʃeɪndʒ/
receipt (n)	/rɪˈsiːt/
tens (n pl)	/tenz/
twenties (n pl)	/ˈtwentiz/

RAILWAY STATION

booking clerk (n)	/ˈbʊkɪŋ ˌklɑːk/
change (trains) (v)	/ˌtʃeɪndʒ (ˈtreɪnz)/
day return (n)	/ˌdeɪ rɪˈtɜːn/
platform (n)	/ˈplætfɔːm/
return (ticket) (n)	/rɪˌtɜːn (ˈtɪkɪt)/
single (ticket) (n)	/ˌsɪŋg(ə)l (ˈtɪkɪt)/

HOSTEL/HOTEL

double (room) (adj)	/ˌdʌb(ə)l (ˈruːm)/
form (fill in a form) (n)	/fɔːm (ˌfɪl ɪn ə ˈfɔːm)/
receptionist (n)	/rɪˈsepʃ(ə)nɪst/
reservation (n)	/ˌrezəˈveɪʃ(ə)n/
single (room) (adj)	/ˌsɪŋg(ə)l (ˈruːm)/

Unit 6

advise (v)	/ədˈvaɪz/
aisle (n)	/aɪl/
beat (You can't beat it.) (v)	/biːt/
behave (v)	/bɪˈheɪv/
behaviour (n)	/bɪˈheɪvjə/
best-behaved (adj)	/ˌbestbɪˈheɪvd/
change one's mind	/ˌtʃeɪndʒ wʌnz ˈmaɪnd/
civilisation (n)	/ˌsɪvəlaɪˈzeɪʃ(ə)n/
complain (v)	/kəmˈpleɪn/
cost of living (n)	/ˌkɒst əv ˈlɪvɪŋ/
cross (between two things) (n)	/krɒs/
cultural (adj)	/ˈkʌltʃ(ə)rəl/
damp (adj)	/dæmp/
defrost (v)	/diːˈfrɒst/
deliver (v)	/dɪˈlɪvə/
deny (v)	/dɪˈnaɪ/
devastating (adj)	/ˈdevəsˌteɪtɪŋ/
disappointed (adj)	/ˌdɪsəˈpɔɪntɪd/
do one's hair	/ˌduː wʌnz ˈheə/
dry-clean (v)	/draɪˈkliːn/
email (v)	/ˈiːmeɪl/
exchange (v)	/ɪksˈtʃeɪndʒ/
feedback (n)	/ˈfiːdbæk/
freezer (n)	/ˈfriːzə/
games console (n)	/ˈgeɪmz ˌkɒnsəʊl/
garage (n)	/ˈgærɑːʒ, ˈgærɪdʒ/
get off (a bus)	/ˌget ˈɒf/
go whale-watching	/gəʊ ˈweɪlˌwɒtʃɪŋ/
groceries (n pl)	/ˈgrəʊsəriz/
hand over	/ˌhænd ˈəʊvə/

hard (be hard on people) (adj)	/hɑːd/
have a say	/ˌhæv ə ˈseɪ/
hesitate (v)	/ˈhezɪteɪt/
homeland (n)	/ˈhəʊmˌlænd/
iced (adj)	/aɪst/
injection (n)	/ɪnˈdʒekʃ(ə)n/
install (v)	/ɪnˈstɔːl/
Israeli	/ɪzˈreɪli/
laze around	/ˌleɪz əˈraʊnd/
mainly (adv)	/ˈmeɪnli/
mean (adj)	/miːn/
nation (n)	/ˈneɪʃ(ə)n/
obvious (adj)	/ˈɒbviəs/
on our way	/ˌɒn aʊə ˈweɪ/
out of the question	/ˌaʊt əv ðə ˈkwestʃ(ə)n/
overall (adv)	/ˌəʊvərˈɔːl/
packed (adj)	/pækt/
pick (flowers) (v)	/pɪk/
plump (adj)	/plʌmp/
politeness (n)	/pəˈlaɪtnəs/
puncture (n)	/ˈpʌŋktʃə/
push off	/ˌpʊʃ ˈɒf/
quote (v)	/kwəʊt/
rediscover (v)	/ˌriːdɪˈskʌvə/
remark (v)	/rɪˈmɑːk/
remote (adj)	/rɪˈməʊt/
rent (v) (TS)	/rent/
repair (v)	/rɪˈpeə/
responsibly (adv)	/rɪˈspɒnsəbli/
sarong (n)	/səˈrɒŋ/
sense (make sense) (n)	/sens/
service (car)(v)	/ˈsɜːvɪs/
sheet (n)	/ʃiːt/
shopping mall (n)	/ˈʃɒpɪŋ ˌmɔːl, ˈʃɒpɪŋ ˌmæl/
side road (n)	/ˈsaɪd ˌrəʊd/
slightly (adv)	/ˈslaɪtli/
snorkelling (n)	/ˈsnɔːk(ə)lɪŋ/
software (n)	/ˈsɒftˌweə/
spicy (adj)	/ˈspaɪsi/
spill (v)	/spɪl/
spin out	/ˌspɪn ˈaʊt/
sunburnt (adj)	/ˈsʌnˌbɜːnt/
Swede	/swiːd/
sweetly (adv)	/ˈswiːtli/
tablet (n)	/ˈtæblət/
take a tablet	/ˌteɪk ə ˈtæblət/
talk over	/ˌtɔːk ˈəʊvə/
the Philippines	/ðə ˈfɪləpiːnz/
towel (n)	/ˈtaʊəl/
tube (n)	/tjuːb/
turn up (clothing)	/ˌtɜːn ˈʌp/
uncomfortably (adv)	/ʌnˈkʌmftəbli/
walk about	/ˌwɔːk əˈbaʊt/
warn (v)	/wɔːn/
wipe (v)	/waɪp/
worst-behaved (adj)	/ˌwɜːstbɪˈheɪvd/
wrap (v)	/ræp/
You're welcome.	/jɔː ˈwelkəm/

RESTAURANT

bread roll (n)	/ˌbred ˈrəʊl/
cash register (n)	/ˈkæʃ ˌredʒɪstə/
cheesecake (n)	/ˈtʃiːzˌkeɪk/
cutlery (n)	/ˈkʌtləri/
dressing (n)	/ˈdresɪŋ/
gravy (n)	/ˈgreɪvi/
ketchup (n)	/ˈketʃəp/
menu (n)	/ˈmenjuː/
napkin (n)	/ˈnæpkɪn/
special (n)	/ˈspeʃ(ə)l/
tablecloth (n)	/ˈteɪb(ə)lˌklɒθ/
tip (money) (n)	/tɪp/
tipping (n)	/ˈtɪpɪŋ/
tray (n)	/treɪ/
waitress (n)	/ˈweɪtrəs/

PHRASAL VERBS WITH IN and INTO

break into	/ˌbreɪk ˈɪntʊ/
come in	/ˌkʌm ˈɪn/
fill in	/ˌfɪl ˈɪn/
give in	/ˌgɪv ˈɪn/
look into	/ˈlʊk ˌɪntʊ/
take in (= absorb)	/ˌteɪk ˈɪn/
turn into	/ˌtɜːn ˈɪntʊ/

ADJECTIVE PREFIX WELL-

well-balanced	/ˌwelˈbælənst/
well-behaved	/ˌwelbɪˈheɪvd/
well-done	/ˌwelˈdʌn/
well-dressed	/ˌwelˈdrest/
well-known	/ˌwelˈnəʊn/
well-off	/ˌwelˈɒf/
well-paid	/ˌwelˈpeɪd/

UNITS 5–6 REVIEW

credit card (n)	/ˈkredɪt ˌkɑːd/
fur (n)	/fɜː/
heavy (traffic) (adj)	/ˈhevi (ˈtræfɪk)/
herder (n)	/ˈhɜːdə/
sweet (adj)	/swiːt/
unpack (v)	/ʌnˈpæk/

Unit 7

according to (prep)	/əˈkɔːdɪŋ ˌtuː/
acknowledge (v)	/əkˈnɒlɪdʒ/
annual (adj)	/ˈænjuəl/
Asian	/ˈeɪʒ(ə)n/
atom (n)	/ˈætəm/
award (v)	/əˈwɔːd/
base (on) (v)	/beɪs (ɒn)/
be given the sack	/bi ˌgɪvən ðə ˈsæk/
benefit (v)	/ˈbenɪfɪt/
brilliant (= very clever) (adj)	/ˈbrɪljənt/
cancer (n)	/ˈkænsə/
catch up (TS)	/ˌkætʃ ˈʌp/
chemistry (n)	/ˈkemɪstri/
colleague (n)	/ˈkɒliːg/
comet (n)	/ˈkɒmɪt/
constantly (adv)	/ˈkɒnstəntli/
decade (n)	/ˈdekeɪd/
deck (ship)(n)	/dek/
deserve (v)	/dɪˈzɜːv/
dialect (n)	/ˈdaɪəˌlekt/
disaster (n)	/dɪˈzɑːstə/
DNA	/ˌdiːenˈeɪ/
do well	/ˌduː ˈwel/
earthquake (n)	/ˈɜːθkweɪk/
educational (adj)	/ˌedjʊˈkeɪʃ(ə)nəl/
electrical appliance (n)	/ɪˌlektrɪk(ə)l əˈplaɪəns/
emphasis (n)	/ˈemfəsɪs/
essay (n)	/ˈeseɪ/
ethnic (adj)	/ˈeθnɪk/
extinction (n)	/ɪkˈstɪŋkʃ(ə)n/
fairly (= in a fair way) (adv)	/ˈfeəli/
fluent (adj)	/ˈfluːənt/
forbid (v)	/fəˈbɪd/
Ghana	/ˈgɑːnə/
half a dozen	/ˌhɑːf ə ˈdʌz(ə)n/
hang (v)	/hæŋ/
honour (v)	/ˈɒnə/
idiom (n)	/ˈɪdiəm/
idiomatic (adj)	/ˌɪdiəˈmætɪk/
increasingly (adv)	/ɪnˈkriːsɪŋli/
ironically (adv)	/aɪˈrɒnɪkli/
jet (n)	/dʒet/
jumbo(-sized) (adj)	/ˈdʒʌmbəʊ (ˌsaɪzd)/
Keep it up.	/ˌkiːp ɪt ˈʌp/
killer (n)	/ˈkɪlə/
know the ropes	/ˌnəʊ ðə ˈrəʊps/
make a deal	/ˌmeɪk ə ˈdiːl/
mark (homework) (v)	/mɑːk/

124

WORD LIST

means (n pl)	/miːnz/
minority (n)	/maɪˈnɒrəti/
murder (n)	/ˈmɜːdə/
nautical (adj)	/ˈnɔːtɪk(ə)l/
Nigerian	/naɪˈdʒɪəriən/
nuclear fission (n)	/ˌnjuːkliə ˈfɪʃn/
oral (adj)	/ˈɔːrəl/
pence (n pl)	/pens/
period (n)	/ˈpɪəriəd/
persuade (v)	/pəˈsweɪd/
platform (n)	/ˈplætfɔːm/
pocket money (n)	/ˈpɒkɪt ˌmʌni/
policy (n)	/ˈpɒləsi/
prejudice (n)	/ˈpredʒʊdɪs/
pulsar (n)	/ˈpʌlsɑː/
race (competition) (n)	/reɪs/
recognition (n)	/ˌrekəɡˈnɪʃ(ə)n/
revolution (n)	/ˌrevəˈluːʃ(ə)n/
sack (n)	/sæk/
shelf (pl shelves) (n)	/ʃelf/
shuttlecock (n)	/ˈʃʌt(ə)lˌkɒk/
slang (n)	/slæŋ/
social (adj)	/ˈsəʊʃ(ə)l/
status (n)	/ˈsteɪtəs/
term (= word/phrase) (n)	/tɜːm/
tool (n)	/tuːl/
tower (n)	/ˈtaʊə/
transform (v)	/trænsˈfɔːm/
twist (v)	/twɪst/
under the weather	/ˌʌndə ðə ˈweðə/
unusually (adv)	/ʌnˈjuːʒʊəli/
user (n)	/ˈjuːzə/
wicked (adj)	/ˈwɪkɪd/
worth (n)	/wɜːθ/
yet (conj)	/jet/

OCCUPATIONS (2)

astronomer (n)	/əˈstrɒnəmə/
bus conductor (n)	/ˈbʌs kənˌdʌktə/
employer (n)	/ɪmˈplɔɪə/
entrepreneur (n)	/ˌɒntrəprəˈnɜː/
linguist (n)	/ˈlɪŋɡwɪst/
salespeople (n pl) (TS)	/ˈseɪlzˌpiːpl/
sociologist (n)	/ˌsəʊsiˈɒlədʒɪst/
street vendor (n)	/ˈstriːt ˌvendə/
travel agent (n)	/ˈtræv(ə)l ˌeɪdʒənt/

COMMUNICATIONS (2)

directory (n)	/dəˈrekt(ə)ri/
engaged (n)	/ɪnˈɡeɪdʒd/
landline (n)	/ˈlændˌlaɪn/
line (n)	/laɪn/
mobile phone mast (n)	/ˈməʊbaɪl fəʊn mɑːst/
network (n)	/ˈnetˌwɜːk/
subscriber (n)	/səbˈskraɪbə/
telecommunications (n pl)	/ˌtelɪkəˌmjuːnɪˈkeɪʃ(ə)nz/

PHRASAL VERBS

call back	/ˌkɔːl ˈbæk/
cut off	/ˌkʌt ˈɒf/
die out	/ˌdaɪ ˈaʊt/
find out	/ˌfaɪnd ˈaʊt/
go on (= continue)	/ˌɡəʊ ˈɒn/
hold on	/ˌhəʊld ˈɒn/
kick off	/ˌkɪk ˈɒf/
pass on	/ˌpɑːs ˈɒn/
pick up	/ˌpɪk ˈʌp/
put through	/ˌpʊt ˈθruː/
put up (on the wall)	/ˌpʊt ˈʌp/
ring up	/ˌrɪŋ ˈʌp/
speed up	/ˌspiːd ˈʌp/
switch on	/ˌswɪtʃ ˈɒn/

VERB PREFIX RE-

reappear	/ˌriːəˈpɪə/
rebuild	/riːˈbɪld/
recreate	/ˌriːkriˈeɪt/
rediscover	/ˌriːdɪˈskʌvə/
repaint	/riːˈpeɪnt/
replace	/rɪˈpleɪs/
replay	/riːˈpleɪ/
retell	/ˌriːˈtel/
rewrite	/ˌriːˈraɪt/

CULTURE Student Life

biology (n)	/baɪˈɒlədʒi/
cash (n)	/kæʃ/
cope (v)	/kəʊp/
cut down (on)	/ˌkʌt ˈdaʊn (ɒn)/
debt (n)	/det/
flatmate (n)	/ˈflætmeɪt/
homesick (adj)	/ˈhəʊmˌsɪk/
live on	/ˈlɪv ˌɒn/
lively (adj)	/ˈlaɪvli/
loan (n)	/ləʊn/
look up (= improve)	/ˌlʊk ˈʌp/
make ends meet	/ˌmeɪk endz ˈmiːt/
nearby (adj)	/ˌnɪəˈbaɪ/
philosophy (n)	/fɪˈlɒsəfi/
pour (with rain) (v)	/ˌpɔː (wɪð ˈreɪn)/
save up	/ˌseɪv ˈʌp/
settle down	/ˌset(ə)l ˈdaʊn/
social life (n)	/ˈsəʊʃ(ə)l ˌlaɪf/
tell off	/ˌtel ˈɒf/

HIGHER EDUCATION

campus (n)	/ˈkæmpəs/
degree (n)	/dɪˈɡriː/
fresher (n)	/ˈfreʃə/
gap year (n)	/ˈɡæp ˌjɪə/
hall of residence (n)	/ˌhɔːl əv ˈrezɪdəns/
lecture (n)	/ˈlektʃə/
student's union (n)	/ˌstjuːdənts ˈjuːnjən/
undergraduate (n)	/ˌʌndəˈɡrædʒuət/

Unit 8

advanced (adj) (TS)	/ədˈvɑːnst/
aftershave (n)	/ˈɑːftəʃeɪv/
alarm (n)	/əˈlɑːm/
amazingly (adv)	/əˈmeɪzɪŋli/
applicant (n)	/ˈæplɪkənt/
application (n)	/ˌæplɪˈkeɪʃ(ə)n/
best-known (adj)	/ˌbestˈnəʊn/
bleed (v)	/bliːd/
broke (= without money) (adj)	/brəʊk/
budding (adj)	/ˈbʌdɪŋ/
cell (prison) (n)	/sel/
chill-out (adj)	/ˈtʃɪlaʊt/
comfort (n)	/ˈkʌmfət/
confession (n)	/kənˈfeʃ(ə)n/
conservation (n)	/ˌkɒnsəˈveɪʃ(ə)n/
crumble (n)	/ˈkrʌmb(ə)l/
daydream (n)	/ˈdeɪˌdriːm/
descriptive (adj)	/dɪˈskrɪptɪv/
do good	/ˌduː ˈɡʊd/
drag (v)	/dræɡ/
endangered (adj)	/ɪnˈdeɪndʒəd/
entrance examination (n)	/ˈentrəns ɪɡzæmɪˌneɪʃ(ə)n/
equation (n)	/ɪˈkweɪʒ(ə)n/
fairly (= quite) (adv)	/ˈfeəli/
fan (n)	/fæn/
fees (n pl)	/fiːz/
fundraise (v)	/ˈfʌndˌreɪz/
gift (= talent) (n)	/ɡɪft/
gut instincts (n pl)	/ˌɡʌt ˈɪnstɪŋkts/
have children	/hæv ˈtʃɪldrən/
headed (adj) (TS)	/ˈhedɪd/
inspiring (adj)	/ɪnˈspaɪərɪŋ/
instant (adj)	/ˈɪnstənt/
interactive (adj)	/ˌɪntərˈæktɪv/
keep an eye on (TS)	/ˌkiːp ən ˈaɪ ɒn/
liberal (adj)	/ˈlɪb(ə)rəl/
living (n)	/ˈlɪvɪŋ/
lock (n)	/lɒk/
long-distance (adj)	/ˌlɒŋ ˈdɪstəns/
make a contribution	/ˌmeɪk ə ˌkɒntrɪˈbjuːʃ(ə)n/
make it (= succeed)	/ˌmeɪk ˈɪt/
mentally (adv)	/ˈment(ə)li/
mid-winter	/ˌmɪd ˈwɪntə/
mother tongue (n)	/ˌmʌðə ˈtʌŋ/
nature reserve (n)	/ˈneɪtʃə rɪˌzɜːv/
opportunity (n)	/ˌɒpəˈtjuːnəti/
perfume (n)	/ˈpɜːfjuːm/
poetic (adj)	/pəʊˈetɪk/
poetry (n)	/ˈpəʊətri/
pressure (n)	/ˈpreʃə/
prize-winner (n)	/ˈpraɪzˌwɪnə/
progress (v)	/prəʊˈɡres/
publisher (n)	/ˈpʌblɪʃə/
quantity (n)	/ˈkwɒntəti/
red tape (n)	/ˌred ˈteɪp/
reject (v)	/rɪˈdʒekt/
relativity (n)	/ˌreləˈtɪvəti/
reliable (adj)	/rɪˈlaɪəb(ə)l/
role model (n)	/ˈrəʊl ˌmɒd(ə)l/
short (of) (= lacking) (adv)	/ʃɔːt (əv)/
short-term (adj)	/ˌʃɔːtˈtɜːm/
single (= unmarried) (adj)	/ˈsɪŋɡ(ə)l/
solar system (n)	/ˈsəʊlə ˌsɪstəm/
spreadsheet (n)	/ˈspredʃiːt/
submarine (n)	/ˌsʌbməˈriːn/
swimmer (n)	/ˈswɪmə/
symbolically (adv)	/sɪmˈbɒlɪkli/
totally (adv)	/ˈtəʊtli/
triathlete (n)	/traɪˈæθliːt/
twin (n)	/twɪn/
unemployed (adj)	/ˌʌnɪmˈplɔɪd/
visualise (v)	/ˈvɪʒʊəlaɪz/
volunteer (n & v)	/ˌvɒlənˈtɪə/
youth (n)	/juːθ/

EDUCATION

approved school (n)	/əˈpruːvd ˌskuːl/
certificate (n)	/səˈtɪfɪkət/
classwork (n)	/ˈklɑːsˌwɜːk/
curriculum (n)	/kəˈrɪkjʊləm/
educate (v)	/ˈedjʊkeɪt/
grade (= mark) (n)	/ɡreɪd/
institute (n)	/ˈɪnstɪˌtjuːt/
Latin	/ˈlætɪn/
physics (n)	/ˈfɪzɪks/
place (eg at college) (n)	/pleɪs/
term (school term) (n)	/tɜːm/
whiteboard (n)	/ˈwaɪtˌbɔːd/

MUSIC and SONGWRITING

chord (n)	/kɔːd/
chorus (n)	/ˈkɔːrəs/
classical (adj)	/ˈklæsɪk(ə)l/
concerto (n)	/kənˈtʃeətəʊ/
lyrics (n pl)	/ˈlɪrɪks/
material (= songs) (n)	/məˈtɪəriəl/
opera (n)	/ˈɒp(ə)rə/
set (= series of songs) (n)	/set/
symphony (n)	/ˈsɪmfəni/
verse (n)	/vɜːs/

PHRASAL VERBS

clean up	/ˌkliːn ˈʌp/
flow out	/ˌfləʊ ˈaʊt/
get on with (= continue)	/ˌɡet ˈɒn wɪð/
go down (well)	/ˌɡəʊ daʊn (ˈwel)/
pull through	/ˌpʊl ˈθruː/
put together	/ˌpʊt təˈɡeðə/
reach out	/ˌriːtʃ ˈaʊt/
shine out	/ˌʃaɪn ˈaʊt/
start off	/ˌstɑːt ˈɒf/

WORD LIST

NOUN SUFFIX -NESS

carelessness	/ˈkeələsnəs/
cleverness	/ˈklevənəs/
fitness	/ˈfɪtnəs/
happiness	/ˈhæpɪnəs/
illness	/ˈɪlnəs/
politeness	/pəˈlaɪtnəs/
sadness	/ˈsædnəs/
thoughtfulness	/ˈθɔːtf(ə)lnəs/
usefulness	/ˈjuːsf(ə)lnəs/
weightlessness	/ˈweɪtləsnəs/

UNITS 7 – 8 REVIEW

criminal (n)	/ˈkrɪmɪn(ə)l/
far apart (adv)	/ˌfɑː əˈpɑːt/
long-lasting (adj)	/ˌlɒŋˈlɑːstɪŋ/
naked (adj)	/ˈneɪkɪd/
perspiration (n)	/ˌpɜːspəˈreɪʃ(ə)n/
phonograph (n)	/ˈfəʊnəˌɡrɑːf/
play back	/ˌpleɪ ˈbæk/
telegraph (n)	/ˈtelɪˌɡrɑːf/
telepathy (n)	/təˈlepəθi/
via (prep)	/ˈvaɪə/

PRONUNCIATION GUIDE

Vowels

/ɑː/	arm, large
/æ/	cap, bad
/aɪ/	ride, fly
/aɪə/	diary, science
/aʊ/	how, mouth
/aʊə/	our, shower
/e/	bed, head
/eɪ/	day, grey
/eə/	hair, there
/ɪ/	give, did
/i/	happy, honeymoon
/iː/	we, heat
/ɪə/	ear, here
/ɒ/	not, watch
/əʊ/	cold, boat
/ɔː/	door, talk
/ɔɪ/	point, boy
/ʊ/	foot, could
/u/	annual
/uː/	two, food
/ʊə/	sure, tourist
/ɜː/	bird, heard
/ʌ/	fun, come
/ə/	mother, actor

Consonants

/b/	bag, rubbish
/d/	desk, cold
/f/	fill, laugh
/ɡ/	girl, big
/h/	hand, home
/j/	yes, young
/k/	cook, back
/l/	like, fill
/m/	mean, climb
/n/	new, want
/p/	park, happy
/r/	ring, borrow
/s/	say, this
/t/	town, city
/v/	very, live
/w/	water, away
/z/	zoo, his
/ʃ/	shop, machine
/ʒ/	usually, television
/ŋ/	thank, doing
/tʃ/	cheese, picture
/θ/	thing, north
/ð/	that, clothes
/dʒ/	jeans, bridge

IRREGULAR VERBS

Infinitive	Past simple	Past participle
be	was, were	been
beat	beat	beaten
become	became	become
begin	began	begun
bend	bent	bent
bet	bet	bet
bite	bit	bitten
bleed	bled	bled
blow	blew	blown
break	broke	broken
bring	brought	brought
broadcast	broadcast	broadcast
build	built	built
burn	burnt/burned	burnt/burned
buy	bought	bought
catch	caught	caught
choose	chose	chosen
come	came	come
cost	cost	cost
cut	cut	cut
dig	dug	dug
do	did	done
draw	drew	drawn
dream	dreamt/dreamed	dreamt/dreamed
drink	drank	drunk
drive	drove	driven
eat	ate	eaten
fall	fell	fallen
feed	fed	fed
feel	felt	felt
fight	fought	fought
find	found	found
fit	fitted/fit	fitted/fit
fly	flew	flown
forbid	forbad(e)	forbidden
forget	forgot	forgotten
freeze	froze	frozen
get	got	got
give	gave	given
go	went	gone/been
grow	grew	grown
hang	hung	hung
have	had	had
hear	heard	heard
hide	hid	hidden
hit	hit	hit
hold	held	held
hurt	hurt	hurt
keep	kept	kept
know	knew	known
lay	laid	laid
lead	led	led
learn	learnt/learned	learnt/learned
leave	left	left
lend	lent	lent
let	let	let
lie	lay	lain
light	lit	lit
lose	lost	lost
make	made	made
mean	meant	meant
meet	met	met
misunderstand	misunderstood	misunderstood
offset	offset	offset
pay	paid	paid
put	put	put
read /ri:d/	read /red/	read /red/
rebuild	rebuilt	rebuilt
retell	retold	retold
rewrite	rewrote	rewritten
ride	rode	ridden
ring	rang	rung
rise	rose	risen
run	ran	run
say	said	said
see	saw	seen
sell	sold	sold
send	sent	sent
set	set	set
shake	shook	shaken
shine	shone	shone
shoot	shot	shot
show	showed	shown
shut	shut	shut
sing	sang	sung
sink	sank	sunk
sit	sat	sat
sleep	slept	slept
smell	smelt/smelled	smelt/smelled
speak	spoke	spoken
speed	sped	sped
spell	spelt/spelled	spelt/spelled
spend	spent	spent
spill	spilt/spilled	spilt/spilled
spin	spun/span	spun
spread	spread	spread
stand	stood	stood
steal	stole	stolen
stick	stuck	stuck
strike	struck	struck
swim	swam	swum
take	took	taken
teach	taught	taught
tell	told	told
think	thought	thought
throw	threw	thrown
understand	understood	understood
wake	woke	woken
wear	wore	worn
win	won	won
wind	wound	wound
write	wrote	written

Macmillan Education
Between Towns Road, Oxford OX4 3PP
A division of Macmillan Publishers Limited
Companies and representatives throughout the world

ISBN 978-1-4050-2950-6

Text © Judy Garton-Sprenger and Philip Prowse 2007
Design and illustration © Macmillan Publishers 2007

The rights of Judy Garton-Sprenger and Philip Prowse to be identified as authors of this work have been asserted by them in accordance with the Copyright, Designs and Patents Act 1988.

First published 2007

All rights reserved; no part of this publication may be reproduced, stored in a retrieval system, transmitted in any form, or by any means, electronic, mechanical, photocopying, recording, or otherwise, without the prior written permission of the publishers.

Designed by Giles Davies Design Ltd
Illustrated by Jamel Akib p26; Paul Daviz pp 57, 61, 106; John Dillow p100; Mark Duffin pp22, 24, 34, 68; Vince Fraser p44-45; Tim Kahane pp52, 80; Katie Mac p59; Andrew Quelch p70; Kate Sheppard pp16, 41, 64, 88; Victor Tavares p25; Gary Wing pp73, 81
Cover design by Sue Ayres
Additional cover design by Lenn Darroux and Anne Sherlock
Cover photographs with kind permission of: Getty Images and Superstock.

Authors' acknowledgements
The authors would like to thank all the team at Macmillan Education in the UK and world-wide for everything they have done to help create *Inspiration*. We are most grateful to Dulcie Booth (Commissioning Editor) for co-ordinating the publication of *Inspiration* 4 with such thoughtfulness, efficiency and enthusiasm, Marion Simon (Managing Editor) for her tenacity and care, Giles Davies (Design) for his great imagination and creativity, Victoria Pullin (Editor) for all her support, and Emily Rosser (Secondary Publisher, Europe) for overseeing the project. We would also like to thank Julie Brett (Editorial Manager), Deirdre Gyenes (Managing Designer), Candice Renault, Maria Joannou and Deborah Hughes (Photo Research), Hazel Barrett and Paulette McKean (Permissions), Xanthe Sturt-Taylor (Workbook Editor) and Lynn Townsend (Teacher's Book Editor) for their invaluable contribution and professionalism. Our thanks are also due to Amanda Bailey and Susannah McKee for writing the excellent Teacher's Book. The *Inspiration Builder* was written by Hannah Fish, Michael Kedward, Nick McIver and Susannah McKee, with Nilgun Demirkaya, Bernadette Harvengt, Agnieszka Mulak, Wayne Rimmer and Adam Trim, editor Clare Nielsen-Marsh. We would also like to thank Jeff Capel for his great skill in producing the recorded material and the actors who appear on the recordings and bring the book to life.

We owe an enormous debt of gratitude to teenage students and their teachers in many different countries who welcomed us into their classrooms and contributed so much to the formation of *Inspiration*. In particular we would like to thank teachers and classes in Argentina, Greece, Italy, Poland, Spain, Switzerland, Turkey and Uruguay. We are equally indebted to participants on teacher training courses in Europe, South America and elsewhere from whom we have learnt so much.

Many individuals reported on the *Inspiration* syllabus and materials, and we would like to express our deepest thanks to all of them, in particular Ursula Bader, Nazan Karakas, Anna Bialas, Maria Birkenmajer, Françoise Etienne, Bernadette Harvengt, Paolo Jacomelli, Sue F. Jones, Antonia Köppel, Annemarie Kortleven, Malgorzata Lombarowicz, Agnieszka Mulak, Urzula Nowak, Katarzyna Pietraga, Peach Richmond, Marta Rosinska, Jean Rüdiger-Harper, Karl Russi, Ursula Schauer, Grzegorz Spiewak, Adam Trim, Maya Tsiperson, Paul Weibel, Ewa Zemanek, and Halina Zgutka.

The authors and publisher are grateful for permission to reprint the following copyright material: Extract from www.snopes.com, copyright © Barbara and David P Mikkelson 1995-2006, reprinted by permission of the publishers. Extract about Philip Pullman', reprinted by permission of AP Watt on behalf of the author. Extracts from 'The Professor and the Ferryman'; 'The Two Painters' and 'Kam's Mirror' all taken from *Stories for Thinking* by Robert Fisher (Nash Pollock, 1996), copyright © Robert Fisher 1996, reprinted by permission of the author. *Spooky* Lyrics by Shapiro/Middlebrooks/Buie/Cobb copyright © Sony/ATV Songs LLC 1968, reprinted by permission of the publisher. All Rights Reserved. Extract about Camilla Naprous, reprinted by permission of The Devil's Horsemen (www. devilshorsemen.com). Extract about 'Virgin Galactic Spaceship', reprinted by permission of the publisher. Extract from 'Explainer: Longitude problem' by James Randerson, copyright © Guardian News and Media Limited 2006, first published in *The Guardian* 25.03.06, reprinted by permission of the publisher. Extract from '2020 vision: live to 120' taken from www.smh.com.au copyright © Australian Associated Press 2004, reprinted by permission of the publisher. Extract from 'How mobile phones are transforming Africa' by Fred Bridgland, copyright © Fred Bridgland 2005, first published in *Sunday Herald* 13.03.05, reprinted by permission of the author. *Every Breath You Take* Words and Music by Sting copyright © Magnetic Publishing/EMI Music Publishing Limited 1983, reprinted by permission of G M Sumner/EMI Music Publishing Ltd, London, WC2H 0QY and Music Sales Ltd. All Rights Reserved. International Copyright Secured. Extract from 'This man is worth £100,000 a year' by David Crystal, copyright © David Crystal 2000, first published in *High Life* magazine June 2000, reprinted by permission of the author. Extract from 'COMMUNICATIONS: Good to talk' taken from *New Internationalist* magazine No 365 March 2004, copyright © New Internationalist 2004, reprinted by permission of the publisher. Extract from 'Fun is my business' by Laura Barton, Susie Steiner, Dominic Murphy, Simon Hattenstone, Kirsty Scott, Caroline Roux and Gareth McLean, copyright © Guardian News and Media Limited 2003, first published in *The Guardian* 09.08.03, reprinted by permission of the publisher. Extract from *Collins Faxfinder: Unsolved Mysteries* (HarperCollins Publishers Ltd, 1996), copyright © HarperCollins Publishers Limited 1996, reprinted by permission of the publisher. Extract from 'It's a man's game' by Jo Tuckman copyright Jo Tuckman 2005, first published in *The Guardian* 05.01.05, reprinted by permission of the author. Extract from *The Lost Continent* by Bill Bryson (Black Swan, a division of Transworld, 1989), copyright © Bill Bryson 1989, reprinted by permission of The Random House Group Ltd. All Rights Reserved. Extract from 'You have so many jokes' by Simon Hattenstone, copyright © Guardian News and Media 2002, first published in *The Guardian* 22.11.02, reprinted by permission of the publisher. Extract from 'Wish they were there?' by Joanna Moorhead, copyright © Guardian News and Media Limited 2006, first published in *The Guardian* 08.04.06, reprinted by permission of the publisher. *Hanging on the Telephone* written by Jack Lee copyright © Chrysalis Music 1978, reprinted by permission of the publisher. All Rights Reserved. Extract from interview with Piers Vitebsky 'Day in the Life' by Sarah Woodward taken from *CAM* magazine no.47, reprinted by permission of Piers Vitebsky. Extract from 'Urban Explosion-The Facts' taken from *New Internationalist* Magazine No.386 Jan/Feb 2006, copyright New Internationalist 2006, reprinted by permission of the publisher. 'Confessions of a Runner' from *Wicked World* by Benjamin Zephaniah (Puffin, 2000), text copyright © Benjamin Zephania 2000, reprinted by permission of Penguin Books Ltd. Extract from 'The School we'd like' by Dea Birkett, copyright © Dea Birkett 2001, first published in *The Guardian* 05.06.01, reprinted by permission of the author. Extract from 'Sarah Bennett: Singer and Songwriter' copyright © Sarah Bennett, taken from www.bbc.co.uk/blast, reprinted by permission of the author (sarahkatebennett@hotmail.co.uk). *True Colours* Lyrics by Kelly/Steinberg copyright © Sony/ATV Tunes LLC 1986, reprinted by permission of the publisher. All Rights Reserved.

Although we have tried to trace and contact copyright holders before publication, in some cases this has not been possible. If contacted we will be pleased to rectify any errors or omissions at the earliest opportunity.

The authors and publishers would like to thank the following for permission to reproduce their photographic material: Alamy/ Cephas Picture Library p16(t), Alamy/ Emilio Ereza p99(bl), Alamy/ Terry Fincher. Photo Int p48(b), Alamy/ foodfolio pp16(b), 106, Alamy/ Robert Fried pp18(tl), 108(8), Alamy/ Jeff Greenberg p67(tl), Alamy/ImageState pp97, 108(10), Alamy/ Indiapicture p68(o), Alamy/ Bob Johns/expresspictures.co.uk p67(b), Alamy/ Celia Mannings pp43(t), 108(6), Alamy/ Antony Nettle p47, Alamy/ John Norman p95(b), Alamy/ Stephen Oliver pp68(m), 108(1), Alamy/ John Powell Photographer p95(t), Alamy/ Simon Reddy p68(t), Alamy /Frances Roberts p14(bl), Alamy/ Masa Uemura p86, Alamy/ Robin Whalley p21, Alamy/ Paul Wood p90(b); Art Archive/ Beethoven House Bonn / Dagli Orti p92(tl); Brand X Pictures p28; Bridgeman Art Library/ Private Collection, The Stapleton Collection p56(l); Corbis pp08-09, 11(5), 14(m), 40(l), 48(t), 76(r), 91(b), 99(br), 92(br), Corbis/ Bettmann pp50(bl), 50(br), Corbis/ Adrian Carroll; Eye Ubiquitous p56(r), Corbis/ Iris Coppola/ Zefa p19(m), Corbis/ Regis Duvignau/ Reuters p14(tml), Corbis/ Free Agents Limited p46-47, Corbis/ Rick Friedman p71, Corbis/ Neil Guegan/ Zefa pp57, 108(7), Corbis/ Hulton-Deutsch Collection pp50(bm), 60, Corbis/ Kelly-Mooney Photography p90-91, Corbis/ Michael Kim p43(b), Corbis/ Justin Lane/ EPA p64(tl), Corbis/ Jacques Langevin p78, Corbis/ Darren Modricker p22(5), Corbis/ Viviane Moos p18(tr), Corbis/ Roy Morsch p22(4), Corbis/ Michelle Pedone/ Zefa p99(tl), Corbis/ Michael Prince p22(2), 91(t), 108(9), Corbis/ David Raymer pp19(r), 108(5), Corbis/ Reuters p92(tr), Corbis/ ROB & SAS p22(3), Corbis/ David Samuel Robbins p76(l), Corbis/ Strauss/ Curtis p84, Corbis/ Josh Westrich/ Zefa p102, Corbis/ Ralph White p35; John Cryan p74(b); Empics/ AP Photo/ Eduardo Verdugo p62, Empics/ Phil Noble/ PA p20(t), Empics/ John Stillwell/ PA p19(l), Empics/ John Walton p63; Everynight Images/ Jamie Baker p72; Getty Images pp06-7, 20, 90(t), 104-105, Getty Images/ DK p88(l), Getty Images/ Amanda Edwards p66, Getty Images/ Alfred Eisenstaedt// Time Life p38(m), Getty Images/ Henry Guttmann pp38(b), 94(b), Getty Images/ David Levenson p24, Getty Images/ Jochen Luebke/ AFP p88(r), Getty Images/ Stone pp12, 14(tr), Getty Images/ Time Life Pictures p94(t); Greenpeace/ Jeremy Sutton-Hibbert2006 p50; Jan Von Holleben p30; Kobal Collection p22-23; Lonely Planet Images/ Krzysztof Dydynski p42-43, Lonely Planet/ Peter Ptschelinzew p18(b); Macmillan Publishers Ltd pp36(b), 75(t),108(2); Maria Joannou pp10(ml), 10(tl), 11(6); NASA p107, NASA/The Hubble Heritage Team, STScI, AURA p32, NASA/ Kennedy Space Center p33; National Oceanic & Atmospheric Adminstration (NOAA)/ National Undersea Research Program (NURP) p34; Naturepl/ Todd Pusser p75(b); Photographers Direct/ Andrew Trask Photography p11(4); Photos. com pp11(1), 11(2), 11(3), 11(7), 11(8), 22(1); Reuters p40(r); Rex Features p64(tr), Rex Features/ Everett Collection p14(tl), Rex Features/ Alex Maguire p67(tr), Rex Features/ Brian Rasic p96; Science & Society/ Science Museum p39; Science Photo Library pp38(t), SPL/ Alfred Pasieka p82(l), SPL/ A Barrington Brown p83; Still Pictures/ BIOS Cassou Jean p98, Still Pictures/ Sebastian Bolesch p64(b), Still Pictures/ Gilles Saussier p54; Tate Images/ Courtesy Chris Ofili – Afroco p20(b); Topham Picturepoint p42, Topham Picturepoint/ Peter Frost p74(t), Topham Picturepoint/ UPPA p92(bl); Virgin Galactic p36(t);Richard Waite pp58(bl), 58(br), 58(t); www.iwantoneofthose.com pp10(tr), 10(mr), 10(b). Photo p20(tl) © Andy Goldsworthy from Time (Thames and Hudson 2000). Commissioned photography by Dean Ryan pp28, 99 and 108.

Printed and bound in Thailand
2014 2013 2012 2011
12 11 10 9 8